THE BEST ARE

CW01499412

Clair Wills's *The Best Are Leaving* is a wide-ranging study of post-war Irish emigrant culture. Wills analyses representations of emigrants from Ireland and of Irish immigrants in Britain across a range of discourses, including official documents, sociological texts, clerical literature, journalism, drama, literary fiction, and popular literature and film. A leading critic of Irish literature and culture, Wills explores a number of received opinions about post-war emigration from Ireland, and the immigrant Irish community in Britain: the loss of the finest people from rural Ireland, and the destruction of traditional communities; the anxieties associated with women emigrants and their desire for the benefits of modern consumer society; the stereotype of the drunken, fighting Irishman; the charming and authentic country Irish in the city; the physical strength of the labouring Irish; the ambiguous meanings of Irish Catholicism in England, both a threatening and a civilising force. She asks why – despite the differences in social background and social outcome for individual migrants – ideas, opinions and representations of the Irish turned on a relatively narrow range of stereotypes. And she analyses the deployment of those stereotypes by writers and artists such as M. J. Molloy, John B. Keane, Edna O'Brien, Tom Murphy, Donall Mac Amhlaigh, Anthony Cronin, and Philip Donnellan.

Clair Wills is professor of Irish literature at Queen Mary University of London. Previous publications include *That Neutral Island: A History of Ireland during the Second World War* (2007) and *Dublin 1916: The Siege of the GPO* (2009).

THE BEST ARE LEAVING

Emigration and Post-War Irish Culture

CLAIR WILLS

Queen Mary University of London

CAMBRIDGE
UNIVERSITY PRESS

CAMBRIDGE
UNIVERSITY PRESS

University Printing House, Cambridge CB2 8BS, United Kingdom

One Liberty Plaza, 20th Floor, New York, NY 10006, USA

477 Williamstown Road, Port Melbourne, VIC 3207, Australia

314-321, 3rd Floor, Plot 3, Splendor Forum, Jasola District Centre, New Delhi - 110025, India

79 Anson Road, #06-04/06, Singapore 079906

Cambridge University Press is part of the University of Cambridge.

It furthers the University's mission by disseminating knowledge in the pursuit of education, learning and research at the highest international levels of excellence.

www.cambridge.org
Information on this title: www.cambridge.org/9781107680876

© Clair Wills 2015

First published 2015

A catalogue record for this publication is available from the British Library

Library of Congress Cataloging in Publication data
Wills, Clair.
The best are leaving : emigration and post-war Irish culture / Clair Wills,
Queen Mary University of London.
pages cm
Includes bibliographical references and index.
ISBN 978-1-107-04840-9 (hardback) – ISBN 978-1-107-68087-6 (paperback)
1. Irish – Great Britain – History – 20th century.   2. Irish – Great Britain – Social conditions – 20th century.   3. Great Britain – Emigration and immigration – History – 20th century.   4. Ireland – Emigration and immigration – History.   I. Title.
DA125.I7W54   2014
304.809415–dc23   2014020958

ISBN 978-1-107-04840-9 Hardback
ISBN 978-1-107-68087-6 Paperback

For Claire Connolly

Contents

Figures

Acknowledgements

I am grateful to the Queen Mary University of London for their continuing support of my research; to the Leverhulme Trust for the award of a Major Leverhulme Fellowship, which allowed me to carry out much of the research and writing of this book; and to Magdalene College Cambridge for the 2014 Parnell Fellowship, which enabled me to complete it. I am especially grateful to Philippa Donnellan and the Philip Donnellan Estate for permission to publish images from Donnellan's 1965 documentary for the BBC, *The Irishmen*, and to Frank Auerbach for permission to reproduce his wonderful 'Summer Building Site 1952' on the cover of this book.

For research advice and discussion I am indebted to Matt Campbell, Bernard Canavan, Nicholas Canny, Jim Chandler, Michael Collins, Claire Connolly, Ultan Cowley, Michael G. Cronin, Mike Cronin, Santanu Das, Sile de Cléir, Julian Deering, Eamon Duffy, David Feldman, Roy Foster, Jason Gaiger, Luke Gibbons, Catherine Hall, Mary Hickman, John Horgan, Paul Keegan, Margaret Kelleher, John Kerrigan, Joe Lee, Ben Levitas, David Lloyd, Paul Long, Ian McBride, Ronan McDonald, Deirdre McMahon, Michael Moriarty, Eve Morrison, John Muckle, Brendan Mulkere, Tony Murray, Deirdre Ní Chonghaile, Micheal Ó-Aodha, Mary O'Callaghan, Diarmuid Ó Giolláin, Eunan O'Halpin, Thaddeus O'Sullivan, Ian Patterson, Lance Pettit, James Ryan, Jim Smyth, Bronwen Walter, Frances Wilson, and my colleagues at Queen Mary, especially Michèle Barrett, Markman Ellis, Paul Hamilton, Anne Janowitz and Jacqueline Rose. For imaginative and efficient research assistance of various kinds I should like to thank John Dillon, Angharad Eyre, Peter Hession, Elizabeth Robertson and Rob Waters. I am grateful to Masami Nakao for her invitation to teach a graduate workshop on this material at the University of Tokyo in 2011, and to Chris Fox and the faculty of the Keough-Naughton Institute for Irish Studies, Notre Dame, for inviting me to take up a Visiting Professorship in the spring of 2012. This provided a great opportunity to discuss emigrant texts with a lively and creative group of graduates, including Evan Bryson, Kara Donnelly, Lindsay Haney, Katy Lattari, Robinson Murphy and Nathaniel Myers. Thanks too to Jacob, Luan and Philomena Wills for their patience and good humour.

Parts of Chapter 2 and Chapter 3 have appeared in previous form in 'Women Writers and the Death of Rural Ireland: Realism and Nostalgia in the 1940s', *Éire-Ireland*, 41:1 (2006), 192–212, and 'Realism and the Irish Immigrant: Documentary, Fiction and Post-War Irish Labor', *Modern Language Quarterly*, 73:3 (2012), 373–394.

Preface

On occasional Sunday afternoons when I was about eight or nine, we children would climb into the back of the Vauxhall Viva ready for my father to drive the hour and a half or so from our home in Croydon to a pub in Shepherds Bush. There my mother would meet her brothers. For me and my sisters these were afternoons of strangeness, if not quite adventure – for a start we were released from the usual purgatory of being left to squabble in the back of the car whilst our parents went for a drink. By some process I judged similar to the territorial reach of Western Europe into West Berlin, the pubs in Shepherds Bush appeared to be outposts of Irish legal terrain so that children were allowed in the bar. There we were treated to endless bottles of red lemonade and packets of Tayto crisps by uncles whose kindness, in the face of our relative unfamiliarity, was just a little bit frightening. At least that is my memory. My eldest sister remembers it differently – as a series of visits to dingy, depressing pubs peopled by men nursing their pints in silence. The afternoons were long and I remember them as awkward. I was used to going 'home' to Ireland every summer, and felt at ease with my cousins and uncles and aunts in West Cork. These London uncles were different – both quieter and harder to know, and louder in company. And there was always the moment, no easier to handle because anticipated, when they would press money into your hand and you would need to be grateful and pleased, as you were, but to make only just the right amount of fuss about saying thank-you.

The awkwardness was not just that of a young girl around grown men. What I chiefly remember about those visits is the journey there and back by car, a journey defined by what I now realise was my mother's edginess. The siblings had left the small farm near Skibbereen within a few years of each other, in the late 1940s and early '50s. But in fifteen years my mother's life had changed almost beyond recognition. She had trained as a general nurse in the newly formed National Health Service, a process which proved a happy meeting between her own desire for change and opportunities for social mobility. Though social aspiration had been no part of a conscious plan – she wanted to travel, and to widen her experience – she made a success of things. A little more than six years after her arrival she had married a local. We lived in a semi-detached house; we had a car; we took annual holidays to Ireland and occasionally even to France; we girls would eventually pass the eleven-plus and go on to university. Apart from the fact that we were Catholic, and nurtured a sentimental attachment to our Irishness, fuelled each summer by our trips 'home', and sustained during the year by listening to Percy French, wearing scratchy Aran sweaters, and baking soda bread, we seemed entirely integrated into English middle-class society. Indeed our Catholicism was proof that my mother's emigration from Ireland had not been a success merely in terms of her own life. If she had cared to dwell on it, she might have reflected that she was a symbol of success too for the Irish church, which in the '50s liked to stress that though emigration was a social evil it might yet be turned into a force for moral good if the Irish 'boys and girls' who left the country by the thousands could be encouraged to bring round the pagan country across the channel. For when my father fell in love with her he fell for the whole lot, Catholicism and all, and converted.

English husband aside, my mother's story is fairly typical of small-farm girls who migrated to Britain in the '50s. There were few, if any, opportunities for girls of her station in rural Ireland beyond domestic service, or work in a shop or small factory if they were lucky. Four out of every five children born in Ireland between 1931 and 1941 emigrated in the 1950s.[1] More than half a million people (from a population of less than three million) left the country between 1945 and 1960. And unlike most European countries, where it was predominantly young men who migrated for work, just as many Irish women as men left home – in some years rather more women than men. Of every hundred girls in the province of Connacht aged fifteen to nineteen in 1946, forty-two had left by 1951.[2] Many of them went into factories, or worked in transport, particularly in the midlands, and a fair proportion trained as nurses. Precisely because nursing in Ireland was still the preserve of well-off farmers' daughters (the training was fee-paying) it retained the professional cachet it was losing in England, where it was becoming associated with hard work and low status. For the many young women without school qualifications who could nonetheless train

---

[1] J. J. Lee, *Ireland 1912–1985: Politics and Society* (Cambridge: Cambridge University Press, 1989), p. 379.
[2] Ibid., p. 377.

in Britain, nursing offered unparalleled opportunities for a career and wider social horizons.

Her brothers were also fairly typical of their class. Small farmer's sons, with nothing beyond a national school education (secondary education was not to expand for the poorer classes in Ireland until the late '6os), and without specific skills beyond those required for the seasonal work on the farm, there was nothing for them but to join the vast pool of Irish unskilled labour which contributed to rebuilding Britain after the war. Many of our stereotypes of the Irish worker in post-war Britain derive from this navvying class. These were men who worked 'on the lump', queuing for work on the building sites on street corners in the early morning, who were paid into the hand at the end of the week, who lived in overcrowded digs and spent their free time in the pub where they drank their pay. Many of them didn't marry; they didn't save, and they didn't 'settle down'; it was marriage itself, almost regardless of to whom, which made the fundamental difference to the immigrants of the 1950s. Unmarried labourers survived their time in England by sticking to their own, barely associating, let alone integrating, with English society; they talked as though they were at any point going to return 'home', but they became increasingly cut off from Irish life through the 1960s. Though the details of any one individual life differed from the stereotype, it was uncomfortably true enough for thousands of Irish men even then. By the time of those Shepherds Bush Sundays it was the late '6os and things were not going to change for my uncles and those like them.

The discomfort I sensed in my mother was not about not wanting to see them. The fondness and anticipation were palpable. Yet her long familiarity with her brothers must have made the consciousness of their different situations acute. The same was true for them, of course – everyone was making an effort to pretend that nothing had changed, that the family at home, neighbours, friends, teachers, authority figures, the whole world they had been brought up to lose, by leaving, was not really lost at all. The good cheer, the remembered stories, the money pressed into the hand, none of it was simply bravado. The sense of injustice was surely bitter, the unfairness of the system – both Irish and British – that had used them and left them behind, impossible to deny. But how could it be acknowledged without condescension towards the lives they had made? It was this feeling I unearthed one day when I asked my mother, 'What does Uncle Thomas do?' Though I can't have been more than ten years old, I vividly remember the slight hesitation and catch in her throat before she answered very deliberately, 'He's a mason.' I had never heard the word and asked her to explain it. For a long time afterwards I imagined Uncle Thomas as a sort of medieval craftsman, carving houses. She would not say builder's labourer. It wasn't that she was a snob, though perhaps she thought I was. She wanted me to be proud of him.

The relationship between these recollections and the chapters that follow is, in several respects, straightforward. I began the research for this book wanting to understand more about the worlds in which my relatives had lived their lives, and more about the ways they may have understood their lives. Historical and sociological research has a vital part to play in making intelligible the social, political and cultural forces which structured opportunities and choices for Irish men and women both at home and after they had made the move to Britain, but so too, I believe, does the kind of cultural and literary reading that I offer here. For – and this is where the relationship between my recollections and this study becomes more complex – it is impossible to extricate historical experience from cultural patterns and representational strategies, which shore up fallible memories and help make sense of our experiences. The scenes I have described are events which actually took place, but their importance – the manner in which I have remembered them, and the fact that they seem to speak of experience in telling ways – has to do with the way they echo and reinforce ideas and images of the emigrant Irish. This book is an attempt to trace the evolution of some of these ideas in the documentary and creative literature of the 1950s and '60s. It is about misrecognition and misunderstanding as much as it is about knowledge and awareness. Experience, after all, is just as dependent on confusion as it is on clarity. The writers, artists, journalists and politicians I discuss were all attempting to be historians of contemporary experience, and the doubled perspective of blind participant and detached observer structures a great many of their responses to emigrant and immigrant life. What might feel like the privileged position of the 'insider', knowing from personal experience at least something of the worlds of the post-war migrants, is put in question but not negated by the evidence and information gleaned from external sources. One contemporary critic called it knowing 'from the inside out', and it is a practice I have tried to learn from the fiction, drama, film and painting which are my subject.

I offer here an analysis of stock formations: the shaping typologies of emigrant and immigrant experience. The chapters track a number of received discourses which formed a core of public opinion about post-war emigration from Ireland and the immigrant Irish community in Britain: the loss of the finest people from rural Ireland and the destruction of traditional communities; the anxieties associated with women emigrants and their desire for the benefits of modern consumer society; the stereotype of the drunken, fighting Irishman; the charming and authentic country Irish in the city; the ambiguous meanings of Irish Catholicism in England, both a threatening and a civilising force. None of these cultural formations remained fixed during the period, and, as the history of 'actual' migrant experience shows, many were widely off the mark. Yet precisely because they may have been in some basic historical sense 'wrong', and failed to offer an accurate picture of migrant life as it was evolving, the remarkable persistence of these formulaic patterns deserves exploration. These pages explore ideas, images and stereotypes of Irish ethnicity as they were employed by a range of writers and thinkers responding to post-war emigration from Ireland and immigrant experience in Britain. Their focus is on the ways in which inherited tropes and stock formations were deployed at a moment of historical crisis and significant social change. The challenge is to acknowledge the culturally determined nature of these representations, and at the same time to account for their historical specificity, to find a way to revisit the history of immigration which both admits and resists the shaping power of culture, which both reads, and reads through, stereotypical representation.

In paying attention to the formation of types and stereotypes, I ask how some experiences became more salient than others, how some stock formations became embedded, as ways of understanding experience, and others did not. In attempting to trace a genealogy of these formations I am wary of the danger of collapsing distinctions between 'lived experience' and the forms in which it is represented – wary of a thoroughgoing type of linguistic determinism, the idea that subjects (and their experiences) are produced discursively. But I do maintain that 'typification' and 'stereotypification' were part of lived experience for emigrants and immigrants, and that this stratum of experience may be opened up to interpretation by a critical reading of the literature.

A further word on the literature, and the practice of critical reading I bring to it, may be in order here. My study of official documents, essays, journalism, drama, fiction and film has been directed at analysing the various ways in which they deploy emigrant typologies, and interpreting the echoes and dialogues between them. Arguably my approach risks flattening out the distinctions between different forms of discourse, and it is true that part of my argument in this book is in favour of a practice of critical reading which can acknowledge the dynamic and symbiotic relationship between texts which were produced with very different purposes, and indeed audiences, in mind. I am interested in overlaps, resonances, and borrowings – in the distorted forms in which discursive patterns can cross from one type of text to another, and in the insights which can be gained from tracking those echoes and distortions. But I do not deny that self-conscious borrowing, and deliberate distortion – strategies characteristic of literary texts – provide a form of knowledge of a different order. The literary texts I analyse here do not purvey stereotypes (in the way that Irish clerical warnings about the dangers of emigration, or British commentaries on the wild Irish immigrant do) so much as interrogate them and put them to use. In so doing they offer up the relationship between discursive formations and lived experience for our understanding, allowing us to see and interpret the stuff of which they, and we, are made.

Introduction
The Crying Game

It isn't a case of staying or going. Forced to stay or forced to go. Never the freedom to decide and make the choice for ourselves. And we're half-men here, or half-men away, and how can we hope ever to do anything.

Tom Murphy[1]

One of the last models of 'city and country' is the system we now know as imperialism.

Raymond Williams[2]

When I boarded the train at Listowel that morning it seemed as if everyone was leaving. It was the same at every station along the way. Dun Laoghaire, for the first time, was a heartbreaking experience – the goodbyes to husbands going back after Christmas, chubby-faced boys and girls leaving home for the first time, bewilderment written all over them, hard-faced old-stagers who never let on but who felt it worst of all because they knew only too well what lay before them.

John B. Keane[3]

John B. Keane left Ireland on the 6th of January 1952, when it appeared that 'everyone was leaving'. The protracted post-war Irish economic crisis had created a situation in which the country was unable to provide for vast numbers of the rural poor. During the 1950s more than 400,000 people left independent Ireland, nearly a sixth of the total population recorded in 1951, and a vastly higher proportion of the working population. The majority left for work in Britain, which would be home to one million Irish-born – then the largest migrant population in Britain – by the late 1960s. Among that million were people of all classes, including middle-class professionals – doctors, lawyers, and aspiring college-educated young

---

[1] Tom Murphy, *A Crucial Week in the Life of a Grocer's Assistant*, in *A Whistle in the Dark and Other Plays* (London: Methuen, 1989), p. 172.
[2] Raymond Williams, *The Country and the City* (Nottingham: Spokesman Books, 2011), p. 279.
[3] John B. Keane, *Self-Portrait* (Cork: Mercier Press, 1964), p. 32.

people for whom advancement had long meant a spell abroad in England - as well as the large army of priests, brothers and nuns whose careers had always involved moving across national borders. But undoubtedly the largest section of the emigrating population stemmed from the poorer rural areas. During the war and in the immediate post-war years young men and women from the labouring and small-farmer classes migrated in large groups to take up work on contract labour schemes building large-scale works, in hospitals, in mines, in factories. Emigration highlighted the division between a traditional Irish small-farming culture in decline and a secular, industrial, modernising, urban British culture which many saw as in part responsible for Irish economic stagnation.

As Keane suggests, the young men and women forced to take the boat were as susceptible as any others to the belief that they were losing all that was valuable by leaving. He goes on to describe the voyage:

> All around us as we left Dun Laoghaire, there was drunkenness. The younger men were drunk – not violently so but tragically so, as I was, to forget the dreadful loneliness of having to leave home. Underneath it all was the heartbreaking, frightful anguish of separation.... The whole scene reminded me of the early Christian martyrs going out to face the terrors of the arena. Laugh if you like, but there was an unbelievable spirit of fraternity, a kind of brotherhood, a communal feeling of tragedy which embraced us all.[4]

The metaphor of being fed to the lions seems wildly exaggerated, yet the overwhelming majority of accounts of leaving Ireland in this period focus on the tears – on the consciousness of irreparable loss and separation. It was, as for Stephen Rea's Fergus, the IRA volunteer turned London labourer in Neil Jordan's film, a crying game. Stories of post-war migration from the West Indies stress hopes and expectations – hopes of a prosperous new life that for the most part were to be cruelly crushed. By contrast Irish emigration, if we are to believe the written accounts, took place in an atmosphere of dread, fear or resignation.

It would be foolish, and insensitive, to deny that real feelings of anxiety and alarm were at play, and that for many of these young emigrants leaving home was, at least initially, experienced as 'tragedy', as Keane suggests. Yet there were also migrants who made the journey in various

---

[4] Ibid., p. 33. See also John Healy, *Death of an Irish Town* (Cork: Mercier Press, 1968), p. 45, where he describes 'the emigrant train': 'The train would pull into Charlestown to a crowded platform. It had travelled about 30 miles from Sligo through Collooney, Coolaney, Tubbercurry and Curry and the young girls who had left these towns and villages were still crying as the train came to a stop.... The Guard's door slamming shut was the breaking point: like the first clatter of stones and sand on a coffin, it signalled the finality of the old life. They clutched and clung and wept in a frenzy.'

degrees of excitement and anticipation of adventure. There were parents who accepted without question that emigration meant profit, and that their children would grow up to make their lives elsewhere. The fact that these experiences are marginalised across the range of records of post-war migration deserves explanation. There appears to be a discrepancy between the particular and varied experience of emigration and the way that it appears in the contemporary record. That disjunction lies at the heart of this study.

When I began the research for this book, I hoped and assumed that it would be possible to offer a fuller picture of the social and cultural history of post-war Irish migrants, by drawing on a range of different representations. I was interested in the ways in which emigrants were portrayed in official documents produced in both Ireland and Britain; in contemporary sociology; in Catholic advice pamphlets; in articles and letters to the newspapers; in popular literature such as serials in women's magazines and *Ireland's Own*; in film, drama, and literary fiction. While this range of representations has certainly illuminated the social history of emigration, and I hope in interesting ways, it has also proved remarkably resistant to historical pressure. However broadly I cast the net, fishing for opinions, images, records and depictions of Irish migrants, I brought up material which seemed to speak more clearly of the persistence of cultural stereotypes, and an ideology, or even fantasy, of Irish migration, than of the experience itself. The implied separation here between representation and reality is a problem, of course. After all, the family history which I outlined in my preface offers a version of experience couched in standard terms – the typical upwardly mobile Irish Catholic nurse, and the typical Irish labourer at the bottom of the pile – which is both 'true' and a product of narrative. Indeed these two cultural stereotypes account for a sizable proportion of the discourse on post-war Irish migrants in both Ireland and Britain. Rather than offering a cultural history of Irish migration, then, the aim of this book is to explore the strange, and mutually reinforcing, relationship between cultural stereotypes and social experience in the post-war years. I trace the evolution of a number of stock formations (including gendered stereotypes of the navvy and nurse) across a range of literatures, at the same time interrogating them for what they may tell us about experience both 'inside' and 'outside' those formations.

One way of interpreting the weight given to loss and tragedy in narratives of emigration is as a form of cultural memory. The emphasis on misfortune derived partly from a kind of folk memory of emigration during the period of the famine and after, when leaving home mostly meant leaving for good, and when the symbolic death of the young emigrant was marked by the 'American Wake' – a sending-off party. Post-war travel had immeasurably shrunk the distances between home and abroad – and mainland Britain was of course much closer than the United States – yet arguably the ceaseless reiteration of departures and short-lived returns reinforced a sense of hopelessness. Separation would always be part of Irish growing up. As the playwright Tom Murphy recalls of his home town in County Galway, repetition increased the emotional rawness of the experience:

> I think the most important feature of my growing up was the emigration from the family. Somebody always seemed to be arriving or going away. A lot of emotion centred around the little railway station in my home town of Tuam.[5]

According to Murphy, a significant portion of that emotion was expended on feelings of guilt. The emigrants of the '50s carried with them shame at having left Ireland and found a home with Ireland's traditional enemy, a sense of inferiority compared to those who stayed on native soil. 'They had a sense of being betrayed by the country of their origin here, but they also felt that they had betrayed that country.'[6] The ability to make it in England, and the willingness to take advantage of work, freedom from authority and all that the welfare state had to offer – free health care, free education, socialised housing, a unionised workforce – was freighted with guilt as much as pride, for it meant having run out on Ireland. These emigrants tended to cling to their national and religious identity, confirming to themselves that they were a people who didn't belong in England. But when they went back home they found they didn't belong there either: they were a people in 'limbo', still 'looking over their shoulders backwards' in the late '60s.[7]

Many contemporary commentators pointed out that these problems of adjustment paradoxically had to do to with the fact that emigration itself was relatively straightforward. There are numerous stories of people deciding to leave on the spur of the moment, jacking in poorly paid jobs one day and taking the bus the next, or travelling over with a friend who was returning to Britain after the holidays, as in this description of a young man from the Aran Islands:

---

[5] Des Hickey and Gus Smith (eds.), *A Paler Shade of Green* (London: Leslie Frewin, 1972), p. 225.
[6] Interview with Michael Billington in Nicholas Grene (ed.), *Talking about Tom Murphy* (Dublin: Carysfort Press, 2002), p. 96.
[7] Hickey and Smith (eds.), *Paler Shade of Green*, p. 227.

He brought a pal to the quay one evening on the cart. They went for a drink to pass the time while they were waiting for the steamer. In the end Cóilín went away with him. He left the horse and cart on the quayside. He left the house door open. He abandoned the dog even, barking after him on the quay.[8]

The journey over by train and boat could be done for less than five pounds, so that people left experimentally, planning to see whether prospects were any better across the water. They could always come back. But this meant that integration in British society was rarely a priority, and people could go for years shuttling back and forth between temporary lodgings in Britain and the family home in Ireland from which they became increasingly estranged.[9] The apparent contradiction between the tears on leaving and the ease with which it was possible to travel back and forth may not really have been a contradiction at all, but a consequence of the continual repetition of departure, the constant reminders of home.

The tension between established narratives of emigrant experience, and the day-to-day reality, in all its variety, is threaded right through the many stages of the migrant encounter. Differences had partly to do with gender – women tended to integrate more easily into British society, not least because they came in contact with it more often, at the school gate, for example. They had to do with personal drive and ambition, and the range of opportunities open to Irish migrants in different parts of Britain. Prospects for those in the more settled, family-based communities which developed around the factories of Birmingham, Luton or Slough were worlds away from the experience of the casual labourer, shifting between temporary camps and lodgings, housing workers building the M1 or the Isle of Grain power station. The ghettoisation of the Irish labourer was, to some extent, chosen, at least in the early years of post-war migration, when the idea of returning home to Ireland having made a packet really did seem possible, and attempts at integration appeared a mere waste of time. But discrimination against the Irish also played an important part. Unreliable, shiftless, drunken, dirty, in the early years flea-ridden – attitudes towards the Irish poor were conditioned by long-held prejudices against Britain's violent and ungrateful neighbours. Those given to bigotry and intolerance had after all recently been proved right about the Irish

---

[8] Richard Power, *Úll i mBárr an Ghéagáin/Apple on the Treetop*, trans. by Victor Power (Dublin: Poolbeg Press, 1980 [1958]), p. 145.
[9] See A. E. C. W. Spencer, *Arrangements for the Integration of Irish Immigrants in England and Wales*, ed. Mary Daly (Dublin: Irish Manuscripts Commission, 2011), where Spencer argues that 'the ease of return acts as a constant deterrent to integration in Britain' (p. 31).

bent towards low-down treachery, when Ireland had remained steadfastly neutral and refused to help Britain during the war.

The Irish were regularly described, in provincial papers, in company memos, in local council debates, even occasionally in Parliament, as lazy workers, unable to turn up on time or stick at a job, as benefit scroungers, as trade union trouble-makers, and as given to violence. On the other hand, they were just as likely to be praised for their willingness to work long hours and take on the hard physical tasks that were failing to draw the English working class. Behind both praise and blame lay fundamental differences in attitude towards time, labour, and even towards the physical body. Though the journey from a farm in the west of Ireland to London or Birmingham or Coventry was short, a vast distance was covered in the move from a still broadly pre-modern rural culture and community to modern, urban, industrial society. Much ink was spilt on both sides of the Irish sea on the need for (and dangers of) 'adaptation' to modernity, rather as though the Irish migrant was a member of a race which was threatened with extinction, and indeed the danger of 'race suicide' was never far from the language of conservative Irish commentators on the emigration crisis.

The difficulty for many of the poorer migrants was that they had been given none of the tools which might make adaptation possible – few were educated beyond the age of fourteen; many had experienced the world of paid employment only through seasonal agricultural work and odd jobs.[10] The lucky ones who got themselves apprenticed to a trade in Ireland were able to find themselves better jobs, if not necessarily higher earnings, when it inevitably came time for them too to emigrate. They generally did rather better in England. But there were plenty who argued that, almost for that very reason, it was better not to equip the Irish poorer classes with skills other that those that would fit them for life in an agricultural society. To train them as carpenters and fitters and mechanics was to train them for the boat. Irish men and women came up against a highly developed class system in Britain, exacerbated in many cases by racial stereotyping and – though they did not suffer to the extent of black migrants – racial discrimination. But they had been primed for it by an equally pernicious, if less visible, rigid social stratification at home – one in which their place was most often on the bottom. Irish parliamentary politics was not, and is not, determined by class in the way that it is in Britain. But the division

---

[10] Education in itself was no failsafe against emigration. In John McGahern's *The Dark*, the scholarship boys from the small farms know as their final exams approach that the options are either to 'get high honours, or go to England' (p. 118).

between what one historian has called 'the possessing classes' and 'the more vulnerable classes' was inescapable for all that.[11] The emigration of vast numbers of young Irish poor was regarded at best with complacency by those a few rungs higher on the social ladder, in safe jobs themselves. Some were happy to spell it out: it was only by ridding the country of large numbers of the unemployed that social revolution, or even social change, could be avoided. At their worst, Irish official attitudes towards the emigrants layered smugness on top of moral censure. The men and women who left Ireland in the '50s were turning their backs on a bleak future, with little prospect of steady employment, or marriage and homes of their own. They were castigated for their folly in abandoning the purity of Irish rural life in favour of the dangers of urban society, and for their greed in daring to prefer a disposable income of their own to slaving for a pittance on the family holding. Their moral failings were indistinguishable from national ones, for those not content with the frugal lifestyle available to them at home were guilty of deserting their nation. It took the major economic crisis of the mid-'50s, when the numbers of emigrants exceeded all previous records, and the sons and daughters of the better-off were also forced to take the boat, for attitudes to shift. For a time in the mid-'60s it was London teams (with London specially designated an Irish county) which took the All-Ireland trophies in the Junior Championships of the Gaelic Football league – there can have been few more damning indictments of the project of national independence.[12]

The migrants themselves – however much they may have eagerly embraced the materialistic society which offered them a living wage, the possibility of a home, healthcare, marriage, and education for their children – stayed oddly silent about the iniquitous social system which had forced them out. There were plenty of people ready with recollections of stuck-up local priests, self-important teachers, or arrogant employers in the farms, shops and factories they had left. There were some who refused ever to go back. But left-wing groups amongst the Irish in Britain who attempted to spotlight the causes of social injustice at home worked hard to gain support. Most people just wanted to get on with their lives, but they were also marked by the fact that, whatever the shortcomings of life

---

[11] See Lee, *Ireland 1912–1985*, where he argues that 'the interests of the possessing classes came to pivot crucially around emigration' (p. 374).

[12] The GAA saw London as key during this era, to the point that they hired Wembley Stadium from 1958–75 for an annual exhibition game, featuring two of the strongest Irish counties in both hurling and football. See Pat Griffin, *Gaelic Hearts: A History of London GAA, 1896–1996* (London: London Co. Board Gaelic Athletic Association, 2011); Mike Cronin, Mark Duncan and Paul Rouse, *The GAA: A People's History* (Cork: Cork University Press, 2009).

back home, they had lost it for good. Donall Mac Amhlaigh, who left Kilkenny in 1951, described a perspective probably shared by the majority of migrants.

> I knew that I'd miss the small ordinary things that I had been used to for so long: the company and the kind chat with the lads down at the corner every night; the good-fellowship and the gaiety of the poor people in the 'four-pennies' at the pictures on pay night; and the excellence of the pints in Larry's after closing time.[13]

They lived in the fissures between the knowable rural communities which had forced them out, and the urban industrial environment which allotted them a place, and they were not about to reject the past that had formed them. As one commentator has put it, 'many of the victims would continue to cherish the values responsible for their own plight.'[14] After all, they were leaving communities where the sense of belonging and kinship was in part derived from those values, where communal bonds often appeared to be at odds with the affluence associated with industrial society, even to be intensified by adversity. Thus the emigrants carried with them pride in the nation that had failed to provide for them. In time this was to develop into a sentimental attachment to their Irishness, and a nostalgia for home which was fed by annual holidays, and social gatherings fuelled by music and dance and drink. The word 'nostalgia' carries with it all sorts of negative connotations, of unreality, and of kitsch versions of the past. But the need to find ways of treasuring a world to which it was impossible to return was real enough. Part of the story of the Irish in Britain is about how the emptied-out Irish countryside became filled with meanings and associations which continue to determine our understanding of Ireland today. It is no accident that many of our stereotypes of Ireland focus on the characteristics of its people, for all that they were no longer there.

From the end of the war until the mid-'60s the Irish kept on coming. How they fared, and the likelihood of whether or not they would 'settle', changed dramatically over that time. By the mid-1960s the stark opposition between traditional and commercial ways of life had begun to break down, particularly in the increasingly urban environment of Dublin. The Anglo-Irish Trade Agreement of 1965 signalled the end of economic protectionism. Industrial development and the educational reforms of the 1960s created an entirely new economic situation for both the migrant

---

[13] Donall Mac Amhlaigh, *An Irish Navvy: The Diary of an Exile*, trans. Valentine Iremonger (Cork: Collins Press, 2003 [1964]), p. 3.
[14] Lee, *Ireland 1912–1985*, p. 385.

and the Irish person who chose to stay at home. Industrial progress in Ireland, and the expansion of secondary education towards the end of the decade, began to improve prospects for the young in search of work, and would eventually narrow the economic gap between the two countries. The advent of an Irish television service in 1961–2, though it was slow to expand into more rural areas, had a huge impact on a still relatively isolated society, as did the back-and-forth movement of the emigrants themselves. 'Traditional' Irish farming culture had long been underpinned by emigrant remittances which furthered a dependent relationship between the two economies. Now, in a strange twist, the empty rural landscape which was one result of emigration became the basis for a new form of commercial exploitation of the Irish in Britain. The emigrant Irish were encouraged to spend their money on nostalgic returns to the unspoilt landscapes which had failed to offer them a livelihood, returning to Britain at the end of the summer with a lump of Connemara marble in their pockets, and the imprint of the Blarney stone upon their lips.

***

These pages do not offer a social history of Irish emigration to Britain but attempt to access the lived experience beneath that history through an analysis of representations.[15] They are informed by a belief in the power of representations – from literary images to social stereotypes to the core assumptions of both Irish and British public opinion – to shape our understanding of experience, at some level to shape experience itself. The attempt to access experience, or even 'history', through representation may seem misguided, or doomed to failure, and it probably deserves further explanation.[16] There have been several absorbing studies of post-war Irish migration in recent years. Mary Daly's analysis of the social and economic background to Ireland's emigration crisis, and the political responses to it, has informed my discussion of the discourses of emigration, just as the work of sociologists, geographers and historians such as Mary Hickman,

---

[15] For the social and economic history of post-war Irish emigration, see Enda Delaney, *The Irish in Post-War Britain* (Oxford: Oxford University Press, 2007), and *Demography, State and Society: Irish Migration to Britain, 1921–1971* (Liverpool: Liverpool University Press, 2000); Mary E. Daly, *The Slow Failure: Population Decline and Independent Ireland* (Madison: University of Wisconsin Press, 2006); Ultan Cowley, *The Men Who Built Britain* (Dublin: Wolfhound Press, 2004); John Archer Jackson, *The Irish in Britain* (London: Routledge Kegan Paul, 1963); Kevin O'Connor, *The Irish in Britain* (London: Sidgewick and Jackson, 1972). For sociologically informed approaches see Mary Hickman, *Religion, Class and Identity: The State, the Church and the Education of the Irish in Britain* (Aldershot: Avebury, 1995) and Bronwen Walter, *Outsiders Inside: Whiteness, Place and Irish Women* (London: Routledge, 2000).

[16] For an influential discussion of theory and methodology in relation to this issue see Joan W. Scott, 'The Evidence of Experience', *Critical Inquiry* 17:4 (1991), pp. 773–797.

Bronwen Walter and Enda Delaney lies behind my interpretation of representations of Irish immigrants in Britain. But there are interesting tensions between the sociological and historical approaches. In 2007 Delaney
argued for the need for a detailed historical narrative of the settlement of
the Irish, to set alongside theoretically informed social science research
on migration and diaspora. Insisting that there was 'no universal historical experience of being Irish in post-war Britain',[17] his study emphasises
the diversity rather than uniformity of individual migrant experiences,
accessed through documentary sources but also oral history, memoir and
other forms of personal testimony.

Delaney's concern to uncover the heterogeneity of Irish migrant experience is well taken, and he delivers an impressive, multi-faceted account
of the history to which I am indebted. Yet the fact that the experiences
were different but the stories told about the emigrant and immigrant
Irish were remarkably similar is something that requires elucidation.
Why, despite actual differences in social background and social outcome
for individual migrants, did ideas, opinions and representations of Irish
migrants turn on such a narrow range of stock formations? Part of the
reason is that there were 'majority' experiences, at least in the early phase
of post-war migration: for the migrants themselves this included leaving rural or small-town communities for large urban industrial centres,
working in factories or hospitals, or as construction workers, and being
Catholic in a non-Catholic country; for employers, landladies and 'the
English' in general there was a similarly narrow range of forms of encounter, in the workplace, in digs, in pubs, in dancehalls, and for English
Catholics, at mass. But part of the reason is that the ways in which these
experiences could be interpreted had already been framed within a set of
narratives and stereotypes derived principally from Victorian discourses
of Celticism, related Revivalist idealisations of rural Ireland, and modernising Catholic discourses of (primarily female) Irish purity and respectability. Put crudely, the experiences of individual Irish emigrants were
overlaid by and fed back into fantasies, or to use a term with different
connotations, ideologies, of emigration, which helped shape the ways in
which those experiences could be understood. The impulse to explore the
mentality of migration cannot afford to ignore the ways in which both
the emigrants' understanding of their own situation, and the responses
of the British population to them, were bounded not only by their social
and economic situations, but also by a set of inherited tropes, amongst

[17] Delaney, *Irish in Post-War Britain*, p. 5.

which ideas of loss, tragedy, the untamed Irish, and the clash between innocence and materialism feature prominently.

As I have suggested, these discursive formations do not map themselves on to the complex and varied social history of immigrants in 1950s and '60s Britain in any straightforward manner. Yet in charting the evolution of formulaic patterns (types and stereotypes) through the population crisis of the 1950s and '60s I have been struck by the continuities between literary representations, popular depictions in magazines and newspapers, and public opinion articulated across a range of documentary sources. Let us take nostalgia for traditional peasant culture, and the fear that the destruction of rural communities through emigration entailed the loss of 'the best' Irish men and women – a set of concerns which I discuss in some detail in Part 1 of this book. These attitudes had long historical roots in ideological constructions of rural and urban Ireland which formed a key element of nationalist theories of Irish exceptionalism.[18] The idealisation of the peasant way of life was central to Sinn Féin and Gaelic League ideologies, at least in their popular forms, and had become closely knitted into independent Ireland's version of itself. There is a substantial body of literature devoted to unpacking the hold which representations (and critiques) of Irish Ireland had in the years immediately prior to the founding of the Free State.[19] From Douglas Hyde, to Patrick Pearse, to Synge, Yeats and Joyce, Irish revivalism – its contents and discontents – is central to an understanding of the literature of the period. The continuing hold of the ideal of rural Ireland throughout the Free State period has also been well documented, for example, through work on the Folklore Commission, or the Blasket island autobiographies, and their influence on generations of Irish schoolchildren.[20] For a number of post-war writers and thinkers it proved impossible to set aside this worldview, to set aside the belief that emigration in itself was anti-national maude in part a consequence of the failure of the Sinn Féin ideals of frugality and self-sufficiency to take hold among a weak and insecure rural populace. This broadly moral framework, couched in its most extreme forms as an ethical interpretation of the economics of revival, lay behind a good deal of post-war documentary and creative literature, although the fact that this was a moral rather than

---

[18] See Liam O'Dowd, 'Town and Country in Irish Ideology,' *Canadian Journal of Irish Studies*, 12:2 (1987), pp. 43–53.

[19] See, for example, P. J. Mathews, *Revival: The Abbey Theatre, Sinn Féin, the Gaelic League and the Co-Operative Movement* (Cork: Cork University Press, 2009); Declan Kiberd, *Inventing Ireland: The Literature of the Modern Nation* (London: Jonathan Cape, 1995).

[20] See, for example, Diarmuid Ó Giolláin, *Locating Irish Folklore: Tradition, Modernity, Identity* (Cork: Cork University Press, 2000).

economic argument was rarely openly acknowledged. Popular forms of art and entertainment such as the plays of John B. Keane and M. J. Molloy, popular songs, stories in *Ireland's Own* and articles in women's magazines, all attest to the continuing concern and confusion over the steady loss of the rural population, and the difficulty of thinking about it in new ways.

Ideas and images of rural purity, and the fall from a rural ideal into the compromises of urban, and later industrial, life, are hardly unusual. They form a core of English as well as Irish literary history. As Raymond Williams points out in *The Country and the City*, arguably they stretch right back to the Garden of Eden. The rural peasant and the urban immigrant are archetypes as much as they are reflections of 'real' experience, or even what Williams calls 'real history.'[21] Yet I take seriously Williams's warning that 'we have to be able to explain, in related terms, both the persistence and the historicity of concepts.'[22] For despite the archetypical framework in which these battles over representation are played out, each reiteration of the rural/urban divide does articulate something historically specific. In the case of the ideas and images of emigration that are my focus here, this means not only tracing their roots in inherited forms, but also accounting for the reasons why they maintain their prominence in the post-war period, despite their divergence from the 'real.'

Part of the answer lies in the nature of the post-war Irish economic and social crisis. The intense flurry of debate over the nature of the Irish community, which formed the background to the emigrant exodus of the 1950s, was one consequence of a period of exceptional crisis and change in the rural economy. Irish attitudes towards emigrants were obviously moulded in part by what appeared to be an unstoppable decline in the Irish population during the 1950s. Emigration was a feature of several European countries in the immediate post-war period, not to mention countries of the European colonial empires, but for the most part the transfer of population was taking place from areas considered to be overpopulated, and with the active encouragement and organisation of the governments concerned. In Ireland, by contrast, the steady decline in population from more than six million just before the famine, to fewer than three million in 1926, showed no sign of ending – quite the reverse. Until the Treaty of 1922 it had been possible to place much of the blame for Ireland's failure to thrive at England's door. Yet the policies pursued by the different governments of independent Ireland had not succeeded in

---

[21] Williams, *Country and the City*, p. 1.
[22] Ibid., p. 289.

halting emigration, even during the war, and it was commonplace for the opposition in the Dáil, the Irish parliament, to point to the continuing loss of population as proof of the failure of government. The association between emigration and tragedy was not simply rhetorical overkill. Rural communities *were* failing; and it was uncomfortably true that many of the poorer emigrants who left in the early post-war years also failed to better their situation in England. Beyond political point-scoring lay genuine anxieties about the effect of emigration on rural areas and, at least in some quarters, genuine concern for the young people unable to find a future at home. These anxieties were, not surprisingly, couched in the terms already available, including apparently common-sense beliefs in the necessity for rural revival, and the Irishness of a rural lifestyle.

Naturally, public opinion about Irish emigration did not remain static in the post-war period. Indeed, the large number of reports, articles, studies and literary representations of the causes, cures and experience of emigration is testament to the fluidity of attitudes towards it. In 1948 the new Coalition government, concerned to distance itself from previous 'complacent' attitudes to the scourge of emigration, set up a Commission whose remit was to analyse 'Emigration and other Population Problems.' Six years later the majority report of the Commission offered a relatively realistic assessment of the causes and possible cures for the leaching of the population out of rural areas. Noting that, for example, between 1926 and 1951 the natural increase in the population of County Mayo was more than twenty thousand, but that the actual population had dropped by more than thirty thousand (meaning that more than fifty thousand had emigrated), the report went on to argue:

> These statistics bring to light two matters of vital significance; first, that conditions in county Mayo failed to provide that economic expansion which would absorb the natural increase of the county, and secondly, that quite apart from the need to create more employment opportunities, in 1951 apparently fewer people were prepared to accept the standard of living attainable in county Mayo compared with the numbers prepared to do so in 1926 ... we are satisfied that, while the causes of emigration have been many and varied at different times, emigration has been due to two fundamental causes – the absence of opportunities for making an adequate livelihood, and a growing desire for higher standards of living on the part of the community, particularly the rural community.[23]

---

[23] *Report of the Commission on Emigration and Other Population Problems* (Dublin: Stationery Office, 1954), p. 131.

This cool assessment, balancing economic and social factors, was sustained through much of the majority report. Economic opportunities were vital, but as the report acknowledged, a further intractable problem lay with people's changing attitudes to their standard of living. Modern lifestyles, driven by consumer culture, were offering alternatives to traditional rural patterns, and further economic opportunities – more jobs – were only part of the answer. The majority report was sanguine about the inevitable consequences of differential standards of living: 'Modern technology can provide rising material standards of life more easily in urban than rural areas and hence, the world over, life in agricultural districts is proving less attractive.'[24]

The papers gathered over the six years of the Commission, political debates, journal articles, and letters to newspapers, offer plenty of evidence of the continuing purchase of the idea of emigration as proof of moral failure, or national 'defeatism.' But they also reveal the pressures on that attitude, and the growing force of a modernising nationalism which sought to offer an ideological alternative to corporatist and conservative forms of Catholic social thought, and practical alternatives to the problems of lack of economic prospects and social malaise.

The 1950s is often viewed as a transformative phase in modern Irish history, in which the post-independence conservative and isolationist nation-building project gave way to a new focus on economic modernisation. A key role was played by pragmatic, reforming civil servants and politicians such as T. K. Whitaker and Sean Lemass, alongside the policy innovations associated with Tuairim, an organisation dedicated to political and economic reform.[25] It is true that as the economic failure of the state deepened through the mid-1950s, and as 'the Irish exodus' gathered pace, the drive to more economic, sociological, 'evidence-based' explanations of the crisis also grew stronger. Moreover, as Anthony Spencer conceded in a 1960 report for the Newman Demographic Survey on 'Arrangements for the Integration of Irish Immigrants in England and Wales', within the Catholic church itself, a more 'realistic' attitude began to take hold. Rather than exhorting intending emigrants to remember their national duty, the hierarchy appeared increasingly ready to accept the economic laws which were forcing people to leave, and increasingly concerned to help them integrate as much as possible after their arrival in Britain. Organisations as various as

---

[24] Ibid., p. 132.
[25] See, for example, Tomás Finn, *Tuairim, Intellectual Debate and Policy Formation: Rethinking Ireland, 1954–1975* (Manchester: Manchester University Press, 2012); Tom Garvin, *Preventing the Future: Why Was Ireland So Poor for So Long?* (Dublin: Gill and Macmillan, 2005).

the Catholic Social Welfare Bureau, which set up an emigrant chaplaincy scheme from the late 1950s, the Legion of Mary, the Columban Fathers, as well as many individual parish priests, became involved in social welfare and missionary work in urban industrial centres. Emigrants were encouraged to integrate into their new parishes in England, to save their souls, but also to participate in the social and political life of the country more generally, to save their health and sanity.[26] Articles published in Catholic journals such as *The Furrow*, *Studies*, and *Christus Rex* were increasingly critical of the preparation provided for intending emigrants. The problem was not only poor religious preparation, which was leading them to lose their faith or 'fall' more disastrously once they left home, but also inadequate schooling and preparation for life. As late as 1967, a young priest engaged in welfare work with the Irish in Britain, Eamon Casey, lamented the fact that 60 per cent of emigrants were leaving with nothing beyond a National School education. Arguing for training in hygiene, deportment, how to dress, and how to speak clearly, he painted a depressing picture of the fate of many of these young people, ill-equipped to deal with the pace of modern industrial society.[27]

In discussing the ideological battles of the 1950s there is an inevitable temptation to side with those who appear to be the liberal, modernising and pragmatic reformers, the drivers of Irish economic progress. It is undoubtedly the case that, in the long run, the policy makers responding to the economic crisis in government departments had far more impact than the neo-revivalist thinkers concerned to preserve an unchanged rural small-farm economy. From a contemporary perspective, the conservative Catholic line on emigration, and the popular literature which promoted it, can read as a hopeless attempt to shore up the traditional values of a dying rural culture, without the economic backing to make it possible. But the temptation to dismiss the neo-revivalists as the rump end of an outmoded worldview, belated adherents of an Irish Ireland ideology which was inexorably losing ground to the liberal modernisers, is mistaken. For a start, such an approach fails to explain why their ideas, about the dangers of city and emigrant life, and the need to preserve traditional rural culture, took such strong hold in the 1950s. It fails to account for the popularity of the post-war literature of rural revival, and the relatively

---

[26] Spencer, *Arrangements for the Integration of Irish Immigrants*. As Mary Daly reveals in her careful edition of Spencer's report, overt criticism of the hierarchy was suppressed when the report was circulated. See also Kieran O'Shea, *The Irish Emigrant Chaplaincy Scheme in Britain, 1957–82* (Dublin: Irish Episcopal Commission for Emigrants, 1985).

[27] Eamon Casey, 'The Pastoral on Emigration,' *The Furrow* 18:5 (1967), pp. 245–256.

widespread acceptance of the narrative of decline through urbanisation, evident in newspapers, popular magazines, and testimony given to the Commission on Emigration.

***

Narratives of decline, of modernisation, of entrapment, of survival: this book traces the evolution of these narratives, and the characters with which they are peopled, across a number of post-war literary genres, including rural social problem plays, popular romance, ethnographic fictions, comedy and satire, realist drama and forms of modernist realism in visual art and film. They investigate the impact of emigration on Irish romanticism and Irish realism, and the transformation of narrative and dramatic modes under pressure from new constructions of family, community and labour.

I begin with writers who sought to deploy popular tropes of emigration in broadly propagandist works which were intended to persuade people against leaving. I focus in particular on the 'neo-revivalist' works of John B. Keane and M. J. Molloy, which I read in the context of developing popular public opinion on the emigrant crisis. One of the strangest critical assumptions about post-war Irish literature is that it does not address the issue of emigration.[28] It is true that apart from Donall Mac Amhlaigh's autobiography and some short stories (mainly by Irish language writers) the experience of waged work in Britain – the majority emigrant experience – is only lightly touched on in Irish prose writing. That said, it would require a particularly one-eyed perspective on the work of Edna O'Brien to argue that *The Country Girls* trilogy does not concern itself with urban migration, whether to Dublin or London.[29] The same is true of the work of Brian Moore and Maurice Leitch – perhaps only in John McGahern's early prose (barring the character of Elizabeth Regan) is the experience of the emigrant reduced to a textual trace. The truth is that almost no picture

---

[28] I refer here to accounts of 1950s and '60s Irish literature in particular. For example, see James Ryan, 'Inadmissible Departures: Why Did the Emigrant Experience Feature So Infrequently in the Fiction of the Mid-Twentieth Century?' in Dermot Keogh, Finbarr O'Shea, and Carmel Quinlan (eds.), *Ireland in the 1950s: The Lost Decade* (Cork: Mercier Press, 2004), pp. 221–232. However, there is a growing body of work on Irish diaspora literature produced in Britain, which has transformed our understanding of the landscape of post-war migrant literature, particularly writing produced from the 1980s onwards. Although I am indebted to this research, the methodological concerns of the literary history I wish to trace in this book differ somewhat from the work of diaspora literary theorists. See especially Liam Harte, *The Literature of the Irish in Britain: Autobiography and Memoir* (Basingstoke: Palgrave Macmillan, 2009); Aidan Arrowsmith (ed.), *Irish Studies Review. Special Edition: 'The Irish in Britain'*, 14:2 (2006); Tony Murray, *London Irish Fictions: Narrative, Diaspora and Identity* (Liverpool: Liverpool University Press, 2012).

[29] For a reading of O'Brien's representation of emigrant experience in the second two volumes of the trilogy, see Murray, *London Irish Fictions*.

of rural Ireland in this period is without its hopeful intending migrant, returned emigrant, letters from emigrants, or stories of disastrous ends in London or Birmingham. And emigration figures centrally in the popular literature of the period, including stories and serials in newspapers and women's magazines. It lies at the heart of the social problem plays of the 1950s, which were popular both on the Abbey stage and amongst the many touring and amateur companies who played to the small towns – plays by Keane and Molloy but also lesser known works such as John Murphy's *The Country Boy*, which enjoyed an extended run at the Abbey in 1958.[30] In these dramas of rural life, emigration is rarely limited to a colourful character or seamy story; instead the plots turn on attempts to prevent young people leaving home, or to keep them at home once they are back in Ireland for their holidays.

While much of this literature is invested in revivalist ideals which seem more fitted to turn-of-the-twentieth-century Ireland, it is also marked by a disillusionment which has more often been associated with the 'counter-revival.'[31] The popular dramatists targeted the failures of the state through a mixture of caustic comedy and sentimental tragedy, but they did so primarily in the name of an older, romantic view of peasant and small-town Ireland, which had very little in common with the critiques associated with *The Bell* and other literary journals. It may be for this reason that their work has been so often sidelined in the narrative of post-war Irish literature. Their romance devices and quasi-arranged marriage plots chimed with semi-official discourses on the causes and consequences of emigration, and in particular underwrote a narrow role for women as wives and mothers, however clever and forthright they were allowed to be. Arguably, because the dramatists worked closely with local audiences on the amateur drama circuit, these plays responded more directly to popular pressures. It is not simply that these works need to be read against the background of debates on the morality and economic costs of emigration, but that they form part of that background, part of the field of representations which in turn shaped the way emigration and individual emigrants were understood.

In questioning the idea of a historical background against which literary texts may be interpreted, I am arguing for a more dynamic model of the relationship between documentary and creative interpretations of

---

[30] John Murphy, *The Country Boy: A Play in Three Acts* (Dublin: Progress House, 1960).

[31] On the counter-revival see especially Terence Brown, *Ireland: A Social and Cultural History, 1922–2002*, rev. ed. (London: Harper Perennial, 2004).

contemporary experience, one in which ideas, images and ideologies fed off and reproduced one another across a range of discourses and artistic media. Yet certain distinctions remain. One of the most important is the distinction between 'emigrant' and 'immigrant' discourse, or between 'Irish' and 'diasporic' representations. Diaspora theorists have long argued for the need to understand the experience of migration as situated in multiple or twinned locations. In my reading of the literature of the 1950s I have attempted instead to stay close to contemporary understanding of the experience of migration, choosing to use terms such as emigrant and immigrant, rather than diaspora or displacement. I have divided the book into two parts, to acknowledge the distinctions between discourses. In the first part, I discuss representations of emigrants, and of the impact of emigration on Irish economic and social life, and my focus is on literature and documentary materials produced in Ireland; in the second I turn to representations of Irish immigrants, and the focus is on writing, painting and film produced in Britain, by and about Irish migrants. My purpose in maintaining these distinctions is not to dismiss the work of diaspora theorists, from whom I have learnt much, but to highlight issues of audience and community. The documentary and literary texts I analyse in Part I were for the most part directed at an 'internal' Irish community; they were part of a home-grown debate about rural decline, class and urbanisation which was fostered and made urgent by the emigration crisis. The ethnography, fiction, drama and film I discuss in Part II is far less certain, and more varied, in its conception of its audience. There is, first of all, the asymmetry that some of these works – Philip Donnellan's 1965 documentary film *The Irishmen*, David Lodge's 1960 novel *The Picturegoers* – are not by Irish writers at all, and are certainly not aimed at an Irish audience, although they nonetheless pick up on stock formations of Irish immigrants. But the 'external' perspectives offered by Donnellan or Lodge are simply more explicit examples of a generalised shift in English-based texts from the representation of varied classed and gendered types in portraits of Irish communities, to the representation of 'the Irish type' in England. In effect, it is a shift from 'typification' to 'stereotypification', where the stereotype feeds off a previous typological discourse developed for very different purposes.

That shift is one that I explore in Part II of this book. I analyse the attempt by ethnographic writers such as Donall Mac Amhlaigh and Richard Power to reflect on the ways in which discursive formations of the best (the most Gaelic) Irish men both fed into and cut across newer, more explicitly class-based constructions of Irish labourers in Britain. I discuss the self-conscious deployment of an Irish stereotype in tragic, satirical and experimental works by Tom Murphy, Anthony Cronin, Michael Campbell and others. I end with artworks which move beyond realist convention to explore, in late-modernist modes, the determining power of stereotype and representation itself, as the fraught relationship between the clichés and the historical experience of migration is brought centre stage. As I do so, I acknowledge there is of course no neat distinction between Irish-based and British-based formations. As I have suggested, the back-and-forth experience of the migrants is mirrored in the literature of immigration, which, while it is concerned to respond to new experiences through new narrative modes, also looks over its shoulder backwards, at the images, beliefs and ideologies of an earlier period. So, when it comes to rural nostalgia, there is no clear separation between the post-war literature of revival and the work of more self-consciously documentary, ethnographic and realist writers. Revivalist ideas and images of the rural peasantry are threaded right through representations of Irish immigrants in Britain, including in work by non-Irish artists such as David Lodge, Frank Auerbach and Philip Donnellan. As Anthony Cronin points out in his 1964 comic masterpiece, *The Life of Riley*, there were plenty of Irish writers in London, many of them attached to the BBC, who were happy to play up to the other-worldly aspects of the Celtic stereotype, the idea that the Irish avoided the worst effects of urban consumerism and industrial anomie. And there were plenty of ordinary Irish labouring migrants who had little option but to inhabit the drunken, violent aspects of Celtic exceptionalism.

Representations of Irish men and women in Britain recycle and adapt many of the images and ideas which structure Irish emigrant texts, but they also borrow from a broader range of sources. Like the ethnographic memoirs by Donall Mac Amhlaigh and Richard Power, concerned to record the experience of Irish labourers in England, Irish realist fiction was influenced by literary developments in Britain after the war, including the working-class realist novel, the vogue for documentary writing, and the British New Wave films of the 1960s. While it is true that the new wave of Irish prose writers in the 1960s owed something to the 'counter-revival' realism of Frank O'Connor and Sean O'Faolain, they owed much more to British working-class realism of the 1950s and '60s. At the same time the ambiguous class position of Irish migrants in Britain, neither securely part of the indigenous white working class nor clearly separated from it, meant that British documentary and realist strategies proved inadequate to express the experiences of the 'half-men' and women described by Tom Murphy.

Both positive and negative features of the caricature of the Irish depended on similar qualities, qualities which formed the core of the literature of emigration: physical strength in the male, purity in the female, verbal eloquence, and above all a resistance to the ordinary as it was defined in post-war Britain. The various ways in which these stereotypes were deployed and adapted by the writers and thinkers under discussion here can tell us something about the particular historical pressures to which they were responding. But they also shape our access to the past. The cultural stereotype is not merely a screen behind which lies the real experience of the immigrant, in some kind of pure state. Rather, it helps form that experience, and thus also what we can learn of it. This book is the record of my attempts to find a way both to acknowledge and to question the forms of recognition and misrecognition which shape the literatures of emigration.

PART I

Emigrants

CHAPTER I

The Best Are Leaving
Fitness, Marriage and the Crisis of the National Family

Let ye marry here for if ye marry foreign, your children will be foreign. If ye want your children to be Irish and of the same mind and knowledge and taste as yourselves, ye must marry in Ireland, and on the land of Ireland.

'Tis mortal hard for a farmer. The few girls in the country are spoiled with working in shops and towns.

M. J. Molloy[1]

I do not blame any young man, contemplating marriage, to leave the locality.... Of course you cannot get the present-day girls to work in the rural areas at all; they find the work too heavy. Consequently, they are all gone to England.

D. Kenney, Chairman Tipperary County Council[2]

The idea that 'the best' were leaving was a commonplace of twentieth-century Irish emigrant culture. Mid-century debates about the demographic crisis are punctuated with laments over the loss of 'the cream of the population', 'the pick of our people', 'the flower of the family', 'the finest of our men.' Like the later sobriquet, 'the brain drain', it was a cliché which could combine feelings of national pride with fears of deepening social and economic decline. Much more than a polite description of the merits of intending emigrants, it carried a warning over the cost to the nation of losing the best. One meaning of the best, in this scenario, was the most dynamic: those least willing to put up with the lack of opportunities on offer in post-war Ireland, those most determined to make something of themselves despite the challenges. As emigrants found work in British industrial cities, put in long hours in order to be able to send remittances back to their families, and returned on their holidays well dressed and

---

[1] M. J. Molloy, *The Wood of the Whispering*, in Robert O'Driscoll (ed.), *Selected Plays of M. J. Molloy* (Gerrards Cross: Colin Smythe, 1998), pp. 111–177.

[2] *Papers of the Commission on Emigration and Other Population Problems.* Arnold Marsh Papers, Trinity College Dublin, Transcripts of Evidence, TCDMSS 8307–8/1.

flush with money, their success appeared to prove the thesis that Ireland was losing those with the talents and potential needed to make good. Just what those qualities were was notoriously hard to define, however. Youth and health were axiomatic, but as the population crisis deepened during the 1950s, and the emigrant net was cast wider and wider, encompassing not just the children of poor farmers and labourers, but of more prosperous farmers, and even shopkeepers, local businessmen, and members of the professions, 'the best' could become code for subtle gradations of class and social status. It meant those from respectable families, with a good education, the social elite of small-town Ireland, who were never meant to form part of the emigrating classes.

But it could also mean the opposite. In other formulations, the best were precisely those who had never been touched by the comforts of town life and to whom the desires for respectability or educational success were largely alien: the 'peasant stock' of the western seaboard. The qualities of excellence held by these people had little to do with professional knowledge or entrepreneurial spirit. It was their physical strength and capacity for hard work which singled them out as the best, qualities which in turn were linked with a frugal lifestyle and a form of moral probity which was understood to spring from that. The long shadow of revivalist idealisations of Gaelic peasant culture falls across these post-war descriptions of west-of-Ireland emigrants, which counter subtle forms of class snobbery (the best as the best educated and most respectable) with subtle forms of 'racial' snobbery (the best as the most Gaelic and least corrupted by alien values). As several critics have demonstrated, aspects of revivalist thinking have their roots in Darwinist theories of racial typology, and fears of racial degeneration clearly inform post-war anxieties over the loss of 'robust rural stock' from Connemara and Mayo.[3] Indeed, the very idea that the population could be separated into superior and inferior types depended on forms of classification, including sub-racial typologies, derived from popular forms of Darwinism.[4] Thus, as I will go on to argue more fully, the best also carried connotations of being the most well fitted to the

---

[3] See John Wilson Foster, *Fictions of the Irish Literary Revival* (Syracuse, NY: Syracuse University Press, 1993); Sinéad Garrigan Mattar, *Primitivism, Science and the Irish Literary Revival* (Oxford: Oxford University Press, 2004); Gregory Castle, *Modernism and the Celtic Revival* (Cambridge: Cambridge University Press, 2001); Gerardine Meaney, 'Decadence, Degeneration and Revolting Aesthetics: The Fiction of Emily Lawless and Katherine Cecil Thurston', *Colby Quarterly*, 36:2 (2000), pp. 157–175.

[4] On the anthropological work of Haddon and Browne in the Aran Islands in the 1890s, see A. C. Haddon and C. R. Browne, 'The Ethnography of the Aran Islands, County Galway', *Proceedings of the Royal Irish Academy*, 2 (1891–1893), pp. 768–830; and the discussion in David Fitzpatrick, 'Synge and Modernity in *The Aran Islands*', in Brian Cliff and Nicholas Grene (eds.), *Synge and Edwardian*

environment. Put crudely, the men of Connemara and Mayo were the best because they had endured physical hardship, and they had therefore developed a mode of survival consonant with that hardship. Once this is understood, the fear of racial degeneration becomes easier to comprehend – the cry, 'the best are leaving', was really a lament that those most able to withstand the arduousness of the life of the Gaeltacht farmer were deserting that life. Who could replace them?

If one meaning of the best was 'those most fitted for survival', that still left considerable latitude over interpretations of fitness – whether physical, psychological, or moral. The best qualities of men and women were also widely divergent. The idea of the physical strength of rural emigrants was hardwired into stereotypes of Irish labourers, on both sides of the Irish sea. The same qualities which fitted men for strenuous labour on the small farms of the western seaboard also matched them to the work of digging and tunnelling through the construction sites of industrial Britain, as monikers such as 'the tunnel tigers' and 'the elite inside the tunnel' attest. Fitness as a discourse of genetics has a particular emphasis on reproduction, and it should come as no surprise that in the context of a demographic crisis, the best women should be those in good reproductive health. Nonetheless, the terms in which women's good qualities were discussed were rarely explicit about physical characteristics, in marked contrast to discussions of men. Instead, neo-revivalist descriptions of the kinds of women most fitted to the rural environment focused primarily on moral and psychological qualities: an ability to cope with poverty, disregard for comfort, and a stoical acceptance of their lot. Stoicism was key. Above all the woman who was to survive the harsh conditions of the postwar ten- or fifteen-acre farm had to be prepared to wait: for goods, a husband, or a home of her own. Like her brothers, the qualities to be prized in her were the opposite of 'the best' defined in terms of social status and middle-class respectability.

Arguments over the physical and mental fitness of the population were intimately bound up with debates about marriage. After all, it was no good just keeping people at home in rural areas; they also had to marry and reproduce. And if traditional small farm culture was to last, tough

Ireland (Oxford: Oxford University Press, 2012), pp. 121–158. On the 1930s Harvard Anthropometric survey, see E. A. Hooton and C. W. Dupertuis, *The Physical Anthropology of Ireland: Papers of the Peabody Museum of Archeology and Ethnology*, 30:1–2 (Cambridge, MA: Peabody Museum, 1995); John Brannigan, *Race in Modern Irish Literature and Culture* (Edinburgh: Edinburgh University Press, 2009), pp. 84–106; Robert Young, *The Idea of English Ethnicity* (Oxford: Blackwell, 2008); Catherine Nash, *Of Irish Descent: Origin Stories, Genealogy and the Politics of Belonging* (Syracuse, NY: Syracuse University Press, 2008).

women were as necessary as tough men. It was for this reason that representations of marriage were so closely tied with representations of emigration during this period. In what follows I explore some of the ways in which 'fitness' was understood, and its impact on ideas about emigration, marriage and rural depopulation in the '50s. I trace a number of attempts to classify, comprehend and offer solutions for the population crisis, focusing in particular on arguments over the optimum qualities of the population, and how these may be preserved. The contradictory and often confused shifts between physical, psychological and broadly 'moral' attributes were one consequence of the impact of the idealisation of 'Gaelic stock' on neo-revivalist and corporatist Catholic social thought. The best were the best precisely because they were most fitted by and for the Gaeltacht way of life, but the fact that they were leaving was a sign of 'national defeatism' or 'lack of will.' And while women were crucial to the idea of the strength of the population, they were also increasingly targeted as the weak link in the chain, the dangerous source of negativity and spinelessness.

'The Survival of the Unfittest'

Some of the bleakest moments in Patrick Kavanagh's 'The Great Hunger' are also the most understated, where the conversational idiom and colloquialisms seem to offer a breathing space to the reader, only to close down all possibilities of a future. One such is the moment when a voice recalls the presence of a young woman, only to realise that the possibility of marriage or a relationship are long gone, just as she herself is long gone from the locality:

> 'Remember Eileen Farrelly? I was thinking
> A man might do a damned sight worse ...' That voice is blown
> Through a hole in a garden wall –
> And who was Eileen now cannot be known.

The hopelessness of Patrick Maguire's existence, and the poignancy of his attempts to find creativity and fertility in the soil in lieu of personal fulfilment, have become touchstones for the critique of the failure of independent Irish rural society. As several critics have argued, the critical realist perspective on mid-century rural Ireland is memorably presented in Kavanagh's work. Frank O'Connor, for example, argued in *The Backward Look* that 'curiously, O'Faolain's influence [was] most strongly marked not on any novelist, but on the poetry of Patrick Kavanagh', which in

'The Great Hunger', 'turned sharply critical.'[5] The sociological turn in Kavanagh's writing is focused on the failure of marriage and generation. With the young women long gone from the rural community, and the old turned to barrenness and bitterness, the neutered life of farmers such as Patrick Maguire barely differs above and below ground. Kavanagh's vision has come to stand for certain aspects of the death of rural Ireland – the spiritual and sexual hunger of the small farm in the shadow of what by the mid-50s would be termed 'the vanishing Irish.'[6]

Such readings situate Kavanagh's work as one of the founding moments of post-war Irish realism, with its concern to excavate a common core of affliction in Irish society: the traumas of family violence, sexual abuse, clerical repression, and the patriarchal authoritarianism of rural Catholic Ireland in mid-century. I discuss 'The Great Hunger' in connection with post-war realist writers such as Tom Murphy elsewhere in this book. For now it is helpful to recall that Kavanagh also wrote a comic version of the failed rural marriage plot (in the novel *Tarry Flynn*), and produced a con-siderable number of articles, ranging from the critical to the sentimental, on rural marriage and community life for the *Irish Press* and *The Standard*, suggesting a more complex landscape of public opinion on the crisis facing the rural population.[7] The combination of realism, sentimentality and melodrama was characteristic of a good deal of writing on rural marriage and the rural family, including the work of Teresa Deevy, Maura Laverty and Edna O'Brien, whom I discuss in the next chapter. The attempt to find an accommodation between personal fulfilment and rural survival marks the most popular literary genres which tackled emigration, notably folk drama and the social problem play. These combined a broadly realist representation of the problems of the decimated rural community with a 'romance' solution to the crisis of Irish society. Dramatists such as M. J. Molloy and John B. Keane focused primarily on the broken community at home. The folk dramas and matchmaker plots characteristic of plays such as *The Wood of the Whispering* (Molloy 1953), *The Bachelor's Daughter* (Molloy 1956), *Daughter from Over the Water* (Molloy 1964), and *Many Young Men of Twenty* (Keane 1961) suggested that resolution and mending of the failed rural community was to be found through romance, which

---

[5] Frank O'Connor, *The Backward Look: A Survey of Irish Literature* (London: Macmillan, 1967), p. 141.

[6] See Patrick Kavanagh, 'The Great Hunger', in Antoinette Quinn (ed.), *Collected Poems* (London: Penguin, 2005); see also John Anthony O'Brien (ed.), *The Irish: The Enigma of the Modern World* (London: W. H. Allen, 1954).

[7] See Antoinette Quinn, *Patrick Kavanagh: A Biography* (Dublin: Gill and Macmillan, 2001), pp. 170–173, for discussion of Kavanagh's journalism and short stories on the ageing rural bachelor.

intervened in the cycle of emigration by keeping young couples at home in Ireland.

The use of static or natural types in these plays – plots hang on the fortunes of three suitors, in almost fairy tale fashion, for example, or revolve around the fates of different 'types' of emigrant – derives as much from social discourses around stock and class as the requirements of folk genre. Neither Keane nor Molloy could imagine an alternative to the ultimate goal of the fulfilled couple settling on the land, and their comic matchmaking plots turn on various devious means of encouraging the right fit between economic needs and romantic aspirations – as all good matchmakers should. Nonetheless these romances had their radical edge. Both playwrights were attempting to critique aspects of the traditional farm system – they were both keen on sexual enjoyment and on romance for its own sake, and they attempted to harness these, along with ideas of personal fulfilment, to the traditional match. And they both targeted the greed and selfishness of those who had already established themselves in rural Irish society. Again and again, the pressure to emigrate, the failure to marry, and the hopelessly mismatched expectations of young men and women are discovered to be the fault of the older generation. Moreover the presentation of the new state as an inadequate and repressive parent is often explored through single motherhood and illegitimacy – a sign of the failure to properly father the younger generation. To take just one example, in Keane's musical *Many Young Men of Twenty*, the central female character is an unmarried mother (the father has disappeared to England) who subsists by working in a bar and is abused by her employer's wife, in a quasi-parental role. The young man who loves her (not the father of her child) is forced to emigrate by his parents, who are looking for remittances. This pattern – the failure of the national family – is repeated across a large number of plays and novels of the period.[8]

Like much of the popular literature of the period, these plays register the tensions within contemporary conceptions of marriage, as traditional Catholic styles of moral theology came under pressure from newer 'personalist' ideas, in which marriage was idealised as a route to psychological and emotional wholeness. While both Molloy and Keane place value on the qualities of companionship and compatibility, neither playwright appears

---

[8] John B. Keane, *Many Young Men of Twenty* (Dublin: Progress House, 1961). Keane's 1959 play *Sive* offers a tragic version of a similar plot. Sive is illegitimate and has been brought up unhappily by her uncle and aunt after her mother died in childbirth. These 'parents' scheme with the local matchmaker to sell Sive in marriage to a rich elderly farmer, in return for several hundred pounds. Sive kills herself rather than endure the match.

comfortable with the idea that the successful marriage should be understood as an ongoing project, a journey from romance to greater intimacy and understanding enabling the family to prosper emotionally. Instead, marriage functions as plot resolution. This was in part a requirement of the genre, certainly, but it also signals a failure fully to comprehend or accept the values of personal self-fulfilment within marriage which were becoming increasing current, and central to a modernising Catholicism as much as to the discourse of romantic individualism.[9]

M. J. Molloy's 1956 comedy *The Bachelor's Daughter* is unusual not only in that it signals the problem of illegitimacy in its title, but for the fact that a poltergeist directs the action on stage. The play is set in a rural farmhouse in County Galway, and the action is precipitated by the arrival of a middle-aged woman and her young servant, Nan, into the locality. Nan's mistress, Kate, who is described as 'domineering and rough' has bought a small farm at a knock-down price for, unknown to her, it houses a ghost called Clurheen. When we meet Nan she is limping and bleeding from the bite of a dog, 'pale and rather thin and nervous.' Kate describes her as 'mentally affected', 'made by some side-of-the-road manufacturer. And her mother left her amongst the leaves, and there my married sister found her.' Despite this provenance, three local men immediately start trying to persuade young Nan to marry them. The poltergeist acts up (throwing the furniture around offstage) whenever anyone it thinks is unsuitable comes courting.[10]

The action turns on the question of whether Nan is, or is not, 'mentally affected.' Her mistress is keen to convince her, and everyone else, that she has some sort of congenital disease, from having been found in a ditch – she doesn't want her to marry so she can keep her a slave. The three suitors try to persuade Nan that she is sane, but this is not just chivalry on

[9] See Michael G. Cronin, *Impure Thoughts: Sexuality, Catholicism and Literature in Twentieth-Century Ireland* (Manchester: Manchester University Press, 2012), chapter 4, on post-war Catholic advice literature, much of which stresses the importance of intimacy and emotional wholeness, and on the formation of the Catholic Marriage Advisory Centre in the early 1960s. One exception to my argument that marriage tends to be limited to plot resolution is Keane's 1969 play *Big Maggie*, in which Maggie's domineering behaviour is shown to be the fruit of the long-term failure and disappointments of her marriage.

[10] M. J. Molloy, *The Bachelor's Daughter*, in *Selected Plays*, pp. 327, 330. The poltergeist was one of the devices Molloy employed for engaging the attention of rural audiences: 'The rural Irish audience is an Elizabethan audience. They're very tough – they come out for a night's fun and if they don't get it from the stage they'll make it for themselves in the auditorium' (p. ix). As Molloy discovered to his cost, urban audiences might be more particular. A later play, *Daughter from Over the Water*, was rejected by the Abbey Theatre because 'the directors were worried that the fake miracle would cause offence among Catholics' (p. xv).

their part. She is repeatedly talked about as the saviour of the rural locale, because she has not enough education to mind being enslaved to the work on a farm: 'Where else can I get a girl who's humble enough to wed into a farm between a bog and a river?'[11]

Humble she may be, but Nan is reluctant to marry at all unless her sanity can be proved. Her concern is over her genetic inheritance.[12] In one pivotal scene the town nurse arrives at the farm to assess her degree of illness. The nurse herself is described as useless for rural life – town bred and used to modern comforts, she threatens to marry the draper unless her farmer fiancé agrees to give up his land and start a construction business in the town. ('She's a deserter from the land of Ireland – like all the women around.')[13] Nonetheless she is presented sympathetically in her encounter with Nan: her modern training comes in useful as she argues that it is only cruelty, beatings and starvation which have made Nan seem unstable. In other words, the source of her trouble is her environment. In the language of Social Darwinism, Nan looks like the weak. She cuts a poor figure on stage – limping, bleeding, poorly clothed, barely socialised and starving. Yet Molloy implies that despite appearances Nan has all the qualities necessary for survival – she is physically able to endure the hard work of the farm because of the harsh way she has been treated. As a true matchmaker, the poltergeist finally gives his blessing to the returned emigrant as a suitable husband for Nan. He has also experienced harsh conditions, 'bulldozing through the London blitz, smothered in dust in the summer, and stuck in mud in the winter.'[14] He too has proved he has the characteristics necessary for survival. Meanwhile the weakness of the most eligible-looking bachelor (affianced to the nurse) is revealed when it becomes clear that he is 'afeard' of the ghost. Molloy twists the idea of the survival of the fittest; he argues in a backhanded way for the necessity

11 Ibid., p. 346. See also *An Lasair Choille*, a play by Caitlin Maude and Michael Hartnett, first performed in 1962 by Taibhdhearc Theatre, Galway. The play features a physically infirm old man who persuades his able-bodied servant Séamus that he does not have the 'mental ability' to emigrate to England.

12 Molloy suffered the long-term effects of tuberculosis, which caused his lameness, and, as I argue below, was influenced by the portrayals of reproductive fitness and ill health in the work of J. M. Synge: 'Without knowing, or as far as I can remember, hearing anything about the doctrines of heredity I surmised that unhealthy parents should have unhealthy children – my rabbit breeding may have put the idea into my head. Therefore, I said, I am unhealthy, and if I marry I will have unhealthy children. But I will never create beings to suffer as I am suffering, so I will never marry.' Synge in Alan Price (ed)., *The Autobiography of J. M. Synge* (London: Oxford University Press, 1965), p. 9.

13 A similar character, Kitty in *The Wood of the Whispering*, suggests that moving to the town is broadly equivalent to having 'gone foreign': 'I'm escaped from the land and from feeding pigs at any rate. I'm behind the counter in Gowlin's drink-shop.' *Selected Plays*, p. 132.

14 Ibid., p. 368.

of adversity – otherwise the population will become too soft to cope with rural Ireland.

Molloy acknowledged his debt to Synge, and in *The Bachelor's Daughter* he was clearly picking up on Synge's representations of physical and mental degeneration. The unadulterated racial distinctiveness of the Gaeltacht populations was axiomatic for much turn-of-the-century cultural nationalism. Synge's Aran Islanders were simply one example of a people blessed by

> the absence of the heavy boot of Europe [which] has preserved to these people the agile walk of the wild animal, while the general simplicity of their lives has given them many other points of physical perfection. Their way of life has never been acted on by anything more artificial than the nests and burrows of the creatures that live round them, and they seem in a certain sense to approach more nearly to the finer types of our aristocracies – who are bred artificially to a natural ideal – than to the labourer or citizen, as the wild horse resembles the thoroughbred rather than the hack or cart-horse.[15]

But such purity was always in danger. As Pegeen Mike points out ruefully in *Playboy*, the western world nowadays is a 'place where you'll meet none but Red Linahan, has a squint in his eye, and Patcheen is lame in his heel, or the mad Mulrannies were driven from California and they lost in the wits.' Her father argues he'd rather die than face the marriage of his daughter to the nervous Shaun Keogh: 'I'm a decent man of Ireland, and I liefer face the grave untimely and I seeing a score of grandsons growing up gallant little swearers by the name of God, than go peopling my bedside with puny weeds the like of what you'd breed, I'm thinking, out of Shaneen Keogh.'[16] The fear that the Irish population was not only dwindling but degenerating was crystallised by one early reviewer of the *Playboy*:

> Why is 'Pegeen' prepared to marry [Shaun]? 'God made him; therefore let him pass for a man', and in all his unfitness, he is the fittest available! Why? Because the fit ones have fled. He remains because of his cowardice and idiocy in a region where fear is the first of the virtues, and where the survival of the unfittest is the established law of life.... We see in [Shaun] how the Irish race die out in Ireland, filling the lunatic asylums more full from a declining population, and selecting for continuance in the future

---

15 J. M. Synge, 'The Aran Islands' in Arrowsmith (ed.), *Complete Works*, p. 323. See Nicholas Grene, *Synge: A Critical Study of the Plays* (Basingstoke: Macmillan, 1985) and David Fitzpatrick, 'Synge and Modernity' for discussions of Synge's awareness of and responses to interwoven aspects of primitivism and modernity on the islands.
16 Synge, *The Playboy of the Western World*, in *Complete Works*, pp. 70, 115.

the human specimens most calculated to bring the race lower and lower. 'Shaneen' shows us why Ireland dies while the races around us prosper faster and faster.[17]

Here lunacy is on the side of degeneration; but for Synge madness was also a figure for the strength of the imagination untrammelled by the dull, conservative impulse to get on in the world. Through his representations of madness (the violent raving of Old Mahon, for example), he both underwrote and questioned the Darwinian language of fitness. It was this nexus of ideas that Molloy took up, fifty years later, when it appeared that crisis point had been reached in terms of population decline. He used the issue of mental or psychological fitness to question the behaviour of those seduced by the modernisation of the towns, those who thought more of their money than greater survival, by which he implied the survival of the race.

There is nothing subtle about the way Molloy figures the relationship between physical and mental health in *The Bachelor's Daughter*. In one scene Kate persuades Nan to agree to be committed to the local asylum, and begins to school her in the deranged behaviour she will need to show when the asylum attendants arrive to collect her. Nan is being tricked by Kate, but her reasons for consenting to committal are partly rational: not only is she persuaded that there really is something wrong with her, but she also believes that in the asylum she will at last be properly fed. A similar play on 'rational insanity' drives *The Wood of the Whispering*, a companion piece to *The Bachelor's Daughter*, which is set outside the crumbling demesne of an abandoned Big House in 1950. The main character, Sanbatch Daly, once a bachelor farmer, has lost his house and farm to ruin and bad weather. Now in his early sixties, and living the life of a homeless tramp, he regrets his failure to marry. The play is peopled by lonely men and women, their health broken, their senses increasingly deranged.[18] The madness induced by the loneliness of rural life is debated

---

[17] 'Pat' [Theatre Reviewer], *Irish Times*, 30 January 1907. For a comparable dramatic text see also Padraic Colum, *The Land* (1905), in which the weaker children stay at home while the strong and intelligent leave. Colum, *The Fiddler's House: A Play in Three Acts, and The Land: An Agrarian Comedy* (Dublin: Maunsel & Co., 1909).

[18] There is an echo here of Synge's Wicklow journal, in which he argues that intense solitude leads naturally to the 'madhouse.' He meets an old man in the Wicklow Hills: 'We had nothing to eat at that time', he said, 'but milk and stirabout and potatoes, and there was a fine constitution you wouldn't meet this day at all. I remember when you'd see forty boys and girls below there on a Sunday evening, playing ball and diverting themselves, but now all the country is gone lonesome and bewildered, and there's no man knows what ails it.' J. M. Synge, *Travels in Wicklow, West Kerry and Connemara* (London: Serif, 2009 [1911]), p. 30.

throughout the play. One character, a girl home from England, argues that rural life is worse for a girl stuck in the country. A man 'can go drinking at night just as good as in England. But what can a girl do, or who can she talk to? There isn't a man keeping house in this village but is part crazy.' The local 'weak' character, Mark, replies equating 'craziness' with the pressure of life, and loneliness, in the rural environment: 'Isn't it you and your likes have made us crazy? Racing off to England and America after plentifulness of money and six nights dancing a week, and leaving us to do a man's work on the farm and a woman's work in the house. How can a man keep evermore working twenty hours a day?'[19] Mental illness and social malaise are calibrated with one another. But, as in *The Bachelor's Daughter*, 'lunacy' also appears in the play as plot device. Towards the end of the play, Sanbatch, the character most concerned to rejuvenate the dying community by encouraging marriage between young people, ties himself to a tree and feigns madness in order to gain admittance to the Ballinasloe Mental Hospital – as less shaming than the poorhouse. But the young couples save him from committal by agreeing to marry and give him a home.

The men from the asylum threaten at the end of *The Wood of the Whispering*, just as they do in Act 3 of *The Bachelor's Daughter*. In both plays renewal of the rural community comes from the 'mentally affected', or rather from those who feign mental illness. It is important to recognise that the behaviour of both Nan and Sanbatch is rational. Nan is tempted by the asylum because she is hungry; Sanbatch's raving is an act. Mark Finnane has argued of an earlier period that mental asylums were less feared than workhouses, and were used by families seeking to unencumber themselves of difficult relatives:

> To the extent that social structures in the West were progressively fragmented by the two-fold impact of emigration and a decline in marriage, the asylum may well have come to absorb some of the casualties of this process.[20]

It was a process that was hardly benign. The threat of the asylum was used as instrument of control, a way of getting rid of drunken, mentally disabled, or merely difficult family members. In *The Wood of the Whispering*

---

[19] Molloy, *The Wood of the Whispering*, in *Selected Plays*, p. 129.

[20] Mark Finnane, *Insanity and the Insane in Post-Famine Ireland* (London: Croom Helm, 1981), p. 163. See also J. M. Synge, *Travels in Wicklow*, p. 41: 'In Wicklow, as in the rest of Ireland, the union, though it is a home of refuge for the tramps and tinkers, is looked on with supreme horror by the peasants. The madhouse, which they know better, is less dreaded.'

Molloy turns this social practice on its head, as Sanbatch manipulates his community by threatening to enter the asylum. In the 'outlier' characters of Nan and Sanbatch, Molloy plays with a version of Synge's primitivism, but his concern is not so much with the qualities of imagination (deemed necessary to rejuvenate society) as of rural robustness. He repeatedly dramatises a battle between the qualities necessary for survival of the rural population and the disappearance of those qualities through town breeding.

The Bachelor's Daughter is a puzzling play, and outside the context of debates about emigration and rural depopulation arguably it makes little sense at all. One way of interpreting the play is that Molloy was attempting to criticise the language of 'fitness.' Nan and her suitor triumph over the social system, which is represented as an alliance between a repressive older generation and the institution of the asylum.[21] Molloy's own experience as a patient in Newcastle sanatorium in 1937, and his lameness from tuberculosis, surely fed into his concern with the meanings of health and fitness and with the intervention of medical experts. A comparable discussion of outmoded ideas of health and hereditary fitness occurs in Michael McLaverty's 1954 novel *School for Hope*. The central character, a newly qualified schoolteacher, Helen Byrne, takes up a new post in a rural townland in Northern Ireland. She is terrified that people will discover that both her mother and sister have died of tuberculosis. As in *The Bachelor's Daughter*, enlightened ideas – held by the various local authority figures, including the priest, the doctor, and the headteacher with whom she falls in love – battle against the superstitions and selfish motives of the local people. The headteacher's sister and housekeeper is against 'marrying into a sickly family':

> The whole affair is against right reason and sound judgement. It'd be madness to marry a girl of her stock. She has no charity in her to allow this to go on.... Miss Byrne doesn't spring from healthy stock![22]

But from the beginning of the novel the reader's sympathies are with Helen, and the selfish schemings of her fiancé's sister are eventually overcome.

McLaverty's novel pitches science (theories of infection) against popular understanding of heredity (theories of blood and stock) in a relatively

---

[21] Elizabeth Malcolm argues that the asylums were used to 'neutralise' strident members of the small farmer class, predominantly male rural labourers. See Malcolm, '"The House of Strident Shadows": The Asylum, the Family and Emigration in Post-Famine Rural Ireland', in Greta Jones and Elizabeth Malcolm (eds.), *Medicine, Disease and the State in Ireland, 1650–1940* (Cork: Cork University Press, 1999), pp. 177–194.

[22] Michael McLaverty, *School for Hope* (London: Jonathan Cape, 1954), p. 217. In Patrick Kavanagh's *Tarry Flynn* (London: Penguin Classics, 2000 [1948]), Tarry's mother tells him to give up dreaming of Mary O'Reilly as her family is consumptive.

straightforward fashion. The battleground is far less clearly delineated in *The Bachelor's Daughter*, though the play has an obviously propagandist intent. Molloy targets the selfishness of the older generation – Kate attempts to manipulate Nan and her suitors by drawing on popular theories of heredity, theories which are debunked by the nurse and the priest. Yet despite the language of modern medicine, and nurture rather than nature, the play as a whole underwrites the language of fitness. The harsh environment in which Nan has been schooled has developed in her the qualities she needs to survive. In terms of genre, Molloy was not quite able to detach his characters from theories of 'type', and the folk models from which he borrowed did not require him to do so. But the significance of Nan's brutal upbringing goes beyond genre. Like many late revivalist thinkers, faced with the unrelenting decline of rural communities, he could conceive of no alternative to bolstering the qualities which had allowed traditional communities to thrive.

Although popular theories of blood, stock and heredity were increasingly embattled by the 1950s (as Michael McLaverty's novel attests), they had by no means been surpassed. There is a strong narrative within contemporary Irish Studies which argues that the moral prescription of acceptable feminine behaviour in the mid-twentieth century, and the institutionalisation of women seen to have breached moral laws, stemmed mainly from the unfettered power of a particular form of sin-obsessed Catholicism. It would be foolish to deny that Catholic moral regulation played a major part – the Catholic hierarchy saw its task as controlling and regulating sexuality and procreation through moral prescription, exhortation and punishment. But this conservative Catholic discourse was threaded through with popular theories of heredity, race and environment derived from Social Darwinist thought, which furthered and anchored anxieties about the loss of particular kinds of stock from Ireland, the loss of particular 'types' of Irish men, and concerns about the sexual behaviour of women. It is in this context that terms such as 'race suicide', used of the population crisis (albeit in certain contexts a euphemism for contraception), have their meaning. There is a tendency within Irish literary scholarship to regard Victorian evolutionary science as something imposed on the Irish from outside (for example, in the work of Haddon and Browne in the 1890s, or later the Harvard anthropometric survey), or else as a particular concern of Irish Protestant intellectuals, including Synge, Yeats or Emily Lawless.[23]

---

[23] See, for example, L. P. Curtis, *Apes and Angels: The Irishman in Victorian Caricature* (Ann Arbor: University of Michigan Press, 1977).

But Catholic moral judgements were also bound up with distorted Social Darwinian arguments about fitness, weakness and the problem of urbanisation.[24] Molloy's unlikely plot was a small fragment of a propaganda war on the part of late revivalist and conservative Catholic thinkers, concerned to fight back against what they perceived as the unrelenting encroachments of modernity into traditional rural Irish society. It was a battle fought (and lost) across the large number of public forums which considered the problem of emigration during the 1940s and '50s, including the work of the Commission on Emigration and Other Population Problems, where questions of physical and mental fitness were keenly debated.

'The Moral Aspect of the Problem'

Public discussion of the post-war Irish population crisis generated a large corpus of works, including official documents, literary representations and personal accounts, which focused on the causes and possible solutions to the problem of emigration and on the men and women who were choosing to leave Ireland. As Mary Daly has argued, emigration gave rise to a wide variety of responses in independent Ireland. Elements in the Catholic hierarchy, as well as some politicians, liked to boast of the huge Irish population outside Ireland which maintained an international profile for both Irish national politics and the Catholic faith. Emigration was also economically useful:

> It provided a safety valve for both the state and Irish society, facilitating the perpetuation of large families and nonpartible land inheritance in a country that was incapable of providing sufficient nonfarming jobs for its children; it enabled Ireland to cling to the myth that it could remain a predominantly rural society; and by reducing the numbers claiming unemployment assistance and other social welfare payments, it saved considerable sums for the Irish exchequer.[25]

There were those who argued that the high rates of emigration should be considered normal, given the lack of productive power in the Irish

---

[24] See Gregory Castle, *Modernism and the Celtic Revival*, esp. pp. 1–39, for discussion of the manner in which 'Irish-Ireland nationalists internalised anthropological and colonialist assumptions about the Irish "race."'

[25] Daly, *Slow Failure*, p. 138.

economy. Ireland had no goods to exchange, only her people.[26] In addition, it was a cheap and simple way of getting rid of troublemakers. In a confidential memo the secretary of the Department of Finance described wartime emigration to Britain as a useful 'safety valve against revolution.' These views were not necessarily kept private. In 1953, a *Leader* editorial acknowledged that many politicians were not unduly disturbed by the emigration figures because '[i]f emigration were to be stopped tomorrow conditions favourable to social revolution might easily arise.'[27]

Levels of complacency were certainly high amongst the better-off classes, those who felt insulated from the effects of economic stagnation and decline, at least in the early post-war years.[28] But explicit defenders and apologists for emigration were a small minority. Majority public opinion broadly asserted that the population was in crisis, that the small-farm culture of rural Ireland could not survive the decimation of its people, and that the high rates of emigration only proved the failure of the independent Irish state. While wartime emigration to Britain could be explained away as the consequence of extreme circumstances, when the war ended and Britain's labour needs continued to draw the increasing numbers leaving Ireland, the problem of emigration began to feature significantly in Irish political rhetoric. In July 1946, Britain removed wartime controls on female employment, enabling women with valid travel permits to travel to Britain in search of work using a visitor visa (they no longer had to go through the British Ministry of Labour). As Daly argues, 'One of the unintended consequences of wartime travel permits was that they provided the first detailed statistics of emigrants to the United Kingdom by age and gender. The revelation that almost two-thirds of travel permits issued in 1946 were awarded to women, and that one-third of these women were in their teens, prompted widespread expressions of outrage.'[29] In October 1947, the Catholic hierarchy wrote to the Taoiseach arguing for, among other things, restrictions on the right to emigrate for those younger than eighteen.

[26] See, for example, James Meenan, 'The Balance of Payments', Lecture to the Institute of Bankers in Ireland, 23 November 1951. TCDMSS 8300/50–51.

[27] Daly, *Slow Failure*, p. 150. See also James Meenan's Minority Report to the Commission: 'In the short run at least, emigration has done a great deal to make life in Ireland more leisurely and less disturbed by class warfare. If it ended suddenly, that life would become much more competitive and much less remunerative.'

[28] See Lee, *Ireland 1912–1985*, pp. 373–387, for a trenchant analysis of the complacency and defeatism at the heart of the political establishment, and the reasons behind the reluctance to acknowledge the economic roots of the crisis.

[29] Daly, *Slow Failure*, p. 156.

The 1948 election was in part fought on the issue of emigration, with the new political party, Clann na Poblachta, led by Sean MacBride, leading with accusations that the Fianna Fáil government was actively encouraging emigration and had no alternative solution to unemployment. Each of the parties promised to tackle the problems of unemployment and emigration; shortly after it was elected in February 1948 the coalition government established the Commission on Emigration and Other Population Problems, whose brief was to examine the problems of emigration and rural depopulation and make policy recommendations.[30] The Commission solicited oral and written evidence from a very wide selections of 'experts', including minor industrialists, county councillors, representatives of employment unions, educationalists, state agricultural bodies, as well as interested individuals – among them the playwright M. J. Molloy.

The level of detail at which recommendations were discussed is striking – the necessity for growing fewer cooking and more eating apples, for example, the dangers of Secondary over Technical education (as less likely to fit youngsters for jobs in their local areas), the impact of Scottish and English trawlers on local offshore fishing, the loss of the country house dance, or the problem of English-speaking factory owners in the Gaeltacht. The Commissioners themselves constituted a broad church. They included former Republicans such as Peadar O'Donnell, the UCD economist James Meenan, the founder of the Central Statistics Office Roy Geary, conservative clerics such as Bishop Cornelius Lucey, Fr Thomas Counihan and Fr Edward J Coyne (these last both Jesuits), and the lay Catholic Aodh de Blacam. The Protestant representation comprised the Quaker educationalist Arnold Marsh, and several other leading Protestants including Rev. A. A. Luce, a Berkeley scholar and vice-provost of Trinity College, and Dr Robert Collis, who was at the forefront of public health in Ireland.

In addition to the evidence gathered by the Commissioners, and the often testy memoranda which they circulated amongst themselves, the Commission generated its own derivative forms of discourse, particularly when the report was finally published in 1954, and local and national

---

[30] *Commission on Emigration and Other Population Problems 1948–1954: Reports* (Dublin: Stationery Office, [1955]). Copies of many of the papers relating to the Commission are held in the Marsh Papers, Trinity College Library, Dublin. For a thorough analysis of the findings and reporting on the Commission see Tracey Connolly, who argues that the Commission's work 'brought to an end the utopian idealisation of life in rural Ireland, by starkly revealing the realities of people's circumstances' (p. 104): 'The Commission on Emigration, 1948–1954', in Dermot Keogh, Finbarr O'Shea and Carmel Quinlan (eds.), *Ireland in the 1950s: The Lost Decade* (Cork: Mercier Press, 2004), pp. 87–104.

newspapers, journals and magazines featured articles and 'symposia' debating its findings.[31] By 1954, the problem of emigration had become acute, and the population crisis was on the agenda in a number of different forums. Cause and cure were discussed in controversial books such as the collection of essays edited by the Notre Dame cleric John A. O'Brien and published under the provocative title *The Vanishing Irish*, the reports of the Catholic Social Welfare Bureau and other philanthropic and welfare organisations, articles in local and national newspapers, and – increasingly through the early 1960s – sociologically informed surveys such as the Limerick Social Survey, the Skibbereen Social Survey and a survey of rural immigrants in the capital, *New Dubliners*.[32]

As the number of different forums for debates on the problem of emigration proliferated during the 1950s so too did the arguments over what caused it and how to deal with it. There are clear distinctions to be made between the arguments put forward by trained economists and sociologists, for example, and the attitude of those for whom emigration, whatever the cause, constituted a national tragedy. Commissioners such as Bishop Lucey, Fr Counihan, Aodh de Blacam and others started from a belief that emigration inevitably meant loss for the individual emigrant. The emigrant narrative was a tragic one – it was couched in terms of exile rather than choice and opportunity. The narrative was tragic too in terms of the loss for the country as a whole, an idea encapsulated in the phrase the 'best are leaving.' A further characteristic was the tendency to analyse what was essentially an economic problem in cultural terms – the solution to emigration for the more conservative sections of the Catholic hierarchy was not the creation of jobs (which brought dangers of 'proletarianisation') but the encouragement of a more vibrant culture at home in rural areas.

---

[31] See, for example, Edward J. Coyne, 'Irish Population Problems: Eighty Years A-Growing 1981–1951', *Studies: An Irish Quarterly Review*, 43:170 (1954), 151–167; R. C. Geary, 'Some Reflections on Irish Population Questions', *Studies: An Irish Quarterly Review*, 43:170 (1954), 168–177; Michael Connolly, 'Rural Depopulation', *The Irish Monthly*, 79:942 (1951), 514–517; 'Symposium on the Report of the Commission on Emigration and Other Population Problems', *Journal of the Statistical and Social Inquiry Society of Ireland*, 19 (1955–56), 104–121; Most Revd. Cornelius Lucey D.D, 'The Problem of Emigration', *University Review*, 1:12 (1956–57), 3–10.

[32] See Jeremiah Newman (ed.), *The Limerick Rural Survey, 1958–1964* (Tipperary: Muintir na Tíre Publications, 1964). For comparable studies with a more clearly defined sociological methodology, see John A. Jackson, *Report on the Skibbereen Social Survey* (Dublin: Human Sciences Committee, 1967) and A. J. Humphreys, *New Dubliners: Urbanization and the Irish Family* (London: Routledge and Kegan Paul, 1966). The *West Cork Resource Survey*, undertaken by the Irish Agricultural Institute, though primarily quantitative in approach, does include some sociological discussion of demographics, particularly in section C, "Economic Aspects of the Survey Area" (Dublin: An Foras Taluntais, 1963).

The cultural and broadly moral framework in which post-war emigration was understood was particularly marked in discussions of female emigration. This was partly a matter of the moral welfare of women. A memo from the Department of Social Welfare in November 1948 enumerated the increasing numbers of girls leaving Ireland, from 10,609 in 1945, rising to 19,205 in 1946, 18,727 in 1947, and more than ten thousand in the first six months of 1948. The tone was anxious:

> The moral aspect of the problem is very serious. Reports are current that a great many young girls who emigrate to Britain become pregnant; many of the reports are alarming and tragic in the extreme.... Girls frequently go in response to advertisements to find that the work is not suitable and drift from town to town in search of employment.[33]

The target here was the 'materialistic and alien way of life' in Britain, for which young Irish girls were unprepared. More than fifteen years later a Radharc newsreel focusing on young female emigrants working in London's hotel industry strongly implied that it was only chance, bolstered by the work of a number of Irish chaplains, which kept girls from falling into prostitution.[34] Though the problem (such as it was) lay in their environment, the sense of moral danger became loosely attached to the women themselves. A characteristic of 1950s attitudes to emigration, clearly identifiable in many of the Commission documents but also a feature of conservative popular opinion in general, was a distinct reluctance to acknowledge that female emigration had economic causes. The majority Commission report acknowledged that the primary motivating force amongst women as well as men was the search for better money and conditions:

[33] Memoranda and Correspondence, TCDMSS 8300/12/1. The reason for the high numbers of female emigrants in the late '40s, popularly known as 'the flight of the girls', was primarily that in the last years of the war it had been somewhat more difficult for women to gain permits for employment in Britain than for men, and parents had been reluctant to allow their daughters to travel to cities and factories in danger of aerial bombing. For a few years the travel permits showed women 'catching up' with men, until a relatively even gender balance was achieved by the early 1950s. See also Caitriona Clear, '"Too Fond of Going": Female Emigration and Change for Women in Ireland, 1946–1961', in Keogh, O'Shea and Quinlan (eds.), *Ireland in the 1950s*, pp. 135–146.

[34] *Hotel Chaplain* (Radharc films, 1965). In a forthright use of montage the camera cuts from an interview with an English hotelier in Paddington lamenting the difficulty of keeping Irish girls in at night ('We found that after a very short period, they met other girls, the next thing that happens is they start to stay out at night, the hours get progressively longer, the results more or less unfortunate'), to panning shots of advertisements for sex posted in phone booths. The voiceover intones: 'The young girl [can be] started on the road which ends up on the noticeboard outside the local newsagents shop, a curiously worded advertisement followed by a telephone number.' The scene shows a number of calling cards: Young Lady Has a Single Room to Let/Would Suit a Gentleman/ For Appointment Phone LAD 1807; CUTIE-DOLL, For Sale, Ring BAY 1503.

Large numbers of girls emigrate to domestic service in Great Britain because they consider that the wages, conditions of work and also the status of domestic service in this country are unsatisfactory. Many others migrate because the opportunities of obtaining factory or office work are better than here, and in the nursing profession numbers leave the country because the remuneration, facilities for training, pension schemes and hours of work in this country are considered unattractive.[35]

But in the face of their own evidence the report went on to claim that 'the purely economic cause is not always so dominant' in female emigration, compared with 'improvement in personal status', and 'better marriage prospects.'

The tendency was to assume that women left Ireland not because they needed employment but because they were looking for husbands, and for an 'easier' way of life. As J. J. Lee argues, part of the problem was the inability of many politicians to appreciate the connection between employment and marriage. 'Emigrants essentially left for the chance of a job that would in turn give them a better chance of marriage than at home.'[36] It was certainly true that women were necessary for marriage, as Patrick Kavanagh's Paddy Maguire belatedly realises, although the idea that women, uniquely, were running off to England in order to find a mate was belied by the statistics. These showed that emigrating to England had the greatest effect on Irish male rates of marriage, who thereby revealed themselves happy to reject a life of extended bachelorhood if the right opportunity arose.[37]

Debates about the failure of marriage in post-war Ireland were, equally, debates about the failure of the Irish state. Marriage was a national imperative if the population was to thrive and expand, but what form of marriage should form the basis of the modern nation? The failure to acknowledge the connection between waged work and marriage was in part a consequence of the failure to understand the ways in which new conceptions of marriage, and particularly ideas of romance and personal fulfilment, were powered by economic change. The expansion of the labour market (through emigration but also through small-scale industrialisation at home) contributed to the redefinition of marriage as an economic unit and the lessening hold of the dowry system. Women were more and more able, and determined, to seek emotional fulfilment as

[35] *Commission on Emigration and Other Population Problems* p. 134.
[36] Lee, *Ireland 1912–1985*, p. 382. The worst year for Irish marriages was 1957, when they numbered only 14,700 (p. 360).
[37] See Spencer, *Arrangements for the Integration of Irish Immigrants*, p. 43.

well as financial security within marriage, as romance, sexual intimacy, and compatibility became increasingly accepted as rightfully part of the marriage contract.

The tensions and contradictions within the modernising marital ideal are perfectly caught in Kavanagh's *Tarry Flynn*, written in the 1940s, but portraying an earlier period in rural Monaghan. Much of Tarry's time is taken up with worrying about the various states of purity of the local women, from the 'amateur' prostitutes, the Dillon girls, to the seemingly sexually available Molly Brady, to the convent girl Mary O'Reilly. His sisters share none of his prudery and seem to have a far less difficult time throwing off the strictures of moral theology in favour of practical and pragmatic responses to their situation. His older sister Mary has no interest in the marriage proposal from an ageing neighbour, enjoys physical intimacy with the local rake, and goes off to the local town rather than accept the limited opportunities on offer in the country. As their mother explains,

> They're thinking of starting an eating-house in the town. Have a better chance of getting a man that way. Since she went to the factory May up the road has scores of young fellas after her. And even if they *are* barefooted gassans at least they're young hardy chaps.[38]

The link between employment and marriage may have been obscure to the politicians, but it seems to have been perfectly clear to many ordinary men and women.

The solutions adopted by Kavanagh's female characters were admirably pragmatic, but for that very reason they constituted a threat to traditionalist conceptions of community. Precisely because of the changes in the status and economic basis of marriage, concerns over the emigration of young women went much further than the simple requirement of marriageable and reproductive bodies. Women were accorded a particular role in the discourse of rural depopulation not only because of their function in the Catholic family, but also because female emigration was understood to undermine the rural Irish economy in a more fundamental way than the migration of men. This was an economy built on ideals of austerity and frugality, on a scarcity of resources which had to be handed down through the generations, and shared, often unequally, among peers. It was an economy which required of the population a stoical acceptance of their lot. Denunciations of women emigrants for desiring an 'easier' way of life, or for choosing 'improvement in personal status', were one way of articulating the fear that Irish people

---

[38] Kavanagh, *Tarry Flynn*, p. 121.

were becoming too soft, physically and 'morally', to cope with rural life. Patience and endurance – an ability to wait for marriage, for a wage, for a productive role – was, for a certain section of conservative Catholic thought, associated in itself with strength and fitness.

'The Weakening of Our Nationality'

In order properly to grasp the meaning of the language of weakness, whether in men or women, we need to understand the language of strength, as it was applied to the population crisis. As I have suggested, it was a commonplace of mid-century emigration that 'the best were leaving.' This idea crops up right across the literature of the period, whether creative or documentary, and it recurs constantly in the papers associated with the Commission on Emigration. What did 'the best' mean? At its most basic it meant those with energy. So the chair of Tipperary County Council wrote in to the Commission arguing, 'Invariably we find that the pick of our people leave the country. If it were possible to keep them at home, judging by their progress abroad they would considerably help in the building of their homeland.'[39] In a similar vein Miss Marion Green, who came from an area in Killarney where the average farm size was twenty-one acres, argued to the Commission that there was no point in starting small industries in the area: 'the people who are left would not bother; the cream of the population is gone.'[40]

The best also meant the most 'respectable.' Among the most revealing of the Commission documents are records of the Rural Surveys undertaken by the Commissioners in which they interviewed prospective migrants at labour exchanges around the country. As Stanley Lyon put it, 'The men interviewed at Waterford and Carrick-on-Suir were all of a very good type personally: they were neatly and cleanly dressed, whereas those presenting themselves at New Ross and Dungarvan were a much inferior type, shifty and suspicious.' And in Enniscorthy, 'The type of men seeking to emigrate were of poor physique, and devoid of ambition, the opposite of the type I met in Waterford.'[41] Roy Geary was told by Gardaí in Letterkenny that '"the best are going", and certainly we were greatly impressed by the fact that a very good type of boy and girl was going.'[42] Others discovered

---

[39] Transcripts and Evidence, TCDMSS 8307–8/1.
[40] Transcripts of Evidence, TCDMSS 8307–8/2.
[41] Rural Surveys, TCDMSS 8306/8.
[42] Rural Surveys, TCDMSS 8306/4.

those intent on leaving to be, variously, 'poor', 'intelligent', 'excellent' or 'shiftless' types.

This typology was partly a euphemism for class, with 'good type' code for the son of a strong or middling farmer, or someone from a respectable labouring family. In addition, the Commissioners were replicating the modes of classification used by British liaison officers who organised the direct recruitment of Irish labour for British factories and construction works throughout the war and early post-war years. These officers selected migrant workers on the basis of physical fitness, intelligence, education, and type of worker and those in the labour exchanges in Ireland would have naturally imitated this system.

There are certainly ways of rationalising this population typology as a form of class distinction, but its roots also lay in theories of the distinct racial characteristics of the true Celt or the true Gael. From the mid-nineteenth century, cultural nationalists had fixed on the remote western regions, and the islands in particular, as the home of an ancient Irish pre-conquest civilisation. At the turn of the twentieth century, Gaelic League ideology popularised the belief that pure Gaelic stock, the best type, was to be found in the more remote areas of the western seaboard, where it had not yet been adulterated or weakened by intermixture with and imitation of English ways. In part, the emphasis on purity and strength was a response to imperial misuse of evolutionary science to argue for the savage and primitive nature of the Celt. In the 1890s, George Sigerson targeted the claim that the Irish languished on a lower rung of the evolutionary ladder by claiming that 'the stock of Anthropoids never went through evolutions in this country. Whatever may have happened elsewhere, the beings who first leapt on our shores must have been the foremost in the developed attributes of manhood.'[43] Over time, revivalist idealisations of peasant culture and the 'primitive' way of life (Synge objected to the more 'civilised' areas of the Aran islands) became so common that the ideology behind them became invisible. They were bolstered by literary discoveries, such as the Blasket island autobiographies, and by the arguments of folklorists, that the richly imagined oral culture

---

[43] George Sigerson, 'Irish Literature: Its Origin, Environment,' in Sir Charles Gavan Duffy (ed.), *The Revival of Irish Literature* (London: Fisher Unwin, 1894), p. 64. Sigerson opposed theories of racial purity and later wrote that 'Irish literature is a literature of many blends, not the product of one race, but of several' (p. 109). On the inversion of imperial racial categories in revivalist thought, see Mattar, *Primitivism*, p. 12: 'The "virtuous" peasantry and the chivalric heroes of the Gael became inscribed in the ideology of nationalism precisely because they were monitory counter-images of the primitive origins of the race.'

of the old Ireland thrived in harsh physical conditions and was alien to urban culture.[44]

In general, the priests on the Commission and conservative lay Catholics such as Aodh de Blacam were more likely to use the language of physical and mental type, of breed, stock, and blood. As Fr Counihan put it bluntly: 'Every endeavour should be made not to allow the Gaeltacht and the County Mayo type of population to die out. They are a very fine stock and would be a great loss to the country.'[45] The Gaeltacht stock was regarded as 'very fine' because it was hardy and robust, strengthened through frugal and simple living. As countless revivalist tirades against the dangers of Anglicisation asserted, it was in danger not only from emigration but also from the 'weakening' effect of modern consumer lifestyles (associated with industrial England). The language of stock and type was extremely mobile, slipping easily from physical to psychological attributes: from bodily strength to 'weak moral fibre.' So, for example, de Blacam noted in his Rural Survey of Dundalk and Carrickmacross that 'England took our best, for mines and foundry', a fact which he glossed by explaining that 'men physically or morally inferior' were rejected.[46] Others insisted it was the morally inferior who were leaving. After conducting a number of interviews in County Clare, for example, Fr Counihan concluded that 'the wrong ones' were going, an opinion he glossed with the information that this meant 'too many agriculturalists', 'too many flower of the family, leaving cripples', and 'too many without the skill and training to get good jobs outside Ireland.' Here Counihan implied that the 'flower' of the family were untrained but able-bodied farmers, in other words, good physical stock. But he went on to list the psychological causes of emigration from County Clare as follows: 'the inferiority complex', 'poor idea of patriotism', 'wrong idea of purpose of life', 'modern craze for pleasure', 'little idea of duty of work and production', 'discontent with monotonous round of duties', 'no shame in idleness', 'no initiative.'[47]

How are we to account for this litany of weaknesses, found in those who above all Counihan would like to keep at home (since 'the wrong

---

[44] See, for example, J. H. Delargy, director of the Folklore Commission: 'Their fate is so hard: an incessant struggle with the stony, unproductive soil and the stormy Western sea, to where harsh laws had banished their ancestors three hundred years ago. Today these poor farmers and fishermen are the only guardians of an ancient heritage. In their Gaelic language, which is their own, and in the rich tradition, which they have preserved, lies the key to knowledge of an old world.' Quoted in Ó Giolláin, *Locating Irish Folklore*, p. 138.

[45] Rural Surveys, TCDMSS 8306/21.

[46] Rural Surveys, TCDMSS 8306/3.

[47] Memorandum, Fr Thomas Counihan, TCDMSS 8304/8.

ones' were leaving)? Throughout the various discourses on post-war Irish emigration the accusation of patriotic or 'national' weakness constantly recurs. 'Lack of nationalism' was a major theme in memoranda and evidence to the Commission, particularly from conservative religious and cultural groups such as An Rioghacht. To take just one fairly representative example of this view, the Comhdháil Náisiúnta na Gaeilge (an organisation dedicated to promoting the Irish language in the Gaeltacht) argued that emigration sprang primarily from cultural rather than economic causes. It was a matter of will:

> The reasons for the present exodus are not purely economic. If Ireland is the only country whose population has decreased sharply in the last century, she is also the only one whose people have largely abandoned their traditions and their nationality during the same period. The Comhdháil firmly believe that there is a distinct connection between the weakening of our nationality and the decline of our population. Unlike other emigrants, the Irish scarcely feel they are leaving home at all.[48]

As the Comhdháil went on to acknowledge however, money did have something to do with it. The problem was not the low standard of living in the Gaeltacht areas, but the fact that, because of infiltration from outside, people were no longer satisfied with that standard.

> Twentieth-century ideas have penetrated the Gaeltacht. No longer are the people satisfied to accept the frugality of past generations, or to suffer the austerity which they suffered. Present-day youth must smoke cigarette (*sic*) rather than pipe; must visit the cinema; must dress in shop-acquired clothes; must possess a bicycle. The provision of these amenities is beyond the income to be derived from the patches of infertile land which comprise the Gaeltacht farms.[49]

Though the language of stock and breed derived from racial typologies and arguably from farming practices, the danger to the stock was less physical than moral. The loss of national hardiness was associated with an 'English' or 'anti-rural' way of life. Frugality and austerity were being undermined by innovations as various as unemployment assistance, commercial leisure pursuits, and modern consumer culture, this last associated above all with women.

The discourse of type, stock and breed was, in part, a popular shorthand for signalling a hierarchy of social groups, a not-very-sophisticated way of articulating class distinctions, which brought along with it all the familiar

---

[48] Memorandum, Comhdháil Náisiúnta na Gaeilge, TCDMSS, 8305/17.
[49] Ibid.

assumptions about the moral failings of the labouring classes, summed up in accusations of greed, idleness and lack of initiative.[50] But there were also attempts to account for the problem of the 'weakening of our nation-ality' in a more thoroughgoing and 'scientific' manner, drawing on rela-tively well-worn theories of degeneration. Throughout the Commission papers there are long and detailed attempts to explain the diversity of the Irish population in terms of the impact of environment on the strength of the population, and on strength of character. Both Protestant and Catholic Commissioners brought forth arguments rooted in popular forms of Social Darwinism, to fuel debates and disagreements on public health measures, the limitation of family size, and the impact of urbanisa-tion on fertility and survival. Though popular theories of race, heredity, environment and mental and physical fitness informed both Protestant and Catholic attempts to respond to the population crisis, unsurprisingly there were clear distinctions between the two.

The Quaker Arnold Marsh, for example, was concerned to elaborate a theory of the impact of the weather and geographical location on the strength of the Gaeltacht population. His attitude was not far from W. B. Yeats's worries in 'Meditations in Time of Civil War' about the effects of a life of 'slippered' ease on his bloodline:

> And what if my descendants lose the flower
> Through natural declension of the soul,
> Through too much business with the passing hour,
> Through too much play, or marriage with a fool?

Marsh had no doubts about the problem of degeneration – if things are too difficult people give up; if too easy they decline, because we all need adversity to thrive. He offered life in Iceland as a model for 'the survival of the fittest.' In Iceland, he argued, 'there was an unusually strong element of natural selection in the propagation and survival of the race. Moral, physical, or intellectual weakness might lead to failure and failure might lead to death. Therefore weaklings usually remained unmarried, or did not live to maturity. Public opinion put a high value on hardihood, but it also recognised the value of things of the spirit.'[51] On the other hand, life in Newfoundland was an example of conditions being too soft – 'weakness

---

[50] Elizabeth Malcolm quotes one record of committal to Sligo asylum in 1898, where the doctor describes the inmate (who was engaged in a familial struggle over his wish to marry) as a 'very low type.' She notes, 'Middle-class doctors, predisposed to regard rural labourers as "low types" seem to have been unable to discriminate between the truly mentally ill, on the one hand, and those in rebellion against family stresses, on the other.' Malcolm, 'The House of Strident Shadows', p. 184.

[51] Memorandum, Arnold Marsh, TCDMSS 8304/12.

mattered less, as escape was easy.' Those who found conditions too inhospitable could move to the consolations of mainland Canada, just across
the gulf of St Lawrence. Applied to the Gaeltacht, the implications were
all too obvious – life in Donegal or the Aran islands should resemble that
in Iceland but it dangerously resembled Newfoundland's comforts, not
least because it was so easy to leave. This concern about easy conditions
echoes that of the conservative Catholic organisations (such as the claim
by the Comhdháil Naisiúnta na Gaeilge that 'The Irish scarcely feel they
are leaving home at all.')[52] A report drawn up in 1960 for the Newman
Demographic Survey made a similar point, though in this case the target
was the failure of Irish Catholic emigrants to participate properly in the
life of Catholic parishes in England. The report lamented the easy, 'experimental' manner in which many Irish emigrated, arguing that it inhibited
integration, as well as encouraging the feckless:

> England is so near, and it is so easy to return home, that emigration is
> approached experimentally; if they like work and life in England they will
> stay, if not they will go back home.... [T]he process of natural selection
> does not operate. Permanent, long-distance emigration does not attract
> the weak and feeble in any community – it captures the imagination
> of the bold, the enterprising and the hard-working. The known ease of
> return thus removes the fears of those unfitted to face the difficulties of
> emigration.[53]

Such points of inter-denominational agreement were outweighed by
implacable religious differences, however. Along with the other Protestant
representatives on the Commission, Dr Robert Collis and Rev. A. A.
Luce, Marsh became involved in bitter exchanges with various Catholic
Commissioners over the most favourable conditions for the survival of
the Irish population in general. Arguing that 'the ideal family is not the
large family but the happy Christian family', and rejecting the distinction
between natural and artificial means of contraception, they objected to
the fact that the question of contraception had not been examined by the
Commission.[54] If it was unlikely that the majority on the Commission
would, in the context of a crisis of depopulation, deem contraception an important or even relevant factor, the fact that the Protestant
Commissioners also argued that allowing divorce ('less sense of doom in
marriage') would encourage younger partnerships and early parenthood

---

[52] The enormous contradiction between this claim and the simultaneous emphasis on the tragedy of
emigration is discussed below.
[53] Spencer, *Arrangements for the Integration of Irish Immigrants*, p. 31.
[54] Correspondence, TCDMSS 8300/52.

no doubt made their arguments seem even further off limits.[55] But their desire to make the case for an 'optimum' rather than a 'maximum' population, given the means of subsistence, was clearly deeply felt. They accused the majority members of the Commission of 'complacent principles', arguing that advocating large families had the effect of subordinating 'the health and happiness of the human person to the lure of numbers.' Robert Collis, who had plenty of experience of the poor health visited on large families living in squalid urban conditions, put forward broadly neo-Malthusian arguments detailing the problems of 'inferior offspring' caused by too many pregnancies, and the effects of poor nutrition, over-crowding and infectious diseases on the health of those with the poorest standard of living.[56]

In some memoranda jointly drafted by Marsh and Collis these public health arguments slid into more overtly eugenicist proposals, including suggestions that the right to marry and bear children should be qualified:

> Excellence is properly sought for not only in character and environment, but also in health and bodily perfection.... It is as desirable and right to avert the occurrence of evil, so far as we can, as it is to overcome it when it has appeared. Physical education is useful in this. Breeding from selected stocks should also be considered.... The difficulty is to devise ways that will not conflict with the preference of young people to marry whom they please, – to devise ways that will result in their choosing to do what is best, and, when married, to have few or many children not wholly according to private desire. The promotion of marriages of the most desirable kind, and of a large number of children as the offspring of such marriages, might be pursued in the first place by financial methods, such as helped to bring about the arranged matches of the past. The deterrent to matches that held the likelihood of poor results could not so easily be financial. They may be especially difficult to deal with. Our duty is not to add to the sorrows of

---

[55] Memorandum, Arnold Marsh and Robert Collis, TCDMSS 8304/16.
[56] Correspondence, TCDMSS 8300/52. Collis's 1942 play *Marrowbone Lane* targeted the combined effects of poverty and slum conditions on working-class Dubliners. In his 1943 Carmichael Prize essay, 'The State of Medicine in Ireland', Collis emphasised the difficulties of providing effective public healthcare for 'the large poor family into which numerous children are born doomed to malnutrition and all the ill health and bodily pain which this means.... Social reformers seldom refer to [the problem] lest they be accused of advocating birth control by unnatural means. The solution is not easy. It consists, on the one hand, in wise limitation by natural means as taught by the Church, and family allowances on the other.' *The State of Medicine in Ireland* (Dublin: Parkside Press, 1943), p. 60. Collis later gained firsthand experience of eugenic experiments on children during the liberation of Belsen, where he adopted five orphaned children; he also played a leading role in transforming attitudes to cerebral palsy. He argued in his later autobiography that 'the only logical response to the Nazis' doctrine of the survival of the fittest, implying the elimination (murder) of the handicapped, is for society to support them in such a way as to give each handicapped child or adult the greatest fulfilment possible during his sojourn in our world.' Collis, *To Be a Pilgrim* (London: Secker and Warburg, 1975), p. 229.

unfortunate people, but to treat them with kindness, at the same time making it plain to them that procreation in their case must be regarded as an offence for which they may expect to be penalised if nothing else will stop them. Social and religious pressures can combine to deter them. Possibly financial inducements might be added. In extreme cases actual prevention may be the only course.[57]

Their claim, that 'Economic and eugenic considerations do operate in the minds of the public-spirited, and ought to continue to do so', should be interpreted in the light of the post-war development of eugenics and the theory of 'social hygiene' in Britain. As Greta Jones has argued, social hygiene emerged 'from a marriage between the hereditarian ideas of the late nineteenth and early twentieth centuries and the public health and sanitary reform movement of the nineteenth century.'[58] Forms of Social Darwinism which stressed heredity, fitness and racial progress merged with practical techniques of social management derived from public health concerns. By the post-war period, arguments claiming the influence of differential fertility on intelligence or the necessity for institutionalisation of the 'feebleminded' to protect the population at large were losing currency in the wake of public concern over Nazi race theory. In the late 1940s, under the influence of thinkers such as Richard Titmuss and William Beveridge, the British Eugenics Society became increasingly focused on welfare and public health as means of improving the population. Nonetheless, claims for the inverse proportionality between fertility and intelligence were sustained, so that, for example, the 1949 report of the Royal Commission on Population (the British equivalent of the 1954 Irish report) argued for a system of graded family allowances (offering more to the middle classes) as well as provision for middle-class educational expenses.[59] As Mathew Thomson has shown, rather than disappearing under the new conditions of the welfare state, eugenic ideas were 'translated' into new areas, including that of mental health:

---

[57] Memorandum, Marsh and Collis, TCDMSS 8304/16. The obvious comparison is with Yeats's notorious comments in *On the Boiler* (Dublin: Cuala Press, 1939), though the memorandum was written over ten years later: 'Since about 1900 the better stocks have not been replacing their numbers while the stupider and less healthy have been more than replacing theirs. Unless there is a change in the public mind every rank above the lowest must degenerate, and, as inferior men push up into its gaps, degenerate more and more quickly. The results are already visible in the degeneration of literature, newspapers, amusements.'

[58] Greta Jones, *Social Hygiene in Twentieth Century Britain* (London: Croom Helm, 1986), p. 5.

[59] Ibid., p. 143. Jones quotes the left-wing *Tribune* of 24 June 1949: 'someone palmed off on the Commission some rubbish about the comparative intelligence of different classes and they swallowed it hook, line and sinker.'

Eugenic anxieties also continued to influence the postwar debate over declining national intelligence. Although the mentally defective were no longer the centre of concern, the debate reflected the continuity of deep-seated moral, social, and eugenic fears that the mentally feeble, dull and backward – and more generally, the 'lower' orders – could not control their profligate breeding, and would therefore dilute the mental fitness of the whole population.[60]

For a host of reasons, the Catholic intellectuals on the Commission had no sympathy whatsoever with the variants of social hygiene put forward by Marsh, Collis and Luce. Not only were divorce and contraception doctrinally off limits, but the overwhelming dislike of 'planning' and state intervention in the social arena, and particularly in family matters which were regarded as the sole responsibility of the Church, rendered the arguments of the public health advocates null and void. Nonetheless, elements of the theory of the 'survival of the fittest', and the honing of characteristics of health and hardiness through just the right amount of environmental adversity, also lay at the heart of conservative Catholic discourse on population in the 1950s.

'Luxurious Living and Modern Sanitation'

There were three principal ways in which theories of racial stock and degeneration were taken up by the Catholic thinkers reporting to the Commission. First, there were the descriptions of prospective emigrants as 'poor physical type', 'poor mental type', 'weak type', 'excellent type' – forms of classification which I have suggested should be understood in part as euphemisms for class distinctions, but which were also a means of referring to those qualities deemed to be enhanced in traditional Gaeltacht communities. Either way, such terms were employed by Commissioners and others in an attempt to test the thesis that 'the best are leaving.' A second strand comprises suggestions for 'positive eugenicist' policies, such as payments to families where children were born to young women, with bonuses for a second birth within eighteen months, or fines for childless women over the age of twenty-five. Such policy recommendations, although not universally supported by the Catholic Commissioners, were

---

[60] Mathew Thomson, *The Problem of Mental Deficiency: Eugenics, Democracy, and Social Policy in Britain c.1870–1959* (Oxford: Clarendon Press, 1998), p. 281. As Thomson points out, the selection of C. P. Blacker, secretary of the Eugenics Society, to produce a plan for future mental health services, was indicative of the continuing reach of these ideas.

broadly similar to Italian and French pro-natalist policies of the 1930s and '40s. As Greta Jones has pointed out, the Catholic Church could live with a version of eugenics which avoided direct intervention in reproduction (whether by birth control or sterilisation) and which did not allow the state to intervene in areas of morality and marriage law which the church regarded as its own preserve. Thus pro-natalism was acceptable – mother-hood, pride in progeny, and the strengthening of the awareness of the social importance of marriage were to be encouraged. To be discouraged were decadence, individualism, pursuit of pleasure and amusement, par-ticularly in women, and the 'artificial' life led by wealthier classes which was leading to diminished fertility. Such anxieties were closely linked to the third strand of degeneration theory discussed by Catholic Commissioners and respondents to the Commission: the belief that the city in itself was a cause of racial degeneration.

Artifice and the 'luxurious living' available to those in large towns and cities were key to this version of degeneration – for they were understood to lie at the heart of both mental and physical weakness. In a 1951 memo to the other members of the Commission, Bishop Lucey complained about the draft of chapter 9 of the report, which laid out policy recommenda-tions to the government eager to find ways of solving the population cri-sis. These recommendations, Lucey argued, did not go nearly far enough:

> I may add that I find the omission of all reference to *rural population as the historic sole source of population increase* in this chapter as inexplicable. If we are even to maintain our present population and if the rural population continues to fall, where are the families of the future to come from? History shows that no urban population anywhere has ever maintained itself over three generations.... Urban populations do not replace themselves over the generations but dwindle and disappear, unless replenished with a constant stream of young blood from the countryside.... In so far as the rural pop-ulation continues to fall and the people crowd into the towns and cities ... it must be regarded as constituting a grave threat to our ultimate survival as a nation.[61]

Lucey was concerned not merely with the survival of a traditional rural way of life, but 'our ultimate survival as a nation.'

The idea that the city in itself was dysgenic was a classic of late Victorian eugenic theory, derived directly from arguments made by Francis Galton. In the 1870s, Galton had conducted a comparative study of the census returns of rural Warwickshire and Coventry, in which he claimed to

---

[61] Correspondence, TCDMSS 8300/53. Original emphasis.

have found that that the people of Coventry had only three-quarters the number of births of those in the surrounding countryside, from which he deduced that within three generations fertility in the cities would cease, unless continually renewed by 'new blood' from the countryside.[62] For Galton and his Victorian contemporaries the idea that the puny, effete town type lacked rural vigour was due to a combination of factors, including the decadence of city life, but also poor public health and the squalor of industrial towns. In the mid-century Irish Catholic discourse under discussion here, public health concerns had been almost entirely suppressed. They had become associated with 'negative' eugenical arguments for intervention in reproduction and the composition of the family (with non-Catholic arguments for contraception). What remained, however, was a strong belief in the detrimental effects of luxury on public health.

Although Bishop Lucey was in a minority on the Commission (he tabled a minority report because he disagreed with the main findings), in the oral and written evidence gathered by the Commission as a whole, his views appear far less isolated. M. J. Molloy sent in an extended written report in which he argued that 'the towns sterilize rural vigour.' Dr P. Moran, superintendent of the Mental Hospital at Ardee, County Louth, argued in his submission that Dublin was 'a cancerous growth on the nation', which was destroying the rural 'foundation stock.' He employed language clearly derived from popular versions of Social Darwinism:

> I think an urban population, even under the best conditions does not make for fertility and survival, and the luxurious living and modern sanitation, etc., do not effect any great change on conditions. I think all history has shown, even in the old civilizations with the best conditions then possible, that the easy living and conditions then achieved did not make for survival in a city.[63]

For Moran it was 'easy living', including the luxury of modern sanitation, which was the root of the trouble, not the poor public health and insanitary conditions targeted by Robert Collis. Though Dublin was a small city

---

[62] See Francis Galton, 'The Relative Supplies from Town and Country Families to the Population of Future Generations, Paper read before the Statistical Society, 1973', in *Inquiries into Human Faculty and Its Development* (London: Macmillan: 1883), Appendix B: 'It is well known that the population of towns decays, and has to be recruited by immigrants from the country.... The more energetic members of our race, whose breed is the most valuable to our nation, are attracted from the country to our towns. If residence in towns seriously interferes with the maintenance of their stock, we should expect the breed of Englishmen to steadily deteriorate.' On Galton and his influence see Greta Jones, *Social Darwinism in English Thought: The Interaction between Biological and Social Theory* (Brighton: Harvester Press, 1980).

[63] Memorandum, Dr P. Moran, TCDMSS 8305/18.

in global terms, it was large in comparison with the rest of Ireland, soaking up about one-sixth of the population, and it was for this reason that it could be associated with unlikely (and rather outmoded) qualities such as decadence and degeneration. Ireland appeared to have become 'top-heavy': 'the foundations, which should rest deep in the soil, are beginning to crumble', as the country 'panders to the gay life of a swollen metropolis.'[64]

Francis Galton and some of his followers were explicit that the science of eugenics was incompatible with Christianity. It was not that Bishop Lucey and others knowingly marshalled eugenic theory in their arguments for a healthy Irish stock; rather, that theories of fitness and weakness, strength and degeneration, had become unmoored from their Darwinian backgrounds and had so infiltrated popular understanding of population diversity and the effects of the environment on health and character that they appeared to be common sense. In particular, Victorian 'social hygiene' concerns over the effects of city life, industrialisation and modernisation had fed into the ruralist ideal beloved of Gaelic League and Revivalist ideologists since the late nineteenth century, and had been popularised by the writings of Douglas Hyde, Patrick Pearse and J. M. Synge among many others.

For this strand of Catholic 'degeneration theory', materialism caused weakening of the stock because it made life too easy. Indeed, it was possible to take this argument further and maintain that economic security in itself was bad for the race – because it was bad for families. Lucey maintained that 'the whole assumption that economic security for parents will ensure large families is not only groundless but positively misleading as well. In point of fact the poor, who have no fear of losing their social or economic status usually have large families, while the well-to-do, who have that fear, tend to have small ones.' It is worth briefly unpacking this statement, which has several strands to it. First, we might notice the reversal of ideas of strength and weakness. Strong families, by which Lucey meant poor ones, were willing to sacrifice their material well-being by having lots of children; weak families, in other words, more well-off, citified types, cared too much about material things and were unwilling to make such sacrifices. An ethical demand for individual sacrifice for the greater good was neatly mapped on to a political and economic discourse of self-sufficient frugality. Lucey was putting forward a marriage between Catholic and Sinn Féin ideologies with which we are relatively familiar.

[64] Fr Patrick Noonan in O'Brien (ed.), *The Vanishing Irish*, p. 48.

But his claim also depended on a belief in the efficacy of adversity – it was not simply that a frugal way of life was necessary in the circumstances, but that hardship was good for you. It was for this reason that Lucey denounced family allowances – the more money you put in a family's pocket, the more they had to lose, and you were in fact pandering to their moral weakness by making their lives more comfortable.[65]

Opposition to Browne's 1951 'Mother and Child Scheme', which would have provided free maternity care and healthcare for children up to the age of sixteen, regardless of income, is usually interpreted as a fear of state intervention in the family, a fear of socialised medicine, on the part of the Catholic hierarchy. It was certainly that. Yet for some thinkers the concern about medical intervention also sprang from a Social Darwinian belief in the benefits of the pressure of the environment. State aid was dangerous because it would inhibit the growth of a large healthy population by making conditions too easy.

Lucey was articulating the uncompromising Catholic view that a large population with a low standard of living was preferable to a small population with a higher standard, because '[h]uman life is valuable in itself', and those who trust in God will be provided for. As J. J. Lee has argued, the belief that emigrants were not really suffering from 'economic want' was deeply rooted 'among the more secure farming, business, bureaucratic and professional classes.' Accusations of unrealistic financial desires were a way of absolving themselves from responsibility for the poverty around them, though in reality 'the interests of the possessing classes came to pivot crucially around emigration.'[66] It would certainly be unfair to accuse men such as Bishop Lucey and Aodh de Blacam of complacency – they were fierce propagandists against emigration, and saw themselves as defenders of the small farmers who were being 'liquidated' by a combination of the forces of commercialised modernity and indifference on the part of the government. What they were witnessing was the death of communities and a way of life which they cherished, as the subsistence economy of remoter rural areas was increasingly overcome by an exchange economy with which small farmers were ill-equipped to deal.[67] Indeed, as James Meenan argued, all such people had to exchange was their labour

---

[65] This argument chimes with concerns voiced earlier by Sean MacEntee and Frank Aiken, that family allowances would have the effect of inducing 'the less fitted to marry at the expense of everyone else in the country', and that 'in order to drive the unfit into matrimony we are to drive the strongest, most enterprising, the best educated of our earners out of the country.' See Lee, *Ireland 1912–1985*, p. 183.

[66] Ibid., p. 374.

[67] See Chapter 2 for a fuller discussion of this issue.

power, so that in effect rural Ireland became part of the British labour market, furthering the emigrant cycle. Yet in the face of economic crisis, the conservative neo-revivalists offered little more than moral exhortation: if people were willing to accept a lower standard of living and eschew the luxuries of urban life, they would not need to emigrate. Their pronouncements must have sounded a good deal like complacency.

The idea that the population failed to maintain its fertility in the city was a version of pro-natalist eugenics – deriving from a belief that civilisation and decadence had reversed the evolutionary process, and there was a need for a return to virile and robust rural stock. But how did this theory account for the weak stock in the countryside, the 'poor types' discovered in County Clare and County Mayo? There were several dangerous routes through which the dysgenic decadent city could begin to creep into the country. Unemployment assistance was one of them. Like family allowances, the dole intervened in the natural process whereby the fittest thrived under the right conditions of adversity. In this view the dole was not merely no help against population decline in rural areas; it was actually counter-productive. As Marion Green argued of her area of County Kerry, 'Every boy at 18 cycles 20 miles to the labour exchange to register for his 'rights'', but the handouts only had the effect of 'injuring enterprise and self-reliance.'[68] Marsh himself, in a comment worthy of his most conservative Catholic opponent, argued against financial assistance to the western seaboard:

> Only an exceptional people could have survived in the Gaeltacht, but their exceptional qualities have been given to them by their conditions of life. If the hard struggle for existence is replaced by scheming for State charity, whether disguised or open, one of the reasons for keeping the Gaeltacht in existence will be removed.[69]

Such arguments – familiar enough today – went back to the introduction of the dole in 1935. As Micheál Ó Conghaile argues in his study of Connemara and Aran, there were two opposing views on state handouts within the Gaeltacht itself. Popular songs are one source of opinions extolling the benefits of the dole, as in the following lines by Dara Beag Ó Fátharta, a poet from Inis Meáin:

> Níor leite ghoirt mhín bhuí é, / It wasn't soft, salty, yellow porridge
> Ach arán breá is im air, / But good bread with butter,

[68] Transcripts of Evidence, TCDMSS 8307–8/2.
[69] Summaries of Memoranda, Congested Districts, TCDMSS, 8301.

Mairteoil agus caoireoil / Beef and mutton
Is pionta i dteach an óil. / And a pint in the pub.[70]

For the desperately poor in the 1930s, without income or farming land, the dole made a significant difference, enabling a line to be drawn between destitution and mere poverty. Yet many of the more educated members of the community argued (with familiar logic) that handouts could only sap the morale of the people, and that work should be provided rather than cash. Pádhraic Óg Ó Conaire's 1972 novel *Déirc an Díomhaointis* seems to have been written largely as a polemic against such state intervention: the title translates as *The Alms of Idleness*. Idleness bred laziness and a sense of defeatism:

> Ag druidim le hoifig an phoist dó chonaic sé slua mór fear ina seasamh le balla. Mheas sé ar dtús gur ar shochraid a bhíodar ach chuimhnigh sé ansin gurbh í an Mháirt í. Lá thar laethanta in Iarchonnacht – lá an dole![71] [Approaching the post office he saw a large group of men standing next to a wall. He thought at first that they were at a funeral but he then remembered that it was Tuesday. The most important day in West Connacht – Dole Day.]

By 1959, the Council for the Revival of the Irish Language (Comhdháil Náisiúnta na Gaeilge) could argue in their report that the lack of employment within the Gaeltacht, coupled with the availability of money, was harming the morale of local communities. There were frequent complaints that skills and the capacity for hard work were becoming lost as people chose to buy their fish from a shop rather than fish for it, or eat shop-bought bread and cakes rather than bake themselves. And by making the people soft, the dole ended up encouraging rather than forestalling emigration, perpetuating the vicious cycle:

> Shúigh agus mheall an imirce an óige as, agus an té atá fágtha níl ag cur imní air ach an *dole*. Táthar ag éirí as curadóireacht, as cearca, as ba bainne, as glasraí. Bainne as veain a bhíonn ag formhór na dtithe anois. Faoi dhó

---

[70] Micheál Ó Conghaile, *Conamara agus Árainn 1880–1980* (Béal an Daingin, Conamara: Cló Iar-Chonnachta, 1988), p. 174. Translation by John Dillon.

[71] Pádhraic Óg Ó Conaire, *Déirc an Díomhaointis* (Baile Átha Cliath: Sáirséal agus Dill, 1972), p. 41. Earlier in the novel Ó Conaire laments the lost art of hard work: "Is geall, is ar éigean atá a fhios ag aon fhear ar an mbaile seo anois céard é lá crua oibre. Údar bróin é ar bhealach nuair a chuimhneofá ar a dhéine a d'oibrigh an dream romhainn; iad ag éirí le giolcadh an éin chun sliabh a shaothrú. [It's for sure that hardly any man in this place now knows what a hard day's work is. It's a sad subject in a way if you remember how hard our ancestors worked; getting up at the bird's chirp to cultivate a mountain] (p. 37). Translation by John Dillon. See also Máirtín Ó Cadhain, *Cré na Cille* (Baile Átha Cliath: Sáirséal agus Dill, 1949), where one of the grave-dwellers insists that another could only afford a plot because of the dole.

sa tseachtain a thagann an vein, í lán de bhuidéil bhainne. Deirtear gur feabhsú ar an saol é, ach ar bhealach éigin níl a fhios agam. [Emigration has coaxed and taken the young, and those who remain are not concerned with anything but the dole. They are giving up tilling, hens, milking, and growing vegetables. The majority of houses now get milk from a van. Twice a week a van comes full of bottles of milk. They say that that is an improvement on life, but somehow, I'm not sure.][72]

It was not only the dole which had made a difference to those wanting to buy their milk from a shop. Emigrant remittances were transforming the lives of family members left behind in Ireland and disrupting a social system built on fine gradations of status and respectability. Cash, whether spent in the grocers, or kept in the Post Office, was beginning to enable the poorest labourer families to 'hold their heads up' in provincial town society.[73]

For conservative Catholics and Gaelic League traditionalists the encroachment of the cash economy was a threat to a whole way of life. More liberal thinkers such as Peadar O'Donnell shared these concerns about the destruction of rural communities, though they strongly objected to the worldview which held that such communities could only survive by maintaining the poverty and social vulnerability of the poorer classes. Belief in the value of moral exhortation was fiercely attacked both from within and without the ranks of Catholic social thought. Canon John Hayes, founder of the Limerick-based rural renewal movement, Muintir na Tíre, for example, strongly defended the value of modernisation, mechanisation and electrification in rural areas, arguing that increasing the levels of comfort and leisure in the countryside was a Christian duty. When giving oral evidence to the Commission, he was challenged by Fr Counihan to agree with him that the loss of the small farm and large family with its 'spirit of hard work' was a loss to rural Ireland. 'Is the idea not creeping in of getting something for nothing?' Hayes's reply was a retort, 'Not slavery, I hope!':

> Of course my experience of the 15 acre farmer is that he worked and lived in slavery. You saw a poor woman with 8 or 9 children, most of them babies, with, perhaps, another expected, milking cows, feeding the hens, and looking after her husband and children.... It's all very well to talk about hard work but these people often worked from 7am–11pm.[74]

[72] Ó Conaire, quoted in Ó Conghaile, *Conamara agus Árainn*, p. 182. Translation by John Dillon.
[73] See John Healy, *Death of an Irish Town*, p. 24. In a final impassioned speech at the end of his 1962 play, *Hut 42* (Dixon, CA: Proscenium Press, 1968), John B. Keane asks his audience to count the human cost of this financial security: 'Every time, boy, you see a sad-faced Irish woman handing an English pound to an Irish shopkeeper, bow your head' (p. 40).
[74] Transcripts of Evidence, Muintir na Tíre, TCDMSS 8307–8/12.

The forms of national 'weakness' that I have discussed in this chapter were understood to have two related causes. First, there was the increasing impact of softer ways of life, associated with the cash economy, and including the dole, shop-bought goods, and commercial leisure activities, all of which encouraged the desire for a standard of living which could not be met on the traditional small farm. As I discuss in the next chapter, this form of consumerist weakness was associated above all with women. The second cause of weakness can be usefully summarised as the 'Newfoundland thesis' – the belief that a spirit of national defeatism had affected everyday life in rural areas because it was now so easy to leave them, in an 'experimental' and offhand manner. Both claims spoke clearly of feelings of anxiety and powerlessness in the face of encroaching modern social structures – rural towns, Irish cities, and British industrial centres were all too proximate for comfort, and becoming increasingly so. The contradictions which lay at the root of these fears were glaring. Since the mid-nineteenth century the majority of the population had lived in towns, rather than in the country, so that the discourse of rural exceptionalism was really one of nostalgia. If it was so easy to leave rural areas, why did young men and women face their impending journeys with dread? Why the feelings of loss and disenchantment? And if rural life was becoming so easy why did people want to leave anyway?

As Canon Hayes was at pains to point out, the problem was not that life was too easy but that the small farmer was being left to fend for himself in unrelenting poverty. It made no sense for him to forgo the wages to be earned in England. It made no sense for his family to turn their backs on modern comforts. Hayes's description of the privations of poverty echoes Paddy Maguire's 'fourteen-hour day', except that Hayes's farmer has a wife, physically worn out by childbearing and the toil of the small farm. It is this future for which Molloy's character Nan, the bachelor's daughter, has been fitted. Who else, other than someone who has never known comfort or affection of any sort, would be 'humble enough to wed into a farm between a bog and a river?' Poorly fed, beaten and abused, with no education, and no experience of ease let alone beauty or luxury, she may be the only type able to survive the adverse conditions of rural life.

It is hard to imagine that Molloy offered his blueprint for saving small farm Ireland seriously – the abuse Nan suffers is graphically shown on stage, underlining the cruelty of a system which requires the stamping out of all signs of individuality and self-fulfilment, at least in women, to survive. Nan's fitness for survival is both physical (she is strong enough for the hard work of an unmechanised farm) and psychological (she has no interest in luxury). Thus she may look like the worst, but she is the best, the most able to endure. While Molloy's portrayal of the ideal wife appears less than flattering, it may also have been intended as a defence of rural girls against the values of the urban middle classes, and particularly urban middle-class professional women. As I discuss in the next chapter, ideals of cleanliness and housewifely propriety were one of the means by which a form of modernising 'good housekeeping' was intended to ameliorate levels of rural poverty and embed aspirations towards a higher domestic standard of living.[75]

The character of Nan, like the various strictures against luxurious living that I have discussed in this chapter, are best understood not as recipes for rural renewal but as representations of impasse. In the absence of economic solutions to the population crisis, conservative thinkers focused on the moral (and morale) aspects of the national emergency. The matchmaker plots of playwrights such as Molloy and John B. Keane were to prove a literary dead end in the 1950s, because the problems could not be solved by pitching the desire for a family farm, however poverty stricken, against the desire for a decent standard of living. As I discuss in Chapter 3, arguably the genres which could answer the crisis were invested in a realism which was economically driven, and about labour rather than love. By contrast, the character of Nan appears as a cry of rage against the disintegration of traditional values and a social system which was still cherished, but whose decline seemed inexorable. For all their denunciations of 'national defeatism' and 'lack of will' therefore, the traditionalists shared in the general feelings of hopelessness. They had nothing to offer but exhortation. The fatalism of the emigrants who saw no alternative and took the train and boat through their tears, the indifference of the older generation, the complacency of the possessing classes, the moral appeals of the traditionalists – arguably these were all responses of the defeated, to whom no practical solution seemed viable.

---

[75] See Caitriona Clear, *Women of the House: Women's Household Work in Ireland, 1922–1961* (Dublin: Irish Academic Press, 2000).

CHAPTER 2

Pink Witch
Women, Modernity and Urbanisation

'Now why do you young people all write about sex now and don't write about money?' and long ago, he was talking about George Eliot, one knew when reading a novel, what that person earned and, you know, who brought the coal up.

Edna O'Brien[1]

Recently my wife had some trouble with a recalcitrant maid who threatened to leave and go to England to take up nursing.

Dr William Doolin[2]

Mary had been going to the convent and Tarry knew that convents taught girls to appreciate the poetic things.

Patrick Kavanagh[3]

We still know too little about the expression of sexuality in nine-teenth- and twentieth-century Ireland to judge the nature of its repression.

Maria Luddy[4]

In a suggestive series of comments in *Ireland: A Brief History of Change*, Roy Foster argues for the link between feminism and secularism in Ireland, defining them as the joint impetuses behind the transformation of attitudes towards authority, and particularly the authority of the Catholic Church, over the last three or four decades. 'Traditional conceptions of Irish society certainly could not survive the revolution in Irish women's attitudes that gathered speed in the early 1970s.'[5] Patriarchy and the Catholic Church were 'under siege' from feminism and secularism after 1970.

---

[1] Edna O'Brien, in Nell Dunn, *Talking to Women* (London: MacGibbon and Kee, 1965), p. 75.

[2] Arnold Marsh Papers, Trinity College, Dublin. Transcripts of Evidence, Irish Nurses Organisation, TCDMSS 8307–8/11.

[3] Patrick Kavanagh, *Tarry Flynn* (London: Penguin Classics, 2000 [1948]), p. 58.

[4] Maria Luddy, *Prostitution and Irish Society, 1800–1940* (Cambridge: Cambridge University Press, 2007), p. 6.

[5] Roy Foster, *Luck and the Irish: A Brief History of Change c. 1970–2000* (London: Penguin, 2007), p. 40.

Foster acknowledges that there were disjunctions between these movements. For example, he argues that the beginnings of the transformation
in attitudes towards the church reach back to changes in Catholic devo-
tions set in train by Vatican II in the 1960s. Then there was the impact
of the mass media, travel, youth culture (arguably, in different ways,
consequences of the Second World War, and the emigrant culture of
the '40s and '50s). These modernising pressures were paralleled by pressure for change in the role and legal status of women, put in train both
by the political establishment, in the guise of the Commission on the
Status of Women which reported in 1972, and by a more radical women's
movement, the most important branch of which was the Irish Women's
Liberation Movement – so that from the 1970s it was possible to point
to significant liberalisation in the laws affecting women and sexuality: the
availability of contraception, the repeal of the marriage bar, the right to
divorce, and, more recently, access to information about and the right to
travel for an abortion.

In this view, shared by many feminist thinkers, the transformation of
women's lives and the changes brought about by secularism are all aspects
of the same process of modernisation. Indeed, in pinpointing the 1970s
as the period when the revolution in Irish women's attitudes 'gathered
speed', Foster acknowledges that the bases for that revolution had been
laid down in the years under discussion here, the 1950s and '60s. There
are good reasons for assuming that historical change for women goes hand
in hand with economic modernisation. Pragmatically speaking, economic
development and social liberalisation, which characterise any advanced
capitalist society, require the equalisation of women's role in society and
the increasing participation of women in the workplace. What is striking about Foster's formulation is not the link drawn between economic
development and the shifting balance of power for ordinary women but
the underlying assumption that women's lives are a better index of modernity than men's. Part of the reason that change for women can be so
easily subsumed under a rubric of economic liberalism is due to the very
specific ways in which women and economic modernisation have been
yoked together in Ireland. Since the Enlightenment, the social status of
women has been used as an index of progress, with all its ambiguities, by
those both for and against it. This is true not only of arguments concern-
ing women's access to the workplace outside the home but also their association with consumerism and with the enjoyment of the fruits of capital
for their own sake. Foster's argument recalls a long history of associations

between women, commerce and modernity in Ireland – and it is a history which is full of contradictions.

Modernisation does not happen more to one gender than another, though admittedly it may be more visible in relation to women, as shifts occur from the family to the workplace, for example. Arguably, the process has been associated so strongly with women precisely because the ambiguity of attitudes towards women's roles is more apt to express ambiguous attitudes towards modernisation as a whole. It is not that women 'stand in' in any simple fashion for the process, but that equivocation and uncertainty characterise both sides of the symbolic equation. One strand of this study focuses on the ways in which the shifting correlation between women and modernisation – whether positive or negative – has been played out in the literature of independent Ireland. In the last chapter I discussed the role of women as saviours of the rural community through marriage in adversity, or frugal romance. Here I discuss not the association between women and austerity but between women and commerce, including commercialised sex. That association, strongly represented though it was across a range of documentary, journalistic and literary discourses, was far from straightforward.

The relationship between female sexuality and commerce, or capital, lies at the heart of some of the most well-known realist texts of mid-century Ireland, including work by Frank O'Connor, Sean O'Faolain and Kate O'Brien: according to members of the literary Censorship Board, it was responsible for the fact that much of this work was banned. In a much-discussed Dáil debate in 1942 the chairman of the Board criticised Irish novelists for turning out stories 'padded out with sex and smut', to appeal to English publishers. Another senator on the Board insisted that the young writers had only themselves to blame if they got banned, for seeking higher sales 'by pandering to the lowest instincts of human nature.'[6]

It was certainly unfair to these writers to suggest that they were 'padding out' their stories with unwarranted sex in order to boost sales. But there may be a case for arguing that some of the sex was extraneous to plot, making an intervention that went above and beyond literary motivation. This should not surprise us, given the social critical edge to much of this writing, the clear intention to mount a liberal realist challenge to

---

[6] *Seanad Éireann*, v. 27, 18 November 1942. http://historical-debates.oireachtas.ie/S/0027/S.0027 .19421118o0006.html. For further discussion of this debate, see Clair Wills, *That Neutral Island: A History of Ireland during the Second World War* (London: Faber and Faber, 2007), chapter 8.

the Free State orthodoxy on women's role in the national family. Writers such as Sean O'Faolain and Frank O'Connor – the most well known of the realist short story writers in the period – chose to undermine images of chaste and wholesome femininity not by exuberant tales of women's power and sexual control but by stories of sexual corruption, disillusion and violence. Sordid affairs, sexual dysfunction, prostitution: above and beyond the realist impulse these representations of debased sexuality are emblematic or even symbolist in nature, much like the portrayal of the prostitute in Joyce's *Portrait*, or the gallery of destitute women and unmarried mothers in George Moore, indeed derived from these representations. Yet while images of debased sexuality may have stemmed from turn-of-the-century realist prose, the neo-realists (much like the neo-revivalists) turned them to very different account. While Stephen's encounter with the prostitute in *Portrait* signifies an opening to the unconscious (her tongue presses upon his brain), for later writers, images of commercialised sexual exchange became primarily a way of signalling the corruption and failure of the Free State.

Moreover, throughout the realist writing of the '30s and '40s we find sex associated with 'abroad', and particularly with France. In the work of self-consciously liberal writers, a character's ability to speak a few words of French, or the ownership of a few French books, was a marker of dissatisfaction with provincial Ireland. In a particularly gothic scene at the beginning of Sean O'Faolain's 1940 novel *Come Back to Erin*, reading Maupassant in Cork cathedral heralds a drunken interlude with a pimp and a visit to a brothel. The bitter tone here is similar to that in Frank O'Connor's 1944 story, 'The Star that Bids the Shepherd Fold', which also couples French books and sex, as the local curate is dragged from his bookshelf to 'rescue' two local girls working as prostitutes on a French boat in the harbour. The implication in both these works is that provincial Ireland has stifled creativity and intellect to such a degree that only corrupt versions of sexuality thrive.[7] In addition to the fact that there does indeed seem to be something gratuitous about these representations of sex, we might also notice the way that the association between women and commerce is being used to undermine that between women and the purity of a national tradition. This particular critique of Catholic nationalist Ireland has fed directly into contemporary debates, not least through the currency of Sean O'Faolain's particular Bloomsbury left-liberal critique of the static and stultifying

[7] See Sean O'Faolain, *Come Back to Erin* (London: Jonathan Cape, 1940); Frank O'Connor, *Crab Apple Jelly: Stories and Tales* (London: Macmillan, 1944).

nature of independent Irish society. The argument is configured as one between liberal realist modernisers and narrow Catholic nationalist traditionalists, with women's sexuality caught between the two.

It is not difficult to mount a feminist critique of O'Faolain or O'Connor. One could argue that to protest against stifling tradition through tropes of women's sexuality as 'exotic' (French), or commercialised, is an indication of not really having come to terms with women's sexual autonomy. It may be that a critique of contemporary mores on the basis of women's sexual independence was simply not on the imaginative or political horizon at that time. Yet one other aspect of these, mostly male, representations of corrupt sexuality is worth mentioning here: that is the way that they pick up on the widespread contemporary discourses of corrupt sexuality in society at large.

There has been a great deal of analysis of the images of ideal womanhood that underpinned the cultural construction of independent Ireland; indeed, I have offered a version of it in the previous chapter, arguing that representations of 'ideal' femininity (even if, like Molloy's Nan, they looked rather less than ideal) were one battleground chosen by the corporatist Catholic social order to fight the impact of modernisation and urbanisation. As Maria Luddy has argued of nineteenth- and early twentieth-century Ireland, narratives of debased sexuality were in part a means of expressing anxieties about the changing nature of Irish society. Concerns about what appeared to be rising levels of immorality, and high rates of illegitimacy and venereal disease, led to a conflation between unmarried mothers, sexually active young women and prostitution in official discourses. The fear over declining moral standards was underwritten by parallel concerns over the need for stricter censorship of the cinema and the immoral press, and stricter controls over dancehalls, contraception, and other invitations to sexual laxity. The 'ideal' Irishwoman was the means by which the Catholic Church could limit the impact of modernisation, and save the 'traditional way of life.'[8] Yet, as Luddy has also shown, one of the consequences of the association between chaste femininity and national purity was, paradoxically, the vast amount of information and writing about corrupt sexuality. Detailed discussion of 'amoral' sexual practices made up the bulk of several government reports, such as the 1926 report

---

[8] Luddy, *Prostitution*, p. 195; see also Maryann Valiulis, 'Neither Feminist nor Flapper: The Ecclesiastical Construction of the Ideal Irish Woman', in Mary O'Dowd and Sabine Wichert (eds.), *Chattel, Servant or Citizen: Women's Status in Church, State and Society* (Belfast: Institute of Irish Studies, Queens University of Belfast, 1995); Diarmaid Ferriter, *Occasions of Sin: Sex and Society in Modern Ireland* (London: Profile Books, 2010).

on venereal disease, and the 1931 report of the Carrigan Committee on juvenile prostitution (which interpreted its brief broadly, investigating the availability of contraception, and the behaviour of single girls, as well as a number of sexual crimes, including incest). The findings of these reports were rarely openly discussed in the Dáil, but public concern about amorality was fed by newspaper reports of sexual crimes, as well as publication of clerical sermons and Lenten pastorals (for example, on the dangers of dancehalls and joy-riding). In *Tarry Flynn* the arrival of a Catholic mission to an area comprising mainly 'old unmarried men and women' has the effect of galvanising old and young in talk of sex:

> She told how a certain girl was raped and another one half raped,
> while Mrs Flynn clicked her tongue, not looking at all displeased.
>
> It was a story of life in a townland of death.
>
> As far as Tarry could gather from his mother's talk about the Mission,
> she had hopes that the Missioners' condemnation of sex would
> have the effect of drawing attention to it.[9]

In true Foucauldian fashion, one consequence of the intense regulation of sexuality was a similarly intense discussion of sexuality. It may be that liberal representations of sex should be read not only as oppositional to but also as echoing public discourses about sexuality.[10] The realist challenge to neo-revivalist representations of rural Ireland depended on the neo-revivalists' own discourse of corruption.

The practice by realist writers of marshalling images of degraded and commercialised sexuality for their critique of the Free State suggests that they too were relying on the forms of classification, and notions of 'type', whether couched in terms of class or more subtle forms of distinction, which were informing the public analyses of sexual behaviours. The discourse of blood, stock and 'nature' hovers around their descriptions of those who have breached moral laws, even if the reader is encouraged to question their attitudes towards them. In Mary Lavin's short story 'Sarah', for example, the sympathies of the reader are all on the side of Sarah, the small-town 'fallen woman', and against her employer, the comfortably off Mrs Kedrigan. But the two women are paired types nonetheless, allowing Lavin to explore the contrasting values of middle-class respectability

---

[9] Kavanagh, *Tarry Flynn*, p. 29. Nearly all the characters in the novel are obsessed with sex, on the one hand, and the difficulties of catching a husband or wife, on the other.

[10] For satirical rather than realist takes on contemporary sexual mores during this period, see the gallery of types created by Dermot Trellis in Flann O'Brien, *At Swim-Two-Birds* (London: Longmans Green, 1939), or the comic portrayal of male characters as lechers in Mary Manning, *Mount Venus* (New York: Houghton Mifflin, 1938).

and earthy 'natural' sexuality.[11] Mrs Kedrigan is a newcomer to the town, a strong farmer's wife whose fertility is in question and who takes trips to Dublin to consult medical experts. She is described as a 'bleached out bloodless thing' by the townswomen, and the narrator concurs, with descriptions of her 'pale papery face' and her physical frailty. Her association with modernity is marked not only by her trips to the city but also by her modern attitudes to marriage, and in particular her insistence on her unshakeable trust in her husband. It is this that leads her to ignore the warnings over Sarah's innate sexual power ('She has a queer way of looking at a man'),[12] and to insist on engaging her to look after her husband while she takes a trip to Dublin. Inevitably Sarah's 'healthy blood' (images of heifers and lambing ewes are never very far away) proves a challenge to the modern companionate marriage.

Lavin's equivocal narrative voice leaves the reader uncertain over the explanatory force of terms such as 'blood', and the target of the story is as much the townsfolk's shifting attitudes towards amorality as it is the character of either of the women ('there being greater understanding in their hearts for sins against God than for sins against his Holy Church').[13] Yet the opposition between an aspiring middle-class mentality and a freer, 'natural' sexuality chimed with public concerns over unregulated sexuality. Sarah represents the dangerous 'amateur' (described by Luddy as 'women who engaged in sexual activity without monetary recompense', thereby causing considerable anxiety to the Carrigan Committee), but she also embodies all the traditional values of hard work and good Catholic Mass-going practice. Most of all she accepts austerity and frugality – she gives up her earnings as a domestic servant to her brothers, and even has sex for free. Her social superior Mrs Kedrigan is the epitome of a good housewife; she bakes excellent bread and cares for her husband, yet it is her trip to Dublin, and her misplaced faith in modern ideas of marriage, which is the direct cause of the tragedy. All the elements of public concern over sexual behaviour and the destruction of traditional community values appear in the story, if in strangely twisted forms: the healthy type accustomed to austerity and hard work, the bloodless type dependant on servants and the city comforts. But the aspect of the story which

---

[11] Mary Lavin, 'Sarah', in *The Stories of Mary Lavin*, Vol. 2 (London: Constable, 1974), pp. 15–23. As I discuss below, one of the reasons Edna O'Brien's representations of women appear so different – and so controversial – is because her characters 'try on' types, rather than are defined by them.

[12] Ibid., p. 16.

[13] Ibid., p. 15.

most explicitly connects it with contemporary public debates is the way
that the struggle over modernity and tradition is located in the bodies of
women.

In my discussion of fitness for marriage I have touched on fears that
women's consumer desires were proving dangerous to the traditional
sexual economy of rural Ireland. The republican virtues of austerity and
self-sufficiency were humanised but also threatened by 'feminine' comforts. There is an echo of this gendered association in the strangely neutered representations of small-town shopkeepers during this period. The
grocers who figure in the work of Brian Friel, Tom Murphy and Edna
O'Brien, for example, are represented as desiccated and isolated individuals who – crucially – lack generosity. Their association with goods and
money sets them in opposition to nature and natural communication –
evoked by memories of a childhood fishing trip in Friel's *Philadelpia
Here I Come*, or the burgeoning landscape in O'Brien's *The Country Girls*.
Just as republican economic autarchy appeared to be threatened by the
importation of lifestyles, leisure goods, fashion, cosmetics, and forms of
popular culture, so republican manly and 'natural' virtues were vulnerable to corruption by the values and practices of commercial exchange.
Both perceived threats were a response to genuine shifts in the rural
small-farm economy.

Under the dowry system women had brought capital and goods with
them on marriage. Not only did the wage economy disrupt this fragile
system, it also reinforced anxieties over rising standards of living, which
could not be accommodated by farmers living barely above subsistence
level. It was these fears that gave rise to denunciations of women's love
of luxury: commerce became associated with feminine pleasures and
self-indulgence, as it appeared to stand for everything opposed to republican austerity. Yet the most acute of the commentators on the crisis of
rural depopulation recognised that what was at issue was not only the
impact of the cash economy on traditional communities but also a revolution in the economic value ascribed to women. It was not that women
were newly allied with money, as Joyce's parallel between marriage and
legalised prostitution reminds us, but that the ways of evaluating their
capital, or stock, had fundamentally altered. For example, so far from
being a drain on parental resources (through the obligation to provide
a dowry) daughters could now prove an investment, if they sent home
regular remittances from their emigrant labour. On the other hand, the
value of those remittances was in danger of depleting rapidly, as worth
became increasingly calculated by spending rather than conserving, and

by accumulating 'artificial' goods rather than land – itself a commodity long associated with women in Ireland.

Toothpaste and Cosmetics

> I'd swear on my oath that poverty is not good enough for him. Heeding that hussy of a clothy of a plótha of a streeleen of an ownshook of a lebidjeh of a girleen that's working above in the bank. And she putting nonsense talk on him. His brains are scattered! He's foolish. But to think that our sweat is not thicker than water! Aren't we all right the way we are? And what have them with the gold to do with us? Now or ever? Let them afford their toothpaste and their cosmetics. Let them afford their love, with their clean long legs. We will stick to our own and the soot, as we did through the centuries. We have a love of our own, and we will keep it![14]

The nonsense talk of the woman who works above in the bank, the young women with their clean long legs, the new generation of women who refuse the privations their mothers have suffered – as Tom Murphy shows in this dream sequence from *A Crucial Week*, the battle was as much as anything between mothers and prospective daughters-in-law. Here John-Joe's mother becomes a comic caricature of the jealous, put-upon housewife who risks losing her one compensation – her son – to the new women of the future. Throughout the play the battle is fought over spending, on new and fashionable clothes, and on leisure and evenings out. Just as the heightened public concern over immorality in post-revolutionary Ireland was a way of articulating fears over the loss of 'the traditional way of life' rather than a response to actually increased levels of dissipation and decadence,[15] so post-war concerns about women's consumerism spoke to anxieties about the Irish economy and its ability to hold its own in the context of Britain's industrial boom. It was commodity culture that was the real target. Yet the fact that these fears were played out in representations and moral prescriptions of women's behaviour built on long associations between ideals of Irish femininity and national tradition, so that the perceived link between new forms of economic exchange and new forms of female behaviour was thoroughly over-determined.

And it was clear that economic opportunities for women were indeed changing, as the emigrant market (the market in labour power) became

---

[14] Tom Murphy, *A Crucial Week in the Life of a Grocer's Assistant*, in *A Whistle in the Dark*, p. 104.
[15] See Luddy, *Prostitution*, pp. 194–200.

increasingly easy to access. M. J. Molloy's representation of the ideal rural wife was uncompromising, to say the least. But he could also acknowledge the social pressures which forced women to leave rural areas – in his social problem comedies, *The Old Road* (1943), *Wood of the Whispering* (1953), and *Daughter from over the Water* (1956), lack of companionship, of available housing, and of social networks are just as much the cause of female emigration as any hankering after luxury and the diversions of city life. The young women emigrants in these plays are sensible rather than giddy or romantic; they have made rational choices about their futures, a fact which made it all the harder to deal with the problematic consequences of those choices as they affected rural Irish society.[16] Yet traditional (and usually negative) associations between women and consumer culture fed relatively easily into attitudes towards women emigrants. It was not only that women were susceptible to the lure of personal consumer goods (with stockings a particular favourite in the lists of things for which a young woman would apparently do almost anything),[17] but that their love of 'things' in general stretched to desirable objects such as ovens and sinks, not to mention electricity and running water. There was little hope of the smallholdings described by John Mogey in 1947 or Jerome Toner in 1955 providing such amenities: on farms of fewer than thirty acres (more than half of the total of Irish farms) it was the norm to have to fetch water from a well, often at some distance; to cook over an open fire; and to do all the work of dairying and poultry-keeping by hand.[18] In 1965, 20 per cent of rural households were still without electricity. Yet for a slew of writers

[16] In *Daughter from over the Water*, the parents engineer a fake miracle (saving the father from near death) in order to persuade their daughter to stay at home after the summer holidays; she marries her English beau nonetheless and the sympathies of the audience are with her (Molloy, *Daughter from over the Water*, in *Selected Plays*.)

[17] As in wartime and post-war Britain, stockings had almost mythical luxury status because of their association with American servicemen. In Ireland, the general shortage was exacerbated by the lack of up-to-date machinery, leaving Irish wool too coarse for fine weaving, so that stockings became the ultimate symbol of foreign luxury. In Pádhraic Óg Ó Conaire, *Déirc an Díomhaointis* (Baile Átha Cliath: Sáirséal agus Dill, 1972), the new stockings figure as another symbol of decline from the old ways of hard work and frugal living: 'Ní fhaca mná óga an bhaile seo tuirne, crann deilbh ná cardlaí riamh ina saol. Níl duine acu a bheadh in ann cliath a chur ar stoca. Nuair a bhíonn stocaí ag teastáil uathu, agus dar fia tá fad maith i stocaí ban an lae inniu, is don tsiopa a théann siad, na stocaí sin cho tanaí go gceapfá gur damháin alla a d'fhigh iad. Cheapfá, amanna, nach raibh stoca ar bith ar chuid acu.' [The young women of this place have never seen a spinning wheel, a warp-frame or teasing cards ever in their life. None of them would be able to darn a stocking. When they need stockings, and by heaven women's stockings are long enough these days, they go to the shop, where they find stockings so fine that you would think that a spider spun them. You would think, at times, that they weren't wearing any stockings at all.] (p.118) Translation by John Dillon.

[18] John M. Mogey, *Rural Life in Northern Ireland* (London: Oxford University Press, 1947); Jerome Toner, *Rural Ireland: Some of Its Problems* (Dublin: Clonmore and Reynolds, 1955).

in the 1950s there was a very fine line indeed between women's rational assessment of the drudgery awaiting them on farms such as these and a problematic self-indulgence.

In Mícheál Ó hOdhráin's short story 'Dúchas', a woman appears to be the cause of most of the misfortune. The story begins as Séamas and Eibhlín are spending time with Séamas's father in the country, attempting to convince him to sell his plot of land and move to Dublin to live with them. The young couple represent change and modernisation in contrast to the father's reference for tradition and 'dúchas', his heritage and home. While the father regrets the 'laziness' of those who no longer work the land, Eibhlín can't wait to get back to the city. "Níorbh fhada anois go mbeadh sí ar ais slán i measc na sluaite agus an fiántas fágtha ina diaidh aici" [It wouldn't be long now until she was safely back among the crowds with the wilderness left behind her.][19] There are elements of the narrative which suggest an attempt to offer a balanced view of the turn away from the land. 'Ní fhéadfadh an fear is fearr ar domhan maireachtáil anseo agus an saol atá ann.' [So Séamas argues that 'The best man in the world couldn't eke out a livelihood in the conditions here.'][20] His father appears at moments to be a pitiable character, unable to adapt to change. Yet what is most interesting about the story is the way in which the bond between Séamas and his father, and his father's almost mystical bond with the land, is destroyed by Eibhlín's deafness to anything but the comforts and noises of the city. Eibhlín's consistently negative attitude to rural life carries the force of the plot, so that it is her character, rather than social and economic forces, which powers urban migration. Just in case we should miss the link between emigration, racial decline and greed, Eibhlín is not only described as unfit and unable to be a mother ('At that time, she had a barren appearance and she was still as thin and barren as a ten-year-old goat.' 'Bhí cuma na seisce uirthi an tráth sin, agus bhí sí chomh tanaí seasc le gabhar deich mbliana fós.')[21] but she is also miserly – frightened that the money gained from the sale of the plot will not come to her and her husband.

Few stories are as upfront as this one about the dire social consequences of women's materialist desires, but they were a common enough theme in the 1950s, and indeed stretched back to earlier representations. Teresa Deevy's 1929 play *Temporal Powers* offers an uncompromising depiction of female 'greed', in the character of Min Donovan, who has been evicted

---

[19] Mícheál Ó hOdhráin, *Sléibhte Mhaigh Eo* (Dublin: Foilseacháin Náisiúnta Teoranta, 1964), p. 185. Translations by John Dillon.

[20] Ibid., p. 183.

[21] Ibid., p. 193.

from a smallholding along with her husband, whom she berates for his
lack of drive. His fault has been his acceptance of poverty, his refusal to
aspire. Homeless and desperate, she is consumed with anger over his dog-
ged acquiescence in austerity, 'workin' an' no thought of what profit was
in it!' The play is interesting for the way the audience's sympathies leach
away from Min, who tries to persuade her husband to take the stolen
money they find by chance and create a new life in America. What appear
at the beginning of the play to be needs (the need for a roof over their
heads and some semblance of comfort) become infected by Min's desires,
so that it proves impossible to distinguish between reasonable and unrea-
sonable demands: 'The kinda man I'd ask is wan that would stand behind
a shop counter quiet and easy the day long, and could be smoking his
pipe in the evening if he'd like, and myself, as was meant, ornamenting
the house.'[22] The play leaves the audience in extreme discomfort, as the
logic of the action means they must reject Min's desires as excessive, which
means siding with the radical renunciations of her husband.

The question of what were reasonable demands, and reasonable aspirations, went to the heart of the problem. The blurring of the line between
necessities and luxuries – between toothpaste and cosmetics – was one way
of avoiding the issue, and laying the blame at the foot of commodity culture in general. For the problem was not only that women were leaving
rural areas in order to reap the benefits of modern consumer culture, but
that modern consumer culture was encroaching on rural areas. Complaints
over the infiltration of the countryside by commercial interests formed
part of the claim that the distinctive culture of the Irish farmer and farm
labourer was being undermined. These complaints were not entirely misplaced. Subsistence farmers, the bedrock of the Sinn Féin ideal of a self-
sufficient republic, were ill-equipped to respond to the increasing demands
for shop-bought goods. As a summary of the memoranda on the congested
districts argued: 'coming to be regarded as necessities are bicycles, cinemas,
cosmetics, professional hairdressing, factory-made clothing, bakers' bread,
tinned foods, radio, reading matter.'[23] Farmers found themselves increasingly operating within a cash economy for which their only resource was
off-farm sales. Farmers with thirty acres found scraping together a regular
income from the land difficult enough. Seasonal remedies such as fattening
turkeys for Christmas went some way towards making the farm pay, but
local county council work on the roads was a vital source of cash for many

[22] Teresa Deevy, 'Temporal Powers', *Journal of Irish Literature*, 14:2 (1985), pp. 18–75.
[23] Summaries of Memoranda, Congested Districts, TCDMSS 8301.

small farmers' sons. For those working holdings of ten or fifteen acres, cash was nearly impossible to come by. For many of the 'relatives assisting' on the farms, their first wages would be earned in England.

For the traditionalists, a whole range of demands that women were beginning to make of domestic life on the small farms – running water, for example, or electric light – were in danger of making rural areas more like the towns, undermining the distinctiveness of the rural, usually western, way of life which was to be prized for the way it maintained a hardy stock. For the conservative commentators, the idea of providing modern conveniences in rural homes, or even cinemas and modern shops in the small towns, in order to encourage young people not to emigrate had the exactly opposite effect – like unemployment assistance, they had the effect of softening up the people, making them fit only for town life. Commissioners often stressed that it was the impact of modern forms of leisure and lifestyle on the local area (rather than the complete absence of modern influences) which caused dissatisfaction with the quality of life which could be had at home. In other words, it was the links with the wages and leisure to be had in England, rather than the distance from them, which encouraged emigration.

There was more at issue here than the emigrant remittances, visits from returning and holidaying migrants, and emigrant letters, which traditionally provided the link between life at home and in England. In contrast to some who argued that emigrants left because of the 'dullness' of rural life, William Honohan suggested that it was, paradoxically, the presence of new leisure activities (along with insufficient money to take advantage of them) which attracted people to life in English cities:

> It may be that, in the past, when standards were lower and perhaps opportunities for spending money not so great in certain areas (no cinema, no dance hall, not so much smoking), many of those now emigrating were satisfied with work in large or short spells from time to time. The modern requirement, however, is a pay-packet of definite dimensions every week, and I think the Commission might well comment on the fact that we are moving away from the time when employers of labour can count on getting men for a couple of days or a couple of weeks at a time and then laying them off. The day of the casual and purely temporary worker – employed directly and not through a contractor – is, to all intents and purposes, passing – a matter which is, of course, aggravated by the attractiveness of full employment in Britain at the present time.[24]

[24] Rural Surveys, TCDMSS 8306/5.

As Honohan pointed out, the growth of the cash economy particularly affected the 'large unpaid pool of relatives assisting.' (He estimated them as 243,000 – 61,000 men and 182,000 women). These men and women, who in the past would not have worked for a wage, could now claim work in Britain:

> It may be that, in years gone by, such persons have been content to live virtually on a subsistence basis, but the cinema, radio, newspapers and friends are now luring them into the attitude that they should not be satisfied with this but should leave home to raise their standards, get married and have homes of their own. Who can blame them?[25]

Although Honohan was sympathetic to the young emigrants, his use of terms such as 'luring' suggests the broadly moral terms in which he understood this process. While Bishop Lucey diagnosed the problem as lack of 'will', others pointed out the fruitlessness of moral exhortation. Marsh acknowledged the problems caused by the desire for 'model kitchens and built-in furniture' – ideals promoted by the radio, the cinema, and newspaper and magazine articles – but argued that it was pointless to hope for a 'moral revolution' amongst the people which would mean they were happy to 'rejoice in hard and frugal living.'[26] The economist James Meenan went further in accepting a link between the increasing commercialisation of rural areas and the rise in emigration. He acknowledged that the farm workers' drift to the towns was part of a shift from a subsistence to an exchange economy. But, he argued, the Irish economy had nothing to exchange, bar its manpower – so that in effect it became part of the British labour market. Again, moral exhortation could have no effect on these conditions.[27]

Meenan's economic laws affected men just as much as women, but in arguing thus he was in a distinct minority. More commonly, 'the flight of the girls' was adduced as a major cause of small farmers' inability to marry and bring up a family at home. The solutions were, at least in part, agreed to be economic ones. M. J. Molloy's arguments in favour of marriage dowries (to be provided by the state) and prohibition of the emigration of women, were of a piece with the views expounded in the '50s plays. 'In rural Ireland', he argued, 'it is not houses that are needed but women.' He reserved especial ire for what he termed the 'extermination through

[25] Ibid.
[26] Memorandum, Marsh and Collis, TCDMSS 8304/16.
[27] James Meenan, 'The Balance of Payments', Lecture to the Institute of Bankers in Ireland, 23 November 1951. TCDMSS 8300/50–51.

emigration campaign', run by British recruiting agents and the 'infinitely more deadly' advertisements for employment in England 'which swamp every newspaper, especially the provincial newspapers, which are bought in every farmhouse.' As he bluntly reasoned, 'What farmer would give his daughter £150 of his hard-earned money [for a dowry] when he could get rid of her for nothing to a respectable job worth £4 or £5 a week?'[28]

The fact that the British post-war recruitment drive was facilitated by Irish newspapers, and Irish labour exchanges was a sore political point throughout the decade. Wartime labour needs had opened up a variety of jobs to the Irish, including catering, factory work, the cotton mills and domestic service. A system of assisted transport and large transit hotels catering for new arrivals made Irish labour an obvious choice for firms trying to fill vacancies in the jobs that British workers had rejected: largely unskilled labour with long hours. Large numbers of Irish men were shipped in to be employed as nomadic construction workers housed in camps, or based at large plants such as Fords in Dagenham or transport projects in Birmingham. Attempts to regulate the flow of emigrants through the Dublin Liaison Office, which had been set up by the British Ministry of Labour during the war, with Irish government approval, proved less and less effective in peacetime conditions. In the middle of 1946, restrictions on Irish women travelling to Britain were lifted, leaving the way open for individual British hospitals and factories to advertise for workers. Typical local newspaper advertisements read: 'Opportunities for Girls to Work in London Factory and Canteen.... Interviews and medical examination will be held in Dublin.' 'Convent Hospital, large English town – Domestic Assistant wanted. All Irish staff. Radio and Television. £4 weekly. Fare paid. Met at Boat.' To the consternation of the British Liaison Officer in Dublin, Mr Toms, some business concerns and hospitals even instigated roving recruitment campaigns. He counselled that employers 'won't be tolerated if they go browsing about Eire trying to persuade Eire girls to come to their hospitals.'[29]

The advertisements appealed to workless young women, of course, but also, as Molloy pointed out, to their parents. The exchange value of women's bodies was fundamentally altered by the prospect of selling their labour. And as Eamon Casey argued, it was not only the parents who might do well out of the exchange: 'I know of a factory where each

---

[28] M. J. Molloy Memorandum, 'The Extermination through Emigration Campaign,' TCDMSS 8305/2.

[29] 'Recruitment of Nurses from Eire.' Eire Government Emigration Policy in Respect of Staff for Hospitals in This Country (1946). National Archives, Labour file (NA LAB) 8/1301.

member of the staff was paid £10 for every girl she succeeded in bringing over from Ireland.'[30]

Such arguments acknowledged the economic forces which were pushing, as well as pulling, emigrants out of rural areas. The dowry system was integral to an economic order which required relatives still living at home to be 'paid off', thereby freeing up the house and land for the marrying couple. But it sat poorly within an exchange economy which encouraged an increase in farm size and transfer from tillage to cattle in order to maximise cash profits. The problem was an economic one, its root the income differentials between Britain and Ireland. Arguing that the farms in his area were not too small to rear a large family, Molloy acknowledged that families were nonetheless turning away from them because 'they are not big enough to out-bid the English and American five or six pounds a week.'[31] Part of his solution was state-funded economic backing for the small farmer, through marriage dowries and other schemes. State intervention was necessary, he argued, because the rural individual, whether male or female, could not withstand the economic pressures caused by the increasing insertion of the Irish countryside into an international exchange economy, all on their own.

The theory that lack of women (and by extension their lack of austerity-willpower) was the principal problem did not go unchallenged. Molloy used a disarmingly simple rule for judging the size of a viable smallholding:

> The simplest definition of an economic farm is one big enough to secure a wife. In this area the economic farm acreage has doubled within the past few years and it will have increased four or five fold in a few years, as marriageable girls become more and more of a rarity.[32]

Yet Roy Geary argued that the statistics showed the marriage rate actually went up during the 'recent spate of emigration to Britain.' Rather than too few women, he maintained the major problem was the lack of houses and waged earnings, particularly for the large pool of 'relatives assisting.'[33] But if lack of women was not the real problem, what was really being articulated in the anxiety over female migrants? The disturbing figures on female emigration revealed by the analysis of travel permits in the late '40s

[30] Casey, 'Pastoral on Emigration', p. 256.
[31] Molloy Memorandum, TCDMSS 8305/2.
[32] Ibid.
[33] Summary of Causes of Low Marriage Rate, TCDMSS 8301. A few years later the statistics analysed by E. C. W. Spencer showed that the male rate of marriage increased most as a result of emigration, not female.

were part of the reason for this concern, yet the belief that female emigration was more pernicious than male persisted even after the mid-'50s
when women were no longer emigrating in greater numbers than men.
The causal connection, less women, fewer marriages, must have appeared
to be common sense. It was common sense too that rural women did not
in fact warm to the life of toil their mothers had known – what William
Honohan, in his Rural Survey of County Kerry, described as the 'understandable reluctance of the modern Cahirciveen girl to marry into a smallholding where nothing but drudgery awaits her.' The evidence of young
women's dissatisfaction with the opportunities offered them was not hard
to find and must have easily outweighed Professor Geary's statistics.

Nonetheless, as I have suggested, the relentless focus on women's desire
for commodities and leisure is best understood neither as a rational diagnosis of the causes of emigration nor as a misogynist attack on women's independence, but as an attempt to criticise the economic forces which appeared
to be destroying traditional communities. The insistence on moral failing –
the idea that people had become 'infected' with consumerist desires and
were unwilling to accept the harsh conditions of former years – was a sign
of the conceptual impasse which greeted the encroachment of a modern
consumer economy, an economy driven above all by spending. Purchasing
power in itself undermined the republican virtues of austerity and self-
sufficiency. Thus women were associated with the dangers of 'conspicuous
consumption' and a drive towards materialist excess, precisely because their
desires for domestic comforts and small personal luxuries were reasonable,
and not excessive. For there appeared to be no way of protecting the traditional small farm economy, and the community life which went with it,
once the principles of consumerism and acquisitiveness were allowed.

The basic critique of women's consumerist desires was that they were
unrealistic – but this was primarily a response to the fact that it was not
possible to accommodate these desires in the small farms and townlands of
the west. By default, girls wanted too much. They wanted stockings, they
wanted a social life, they wanted to go to the cinema, they wanted their
hair done. In *The Wood of the Whispering* one of the male characters talks to
his brother about whether he can afford marriage (he is in his seventies, so
he has proved he can wait) – he tots up the cost of fancy furnishings, exotic
drinks, and outings to the town, but is finally put off the idea of marriage
when he reminded of the cost of 'the hair-docking – what they do call the
perm.'[34] The problem was not so much the women as the spending.

[34] Molloy, *The Wood of the Whispering*, in *Selected Plays*, p. 128. Any doubts about the prevalence of
the language of breeding as it was applied to rural Ireland should be allayed by the word 'docking':

This comes into focus more clearly when we reflect on the forms of acquisition which were considered compatible with the small farm economy. Concern over the impact of capitalist modernity on rural Ireland was by no means the exclusive terrain of conservative thinkers. Peadar O'Donnell, for example, wrote of the small farmers as a revolutionary class, and, like the members of Muintir na Tíre, was far from antipathetic towards the modernisation and industrialisation of rural areas. In the early 1960s the 'Save the West' campaign, protesting the ineffectiveness of state policies for rural renewal, put forward co-operative organisation and collective self-help initiatives as a means of creating jobs and furthering the industrialisation of rural communities.[35] These were broadly anticapitalist and corporatist ventures. Most critiques of consumerism relied on a somewhat contradictory idea of frugal ownership. In this view the ideal small farmer operated a form of austere capitalism, accumulating only sufficient goods and machinery to work the land effectively. In such a context, spending on luxuries (fashion, the cinema, hairdressers) appeared to be evidence of a creeping individualism and creeping modernisation which was affecting rural areas, driving down the birthrate, and making it more, not less, likely that people would emigrate.

This opposition between a stoical manhood content with simple pleasures and a giddy femininity unable to control its desires did not, of course, go unchallenged even within the ranks of the Catholic hierarchy and amongst Catholic lay intellectuals. What appeared on the

---

while for Synge and Yeats the Darwinian model was explored through a rhetoric of thoroughbred horses, for the small farmers it was cattle farming.

[35] O'Donnell 's 1955 novel *The Big Windows* (London: Jonathan Cape, 1955) explores a woman's ultimately positive modernising influence in a turn-of-the-century rural townland. See also Peadar O'Donnell, *The Role of Industrial Workers in the Problems of the West* (Dublin: Distributed by Dochas Co-operative Society, [1965?]) and *Challenge: A Journal of the Worker-Small Farmer Alliance*, first published in February 1968. For a discussion of O'Donnell's post-war interventions on emigration and the rural economy, see Donal Ó Drisceoil, *Peadar O'Donnell* (Cork: Cork University Press, 2001), pp. 115–124. For the Save the West campaign, see Tony Varley and Chris Curtin, 'Defending Rural Interests against Nationalists in 20th-Century Ireland: A Tale of Three Movements', in John Davis (ed.), *Rural Change in Ireland* (Belfast: Institute of Irish Studies, 1999), pp. 58–83. As Varley and Curtin point out, however, though the impetus behind Fr McDyer's campaign may have been towards co-operative industrialisation, McDyer himself shared many of the concerns about the impact of emigration and 'easy money' that we have discussed. They write of a debate in a 1963 County Mayo public meeting: 'Collective self-help initiatives may have held much of the answer to the west's rural problems, but the many obstacles that lay in the way of effective local initiatives were not ignored. Among the difficulties that would have to be tackled were those created by the authoritarian educational system, the tendency for emigration to result in the weaker elements being left behind and the dependency and apathy that were part and parcel of the 'dole' mentality' (p. 71). See also James McDyer, *Fr McDyer of Glencolumbkille: An Autobiography* (Dingle: Brandon Books, 1982).

surface as an opposition between the ability to endure, on the one hand, and gratification and indulgence, on the other, was exposed by several commentators as simply a contrast between two rival versions of desire. Women may have wanted a social life and some of the perks of modern consumer society, but their desires were easily matched in intensity by men's desire for a larger farm or more livestock. Seen from this perspective, waiting for marriage had very little to do with a hardy ability to withstand the demands of a frugal way of life, but was in fact all about greed – a desire for more land, a larger farm, perhaps even the neighbour's farm, which outweighed the costs and benefits associated with raising a family.

The portrait of the Irish farmer as parsimonious, lazy, devious, and envious of others' success paradoxically went hand in hand with the portrait of his womenfolk as would-be spendthrifts. It lies at the heart of criticisms of the greed of the older generation who are too mean to give up control of the farm to their children, thereby forestalling emigration, or those who are so hungry for remittances that they actually encourage the young to emigrate. For all his strictures on the behaviour of young women, Molloy was clear-eyed about the forces ranged against them: 'The Irish farmer's ambition is twofold: to have as much land as possible and to do as little work as possible.'

A similar argument about the clash between the sexes underpins much of John O'Brien's *The Vanishing Irish,* a 1954 collection of essays on the emigration crisis which included contributions by writers and commentators such as Sean O'Faolain, Paul Vincent Carroll, Arland Ussher, Bryan MacMahon and Shane Leslie, many of whom had been associated with the liberal Irish literary journal *The Bell.* Many of the essayists blamed the system of inheritance and the relationship between the sexes for the failure to marry and the emptying of the countryside. The practice of waiting until parents were ready to relinquish their control of the farm was targeted by nearly all the contributors as causing harm to both young women and young men. According to Shane Leslie, 'marriage is dreary on Irish farms, where the old folk cling on and expect sons and daughters-in-law to act as unpaid servants.'[36] But much more focus was laid on male behaviour as a contributory cause of the crisis. Women were being asked to wait too long for marriage not only by their future mother-in-laws, but by a breed of

---

[36] Shane Leslie in O'Brien (ed.), *The Vanishing Irish*, p. 79. See also Sean O'Faolain in same volume: 'old Irishmen never die, they just fade away at ages of such fantastic antiquity that their offspring are by then too old to start fruitful lives of their own' (p. 107).

uniquely 'marriage-shy' Irishmen, reluctant to give up the freedoms of an extended bachelorhood:

> Call it selfishness, lethargy, indifference, love for independence, laziness, the fact of the matter seems to be that Ireland's young and not so young men are at fault more than the women or economics or any other cause one might suggest.[37]

Moreover, once these hesitant males had been persuaded to accept the married state, they often proved less than exciting partners, loath to allow their wives any enjoyment. Sean O'Faolain, well known for his critique of the ruralist ethos, quoted from a number of supposed letters from Irish men outlining the reasons they were happy to wait until a mature age before marrying. These included the fact that men don't lose their looks as they grow older so they can afford to wait, as well as scepticism that a modern Irish woman was up to the task of supporting her farmer husband, since contemporary girls were 'flighty flibbertigibbets', more interested in makeup and the cinema than hard work. But why, O'Faolain asked, should women not be allowed their drinks in the pub and their visits to the cinema? While acknowledging the costliness of marriage, he argued that the real problem was the men's greed for land and livestock. In this interpretation, the crisis of marriage derived not from the rise of materialism, pitted against the traditional values of Christian austerity, but from a clash of materialisms. Two kinds of acquisitiveness were in conflict with one another – the material farm and the 'luxury' commodity.

Toffs and the Poorer Type of Girl

'One wonders why so many young girls leave Ireland for England when there seems to be sufficient work for them at home. The lack of parental control and the facilities for plenty of freedom and amusement and adventure would seem to be a predominant attraction.'[38] Despite the fact that the Population Commissioners could appreciate 'the reluctance of the modern Cahirciveen girl' to embrace the drudgery of the small farmer's wife, and acknowledge the drear and often unfulfilling prospects for the ranks of the 'relatives assisting', their overall judgement of the causes of female emigration came down firmly against the flightiness of country

---

[37] Ibid., p. 70.
[38] Rural Surveys, 'Employment and Living Conditions of Irish Workers in Great Britain', TCDMSS 8306/24.

girls.[39] Lyons's claim that there was sufficient work for young women in the rural areas suggests that he considered part-time and seasonal employment to be enough, for the women if not for the men. The idea that women may have wanted, and indeed needed, full-time paid work, let alone a career, was fundamentally alien. In a situation of long-term unemployment the male breadwinner naturally took precedence – after all, this was a society in which women were still obliged to give up their civil service and teaching careers on marriage.

The assumption that women required only casual and part-time work was countered by representatives of women's unions and other organisations, who argued bluntly that 'Poverty and lack of opportunities for employment or the building of a career are primary causes of emigration for women as for men.'[40] The Irish Women Workers' Union tangled with an apoplectic de Blacam in maintaining that women worked under better conditions in England. Mrs O'Neill, of the Irish Countrywomen's Association, insisted there were only three reasons for emigration: 'higher wages, lighter work, and more time off.' Girls preferred hotel work and employment as domestics in hospitals over Irish domestic work, 'because there they are better fed.'[41] But such claims were largely dismissed. Apart from these lone voices, and the testimony of members of the Irish Housewives Association, who did emphasise economic need on the part of female emigrants, there was little sympathy with the women leaving Ireland, at least amongst the experts approached by the Commission.

It is not too much to say that if it was the best men who were leaving, it was the worst women. The debate occasioned by the oral evidence given by the Irish Nurses' Organisation offered opportunities for this claim to be made explicitly. In a long submission to the Commission, the Nurses' Organisation outlined problems of resources and scale. Irish hospitals trained approximately 500 nurses every year, but more than twice that number left to train in Britain; in addition, the shortage of nurses in England meant that young nurses trained in Ireland were likely to emigrate as soon as they had finished their course, as they could not be absorbed into Irish hospitals. But these economic criteria were overlaid by defensive arguments over the relative value of training and conditions in the two jurisdictions. As Dr Doolin, one of the Commissioners,

---

[39] Summaries of Memoranda, Congested Districts, TCDMSS 8301.
[40] Transcripts of Evidence, Irish Women Works Union, TCDMSS 8307–8/8.
[41] Transcripts of Evidence, Irish Countrywomen's Association, TCDMSS 8307–8/3.

insisted, it was the worst type who went to England, those who would not be accepted into Irish hospitals, who would not make the grade. 'Those who go and are accepted for training in Secondary Institutions are girls who have been refused by Irish matrons as unlikely to make good nurses.' The nurses interviewed broadly agreed with this view, arguing against the introduction of an Assistant Nurse grade for 'the poorer type of girl.' This is an instance where the habit of classification into 'types' maps very clearly onto class. The Nurses' Organisation evidence smoulders with prejudice against the slovenly, uneducated, poor type of girl (often labourers' daughters, or even, to Dr Doolin's horror, his own maids) who were contrasted with the convent-educated, strong farmers' daughters paying for their training in Dublin hospitals.[42]

The open snobbery of the Irish medical establishment was one sign of the tension produced by the impact of the wage economy on traditional social structures. It was of a piece with the cash-induced transformations in social status described by John Healy in his portrait of Charlestown, County Mayo, although his focus was on male emigrants returning home for the holidays flush with money: 'Now they could drink in The Hotel with the best: they could buy drinks with the best in the best lounge bar in town. Their money and their earning power was as great, if not greater, than the social hierarchy of the town.'[43] Paid employment, whether it was available in Ballina or Birmingham, had the effect of closing the income gap between the 'possessing' and the more 'vulnerable' classes, and gave rise to anxieties about the closing of the social gap. Reactions included the condescending attempt to insist on social distinctions (as among the established nursing sorority) as well as paternalistic concern for those not fitted for life outside their communities. All too often these attitudes were combined. Paradoxically, the processes of emigration, which were seen as

---

[42] Transcripts of Evidence, Irish Nurses Organisation, TCDMSS 8307–8/11. This attitude was common in official British discourse too. In 1944 a request was sent to the Ministry of Labour arguing the need for an official to check out the girls before they left Ireland: 'There is at the present time a very considerable volume of recruitment in Ireland for hospitals in this country. The great majority of the applicants are accepted on a written application and testimonials only, though doubtless in many cases the applicant is introduced by a present employee of the employer. We know that the better class of hospital, which is not in desperate straits for staff, declines to engage girls on this basis. We also know that girls who are accepted are quite often not suitable and that a fair amount of false pretences goes on.' 'Recruitment of Nurses and Volunteers for Nursing in Eire: Proposed Appointment of Technical Nursing Officers to Be Stationed in Eire' (1944–1947). NA LAB 12/284. In 1951, a series of interviews with Irish nurses in England published in *The Irish Democrat* and entitled 'They Treat Us Like Dirt', suggested that attitudes had not changed: '"When I came over here," one of the Irish girls was saying in her attractive Kerry accent, "Matron asked me would I be able to mix with the other nurses without having had a secondary education. She doubted if I would be tolerated at all."' *Irish Democrat*, April 1951.

[43] Healy, *Death of an Irish Town*, p. 26.

bringing rural women into ever closer contact with dangerously modern urban mores, became one of the flash points through which rural standards could be exposed to view and criticised by the urban middle class. The process was reminiscent of the case of urban working-class British children who turned out to be lice-ridden and malnourished when they were evacuated to the countryside during the Second World War, but with the roles of country and city reversed. Anxieties about the health of rural emigrants were partly driven by British concerns, particularly with regard to tuberculosis and typhus. From 1943, the 'Health Embarkation Certificate' was issued to Irish migrants before they left the country, after a medical inspection which included a thorough check for 'vermin.' In 1944, a British nursing recruitment officer on a visit to Dublin claimed that even among the 'better class' of applicant the rate of women found to be verminous was 85 per cent. ('I was very exercised in my mind about the advisability of requiring women coming over for nursing to undergo this ordeal, but when I saw the records and realised that 85 per cent of the women were dirty, I felt it was most essential that they should be examined, even if they are quite a different type from the women being submitted for work in factories.')[44] By 1948, the Dublin authorities were arguing that there was no further need for medical examinations, since most women left under their own steam (and therefore did not go through the Liaison Office procedures), and the threat of typhus was negligible. But the Ministry of Labour was supported by Irish medical opinion which argued that louse examination should be continued as part of the tests for general 'fitness.' According to Dr Ethna McCarthy: 'Poverty, as indicated by underclothing, is no guide as to the likelihood of infestation. I have seen silk clothing crawling with vermin, and girls in miserable rags scrupulously clean.' Elsewhere in her 1948 report, however, she implied that rural customs and education militated against basic cleanliness.

> The standard of cleanliness among women emigrants is low. Although aware that they are presenting themselves for medical examination and have presumably come prepared, many appear engrained with dirt, while a vintage accumulation in the umbilicus is common even in otherwise clean people. A considerable number, in spite of brand new clothes, have made no attempt to wash their bodies at all. From enquiry 'washing' refers only to the face and hands; daily washing cannot be assumed. One girl boasted that she 'washed once a fortnight', a statement that was meant to impress.[45]

[44] 'Recruitment of Nurses and Volunteers for Nursing in Eire', NA LAB 12/284.
[45] Ethna MacCarthy, 'Public Health Problems Created by Louse Infestation', *Irish Journal of Medical Science* (February 1948), pp. 65–78.

With tales of unembarrassed girls so infested that the lice lay like sand in the bottom of the bath after washing, McCarthy put the dirt down not to lack of running water but to rural custom and old wives' tales, such as that their rashes were caused by food or menstruation, or the belief that washing 'weakens' children. For McCarthy, dirt was a matter of 'national prestige' – as it was for M. J. Molloy, except that in his portrait of an unwashed, lame, and unfit rural woman he tried to argue for a reversal in the value ascribed to it.

The point of concern shifted from social class to physical cleanliness to moral fitness in predictable fashion. In the Commission papers as a whole, the 'poorer type of girl' was overwhelmingly associated with the girl who left Ireland pregnant, or was likely to fall pregnant while in England. Many of the discussions of 'weakness' in relation to female emigrants were thinly veiled anxieties about sexual behaviour and falling away from religious duties (though nurses, to some extent controlled by the matrons with whom they lodged in the Nurses Homes, were often exempted from this particular moral failing). Evidence was adduced from the governor of Holloway Gaol, who argued that Irish girls 'who are lonely easily get contaminated', from a priest in Manchester who complained of the 'weak moral fibre' of female emigrants, from a Southampton cleric who regretted the 'very poor type' of girls then looking for work as domestics, and a canon in Holloway who argued that 'the girls were good enough for a while but their living conditions contaminate them.'[46] In 1955, an editorial in the *Irish Democrat* noted the appearance of recent scare stories about the unreliable Irish published in newspapers with very different political standpoints, including the *Kerryman* (which described immigrants as 'weak characters, lacking in moral fibre, and unstable'), the *Manchester Guardian*, the *Daily Herald* and *Reynolds News*, then the organ of the Co-Operative movement. The editor, Desmond Greaves, held that these stories heightened anti-Irish feeling and were irresponsible, more particularly since 'many Irish girls better themselves in England.'[47]

---

[46] Increasingly, reports on emigrants in England blamed the fact that they could be so easily 'contaminated' on the poor preparation they received in Ireland. In the Radharc newsreel *Hotel Chaplain*, Fr Joe Kennedy opined, 'The preparation they got in Ireland made no provision for life in this amoral and almost pagan society of England', a way of life that was 'inconceivable' to the average young Irish person. *Hotel Chaplain* (Radharc films, 1965). See also *Oldbury Camp* (Radharc films, 1965) and *Boat Train to Euston* (Radharc films, 1965).

[47] Editorial, *Irish Democrat*, June 1955. See also 'Birmingham Spotlight on the Irish', published in *The Irish Digest*, 1956, an article which summarised and quoted coverage of Irish migrants in a number of local Birmingham newspapers: 'Irish girls found living with coloured men and Poles'; 'Irish boys living in illicit association with their landladies and divorced women'; 'Coloured landlords' have offered sums of 20 pounds, through adverts in Irish newspapers, for Irish girls to be

The general climate of opinion on the dangers associated with the single girl were not so different from stereotypes of the newly independent shop girl which were common in turn-of-the-century Britain and France. In both cases women and girls were suspect merely by virtue of living alone and undertaking employment. Good women – such as those training to be nurses in England – could easily be discovered to be 'poor types' in reality; 'good enough' girls could quickly become contaminated. The ease with which women could be assigned to such varied social roles was in part a consequence of the long historical obsession with female purity as the basis of national strength. But it was also a consequence of the way that women's earning and spending power attacked the class-based distinctions that had helped define the differences between rural and urban Ireland. Shopping for ready-made fashions was, by default, a city-based activity in the years before the Second World War. High-end department stores such as Switzer's and Brown Thomas's catered to the upper-middle classes while smaller chain stores such as Cassidy's and Newell's, with several branches in Dublin, sought to attract young women who were earning their own money for the first time.[48] In smaller towns and rural areas, clothing was made up at home or by tailors and seamstresses (often using patterns published in newspapers and women's magazines as well as commercial patterns such as those produced by Butterick and McCall which were available over-the-counter in regional drapers' shops). As Orla Fitzpatrick has argued, 'A comparison of fashion plates and photographs from Britain with the clothing advertised in Ireland reveals little sign of a time-lag with regard to the adoption of styles. Slouch hats, shirtwaister dresses, rayon suits, Cuban-heeled shoes and a silhouette of square shoulders are all to be found in Irish advertisements and family photographs from the period.'[49] Modern fashion for women also included trousers, made popular initially as sportswear, and designed specifically for the leisure activities of the middle class such as golf and sailing. An interest in fashion was further associated with membership of the anglicised middle class, as Dublin in the post-war years became a popular shopping destination for well-off English tourists, seeking to escape an uncomfortable austerity regime at home. Dublin's city lights were thus

---

brought over as 'housekeepers' where they become trapped into 'working in houses little better than brothels.'

[48] See Orla Fitzpatrick, 'Coupons, Clothing and Class: The Rationing of Dress in the Irish Free State, 1942–1948', *Costume*, 48:2 (2014), 236–259.

[49] Ibid., p. 241. It should come as no surprise that in *Girl with Green Eyes*, Cait Brady's astrakhan coat (the ultimate luxury, anti-pastoral commodity, in that it is made from the skins of fetal lambs) is bought for her in a posh shop by Eugene Galliard, the dangerous foreigner to whom she ends up losing her virginity.

seen as a contributory factor to the decline of traditional rural communities caused by 'foreigners', many of them seeking to evade Labour's tax
regime, buying up land in Ireland.

'Love of luxury' made it hard to tell the difference between rural and
citified types. As Father Patrick Noonan argued, 'The combined influences of emigration, the tourist influx, the craze for pleasure, and all the
modern trends in thought and conduct have well-nigh transformed the
traditional colleen into a sophisticated miss.'[50] Women could be castigated
for being at the same time too slovenly (lice-ridden) and too sophisticated
(wearing silk underclothes), too poverty stricken and too well educated.
As Stanley Lyons argued following his survey of Waterford, Wexford
and Carlow, traditional class distinctions, such as those cleaved to by
the Nurse's Organisation representatives, were giving way to more varied
social divisions. Lyons singled out the convent schools as major actors in
this drama:

> It would appear that, in coastal towns, the temptation to go to England
> amongst young girls is very strong; it seems to be, as it were, in the blood
> and large numbers have no other thoughts after leaving school. The stan-
> dard of education, particularly in the Convent Schools, is high, and tends
> to make girls dissatisfied with home conditions, particularly so in the case
> of those living in poorer localities, with few-roomed houses and large
> families.[51]

On the surface, the point was that educating the young was no proof
against their desire to leave – rather the opposite. Arguments to this effect
were relatively gender neutral. Secondary education was also targeted in
more general terms as a cause of rural weakness, in that it trained young
people out of the habits of physical labour, for example, and gave them
'ideas.' M. J. Molloy put it with characteristic bluntness: 'Education is
anti-rural and the more there is the worse it will be.'[52] But just as fundamental to Lyons's point was the ambiguous role of the convent schools
in enabling girls to access forms of social mobility through education.
However hard the convent regime attempted to preserve social distinctions between the better and poorer classes of girls, the schools became
minor agents of social change. 'Oh, you'll be a toff from now on', says
Hickey the farm hand when he hears of Caithleen's scholarship, at the

[50] Patrick B. Noonan, 'Why Few Irish Marry,' in O'Brien (ed.), *The Vanishing Irish*, p. 52. Noonan
    advocated marriage and family allowances and graded taxation 'affecting 'old maids (over twenty-
    five) and bachelors (over thirty)' as partial solutions to the problem.
[51] Rural Surveys, TCDMSS 8306/8.
[52] Molloy Memorandum, TCDMSS 8305/2.

beginning of Edna O'Brien's *The Country Girls*. When the farm is sold, Hickey leaves for London and a job on the buses, and Caithleen for her convent education, which will eventually lead her to Dublin.[53]

There was an entire sub-genre of popular literature of emigration dedicated to the respectable convent girl and her civilising role. Magazines such as *Ireland's Own* and *The Messenger of the Sacred Heart* recycled stories (often written by the same people) of well-educated Irish girls facing personal and moral crises in London and Birmingham, but winning through due to their strong faith and sure, traditional principles. In 'The Rosary', for example (published in *The Messenger* in 1951), a student-nurse is censured for placing the rosary in the hands of a dying man, victim of a road accident, and saying prayers for him. Sometime later, after she has left the hospital, she meets him, fully recovered (thanks to the intercession of the Sacred Heart), and discovering that he is luckily a Catholic, they happily marry. In 1956, the *Messenger*'s year-long serial 'The Young Emigrant' followed the fortunes of Rose, eldest daughter of 'a comfortably off farmer' who 'was giving his children a good education and fitting them for responsible positions.' Rose has been trained as a hospital almoner in Dublin and is due to marry her beau, the newly qualified local doctor, but plans to spend a year working in London first. There she meets the silent but deep Dr Martin, a psychiatrist, and after encountering him by chance at Westminster Cathedral she discovers he is a Catholic. Eventually they confess their love, but their marriage is put in doubt when Rose's former fiancé, David, is blinded in a chemistry accident, and Rose feels she must stand by him. Bravely David releases her from her promise, to allow her to become an upstanding Catholic wife in England. These stories trade on the virtues of respectable and pious Catholicism and take it as read that Irish women's role is to civilise and humanise life in 'pagan and materialistic England.'[54]

---

[53] In John B. Keane's 1959 play *Sive* the aunt's rage against her niece is crystallised in her resentment of her education. Sive has cookery classes at the convent where they learn to make 'fricasee with dartois for dessert', to which her aunt retorts, 'Out working with a farmer you should be my girl, instead of getting your head filled with high notions.' John B. Keane, *Three Plays: Sive, The Field, Big Maggie* (Cork: Mercier Press, 1990), p. 13.

[54] Circulation records for *The Messenger* were not kept. Judging by the published thanksgivings, women appear to have been more active in writing to the magazine and to have engaged more strongly with the publication. Many of the thanksgivings focus on education and business success, but this bias may have been formed in part by the Jesuit priests who were keen to promote devotion to the Sacred Heart among students and teachers, and may have prioritised the publication of these letters. Sile de Cléir's research into the publication suggests that the readership for the magazine was much wider than the published letters suggest, since it was available in schools, convents and the Catholic Truth Society stands in parish churches, and each issue would have been picked up and read by a range of family members, neighbours and relatives. Private correspondence from Sile de Cléir.

It seems unlikely that readers took these moral parables seriously, but the intention behind them seems to have been sincere enough. A 1953 *Handbook for Catholic Men and Women Going to England* (handed out to migrants at the boat, and specially pocket sized so it could be carried about and referred to as necessary) pointed out some of the most frequent pitfalls across the water.[55] These included the fact that Protestant churches looked very like Catholic ones and the faithful would need to be on their guard to avoid wandering into the wrong establishment by mistake. What is most striking about the *Handbook*, however, is the way that it is really directed to women as the guardians not only of their own but of everybody else's conscience. The fact that women even from the poorer classes had, in general, a slightly better, longer, education than their brothers was one reason for this. But that longer education was also a problem – the danger, particularly for convent-educated girls, was that they had been introduced to all sorts of luxuries, such as piano lessons or how to make sponge cakes, which were going to be difficult to accommodate on small, poorly serviced rural farms. Women's civilising role, which should be their strength, turned out also to be their weakness, as it encouraged emigration.

The argument that women left home not because they needed jobs or lacked economic security but because they were weak (they loved 'a good time', they were easily led, they were looking for husbands, and they were not able to withstand the rigours of rural life)[56] was a way of expressing concern about the impact of modernity and commodity culture – a way of articulating the forms of loss and decline which went along with progress and improvement in the rural community. The small farmer economy required patience of both men and women; both men and women had to be prepared to wait for siblings to grow up, to emigrate, and for parents to die, in order that they might inherit and set up productive family units of their own. The assumption of female impatience, their greater susceptibility to the lures of modern consumer society and amoral, hedonistic lifestyles, was not, of course, an accurate diagnosis of the breakdown of the rural economy. It goes without saying that the numbers of extra-marital pregnancies indicated impatience in both men and women. By the mid '50s, both men and women were refusing to wait

---

[55] *A Catholic Handbook for Irish Men and Women Going to England* (Dublin: Catholic Truth Society of Ireland, 1953).

[56] See Lucey on fun-loving mothers: 'They see no sufficient reason why they should give up going out to pictures, dances, races, clubs, or perhaps jobs, for the sake of the children. Having a good time and looking after a family are incompatible with their way of thinking – as indeed they are, when only material considerations are taken into account.' Correspondence, TCDMSS 8300/54.

around in rural Ireland in roughly equal numbers. But female emigration remained a large part of the focus of population anxiety. This was in part because the idea of emigrating for 'modernity' or 'materialism' was more threatening. If men were emigrating for work, then this could be cured by introducing industry to rural areas (though there were those, including Aodh de Blacam, who argued that industry merely accelerated the rate of 'proletarianisation' and therefore also encouraged emigration). But if girls were emigrating for the nebulous benefits of modern urban life, what could be done to stop that?

'Love and Things'

Bicycles, cinemas, cosmetics, professional hairdressing, factory-made clothing, bakers' bread, tinned foods, radio, reading matter – all these objects of desire feature in Edna O'Brien's 1960 novel *The Country Girls*, a novel which effectively breaks down the distinction between the 'poorer' and the more respectable type of country girl. O'Brien's two heroines, Cait and Baba, are relatively well-off, convent-educated types who nonetheless 'fall' even before they get to the city, and long before they emigrate.

In a 1965 interview, O'Brien reflected on the apparent shift away from classical realism in the contemporary novel. She had met someone at a party who asked, 'Now why do you young people all write about sex now and don't write about money? And long ago, he was talking about George Eliot, one knew when reading a novel, what that person earned and you know, who brought the coal up ... ' Certainly money, or the lack of it, figures large in the trilogy, but it is not so much the cash earned through labour as that earned through sex, or what the young Caithleen still thinks of as romance, which powers the narrative. The darkening tone of the trilogy as a whole is in part a consequence of O'Brien's growing attempt to analyse rather than simply register the relationship between money and sex, as well as the developing aura of naturalistic determinism which hovers over Caithleen's fate. But the sexual economy had always been central to her portrait of rural Ireland.

Caithleen comes from a world which should be well insulated from the desperate economic calculations of the rural poor. She lives on a 400-acre farm in a big red, cut-stone house, but, because of her father's drinking, the place is 'going to ruin.' Rather than being a productive enterprise, the farm economy is based on hoarding. While the natural world offers a model of growth and abundance, the finances of the farm have become stagnant. Caithleen's father spends only on himself, using up resources on drink; the rest of the family, including the hired hand, operate an economy of hiding, and squirrelling away:

> In our house things were either broken or not used at all. Mama had a new clippers and several new coils of rope in a wardrobe upstairs; she said they'd only get broken or stolen if she brought them down.[57]

Caithleen and her mother keep sweets and bars of chocolate under the pillow to eat at night. The Doulton plates on the dresser 'were a wedding present, but we never used them in case they'd get broken. There were bills stuffed in behind them. Hundreds of bills. Bills never worried Dada, he just put them behind plates and forgot.'[58] Mama's definition of life is that 'some work and others spend', even when there is nothing to spend. Her distinction reveals the Brady holding to be a grotesque caricature of the traditional hard-working and austere farm economy, based on the communitarian exchange of goods and services, and untainted by money. For what they need is cash, and in order to get it they have to exchange the farm itself, and even offer themselves for sale. Dada has been given so much credit at the local hotel that in return ten cows graze on their land for life. Even Caithleen's mother is returned to the marketplace because of the economic failure of the farm – she is unable to reject the advances of the shopkeeper Jack Holland, who eventually buys up the house and land. When Mama dies, Caithleen finds herself subject to his offers of marriage, with the promise of living in her old home again. As a form of bribery it mirrors his former offers of a glass of juice in return for a kiss – it is not so much that women are objects to be bartered in a series of exchanges between men, but that women are expected to barter themselves in exchange for the goods they want. It is no surprise that Caithleen's romance with Mr Gentleman begins on a shopping trip. He buys her lunch and gets to hold hands with her in return, just as later, in Dublin, dinner of roast lamb and mint sauce comes with a price to pay.

One way of reading *The Country Girls* is as a rewriting of Maura Laverty's 1942 novel, *Never No More, the Story of a Lost Village*, with its popular mixture of realism and romance, and notably its obsession with food set against the blossoming sexuality of a young country girl.[59] *Never No More* was an idyllic story of growing up in a village on the edge of the Bog of Allen, and at the same time a sort of cookery book in which

---

[57] Edna O'Brien, *The Country Girls* (London: Phoenix, 2007 [1960]), p. 4.
[58] Ibid., p. 7.
[59] Maura Laverty, *Never No More: The Story of a Lost Village* (London: Longmans, Green, 1942).

Laverty sang hymns of praise to culinary innovations such as peas and carrots, offered detailed instructions on how to salt and dry ling, and how to cook it (fried, or coddled) once you had it hanging in your back kitchen.[60] As the title insisted, the story focused on a lost world – in which the fictional 'Gran' figured as a source of plenitude and fulfilment, her cooking a figure for unconditional love and the stability of the forgiving village community. Gran's mastery of pre-oven cookery and traditional herbal remedies harked back to a lost, indeed impossible idyll, but it also conjured a domestic world which more and more town-bred women were facing as reality during the war: cooking over turf rather than gas or even coal, having to create meals from scarce supplies and to find alternatives to basic foodstuffs, medicines and fuel. The not-so-subtle message of the novel, that folk practices and country lore could enable a balanced integration of modern and traditional Irish life, offered little resistance to the state's line on traditional, but increasingly regulated, small-town Ireland. Its appeal undoubtedly had to do with its unbridled nostalgia for an unspoilt Ireland, the simplicity of childhood and youthful innocence, and a land of burgeoning plenty. The elements of rural custom, neighbourly co-operation, petty jealousies, first dances, and above all lack of want, compared especially to the unhappy life of the towns, were replicated in a score of less-accomplished fictions – all catering to the needs of a generation of readers newly living in urban surroundings. The novel's nostalgia was not for the life of a parent's or grandparent's generation, but for an unspoilt childhood not much more than a few years in the past. (The story spans the years 1920 to 1928, though the central character grows from fourteen to only seventeen years of age in those eight years).

Romantic it may have been, but the novel was also read for its 'realistic' depiction of contemporary country life. In 1942 it was referred to in the Dáil in a debate on tuberculosis. Laverty's description of a young man dying in a cottage on the Bog of Allen, having waited too long for a place at Newcastle sanatorium, was used to highlight the problems of underfunding and lack of equipment in the treatment of tuberculosis.[61] And it was hardly coy about the facts of sexuality. Laverty's local anecdotes include at least four stories of illegitimacy (including the rape of a child leading to pregnancy), prostitution (servicing men on the canal boats),

---

[60] For a discussion of the relationship between the novel and 'emergency' realism, see Clair Wills, 'Women Writers and the Death of Rural Ireland: Realism and Nostalgia in the 1940s', *Éire-Ireland*, 41:1 (2006), pp. 192–212.

[61] See comment by James Dillon, *Dáil Éireann*, v. 87, 16 June 1942. http://debates.oireachtas.ie/DAIL/.

desertion, infidelity, women's physical pleasure in their own bodies, explicit reference to puberty, and sexual desire.

Laverty presents the burgeoning sexuality of young men and women
as integral to her romantic utopian vision of rural Irish life. She writes of
a community full of appetite, for food and for love, of a village teeming
with sexual impulses – both loving and brutal – and with generation. As
Caitriona Clear has argued, those characters who hoard (their food, their
youth, their bodies) go unrewarded. Women who have saved for years to
marry prudently die in childbirth, while life for those who have given way
to their impulses never turns out badly (bad husbands die; illegitimate
children conveniently disappear or are accepted into the community).[62]
For all the sex then, the novel offers a deeply unrealistic representation
of rural Irish society in the 1920s. It is the saintly character of Gran who
manages to hold the realism and the romance together. Gran's Christian
generosity and forgiveness – and not the moralising religion of the priest
who comes out badly in the novel, and to a literally sticky end when his
dropsical body explodes the evening before his burial – is the principle
by which this community can continue to thrive. In the context of public concern over the inevitable decline of rural communities in the face
of commercial commodity culture, Laverty's utopian vision can be interpreted as a radical intervention. She argued for the need to recapture and
reinvigorate nostalgia for pre-modern social forms – her lost village echoes
aspects of Goldsmith's deserted one – but at the same time she embraced
modern trends, not only of sexual but of socio-political behaviour. She
rejected the forms of republican austerity which were underwritten by
conservative moral codes, championing instead a sense of community
based on generosity.

Many of the ingredients in Laverty's novel reappear in *The Country
Girls*, including a violent father, drink, illness from tuberculosis, and tales
of disaster told in matter-of-fact terms (such as the description of Molly
the maid's mother's death, burnt to cinders while throwing paraffin on
the fire to boil up the potatoes for tea). Most of all *The Country Girls* echoes the failure of the nuclear family, with a shift to an alternative mother
figure in the first chapters of the book. But Laverty's broad underwrit-
ing of good housekeeping as a form of civic duty, as a means of healing
the rift between the traditional rural extended familial community and
the urban, increasingly nuclear, housewifely domain, is entirely undercut

---

[62] See Caitriona Clear, "'I Can Talk About It, Can't I?": The Ireland Maura Laverty Desired, 1942–
1946', *Women's Studies*, 30:6 (2001), pp. 819–835.

in O'Brien's narrative. Where Laverty's heroine manages to locate in her grandmother a lost world of communal values that is still somehow current, Cait goes to stay with the almost obscenely irreverent Mrs Brennan. Where Gran, the archetypal nurturer, feeds the village with wholesome dishes and country lore, Mrs Brennan wears velvet shoes, drinks red wine, and eats chicken and trifle in bed to hide it from her hard-working husband. Though the Brennan household is financially sound (Mr Brennan, the local vet, brings in good money, which he supplements with all sorts of extra finds, such as road-kill rabbit and fresh peas), the economy mirrors that of the failed Bradys, in that it is based on hoarding.[63] The only difference is that the younger Mrs Brennan can enjoy her private world, and she makes a virtue too, of the economic value of being female:

> Martha was what the villagers called fast. Most nights she went down to the Greyhound Hotel, dressed in a tight black suit with nothing under the jacket only a brassiere, and with a chiffon scarf knotted at her throat. Strangers and commercial travellers admired her. Pale face, painted nails, blue-black pile of hair, Madonna face, perched on a high stool in the lounge bar of the Greyhound Hotel, they thought she looked sad. But Martha was not ever sad, unless being bored is a form of sadness. She wanted two things from life and she got them – drink and admiration.[64]

To consume and to be consumed – apart from the nuns in the convent school who set themselves up in exaggerated opposition to this economy, by refusing wholesome food, and especially sweet things, and denying physical pleasure – the lives of all the women in the book are defined by these twin obligations. Rather than associate the city, either Dublin or London, with the excesses of consumption (though Baba fittingly contracts tuberculosis after a season of city pleasures), O'Brien suggests that there is no difference between urban and rural when it comes to the female economy. The young Caithleen reads almost as a caricature of an easily led, romantic young woman, but it is at home in the country, under the very noses of her family, that she falls for the citified, naturally French, Mr Gentleman. ('Paris? I thought of girls and sin at once.') With her options neatly divided between selling herself for her own inheritance (through marriage to Jack Holland, which would reinstate her ownership of the farm) or true romance with a rich married man, whichever way she turns

---

[63] The lower-middle-class economy in Dublin is also based on hoarding and recycling: the grocer's wife Mrs Burns hides food and gives herself the best dinner; Joanna the landlady fishes Cait and Baba's old bras out of the bin and uses them instead of money to pay the cleaning lady.

[64] O'Brien, *Country Girls*, p. 40.

she is for sale. Baba keeps her 'sane' because she has no illusions about this state of affairs.

One way of reading the arc of the trilogy as a whole is that the style shifts from naturalism to decadence, as the characters become caught up in urban consumerism and the 'artificial' relationships associated with the metropolis: failed marriages, affairs, one-night stands. But O'Brien dispenses with the martyr mother figure really early on as though to emphasise that she doesn't exist – the woman who lets you keep chocolate under the pillow and supplies cake for your lunchbox is always a nostalgic projection. All the women in the novel, and therefore too all the men, are washed through with the corruptions of commercial exchange. Cait is prone to comparing the city to food and nature in the country and particularly the dead mother, but this form of nostalgia has already been queried in the novel as it mirrors the forms of romantic association indulged in by both Jack Holland and Mr Gentlemen. Jack Holland's romantic nostalgia is expressed by quoting Colum and, tellingly, comparing Caithleen, 'an Irish colleen', to 'the woman with the face on the pound note' – a perfect union between an idealised projection of Ireland as a woman, and her commercial value.[65] Mr Gentleman's is more subtle. He tells her he prefers her without lipstick and praises her naturalness, while earning his right to do so in lavish lunches and candle-lit dinners. Either way, men treat women like tourists treat the countryside, paying for it to be, or to seem, pure.

In O'Brien's travelogue *Mother Ireland,* the armchair tourist is positioned as the obtuse consumer of a nurturing Mother Ireland and her home baking: 'Romantic Ireland, quite dead, you say, when you are sitting down to high tea in Athlone, imploded with drop scones, apple pie and soda bread.'[66] Romantic Ireland is still there for those who have the money to access it. But for those who live in it, it never had value: 'There was porter cake or the treacle cake that one turned one's nose up at, but a shop cake, or a swiss roll say, stale as rice paper, spoke of another world.' Cait has no regrets about turning her back on rural Ireland in favour of the 'neon fairytale' of Dublin, but even her willingness to leave is couched in terms of the failure of the country to live up to her nostalgia: 'I was not sorry to be leaving the old village. It was dead and tired and old and crumbling and falling down. The shops needed paint and there seemed to be

---

[65] The portrait of the woman on the pound note is believed to be Lady Hazel Lavery, wife of the artist Sir John Lavery.

[66] Edna O'Brien, *Mother Ireland* (London: Penguin, 1978), p. 20.

fewer geraniums in the upstairs windows than there had been when I was a child.'[67] Throughout the trilogy she will be caught by moments of wistfulness and longing for a place and time she acknowledges never existed. But rural Ireland does its best to maintain the tourist image of purity. Early on in *The Country Girls* Caithleen can see the difference between the reality of her unhappy home and its visual projection:

> A stranger going the road might have thought that ours was a happy farm; it seemed so, happy and rich and solid in the copper light of the warm evening. It was a red cut-stone house set among the trees, and in the evening-time, when the sun was going down, it had a lustre of its own, with fields rolling out from it in a flat, uninterrupted expanse of green.[68]

By the middle of *Girl with Green Eyes* the village is doing its best to live up to its reputation as a rural, Catholic, idyll: Jack Holland joins forces with her father and Mrs Brennan starts going to Lourdes and putting fake flowers around the house.

It is a far cry from her earlier advice to 'Get out of this dive – be something – somebody. An actor, something exciting …' The fantasies of escape rarely focus on educational opportunity, even for Caithleen the scholarship girl. Instead they are formed by dreams of romance shaped through Hollywood films, and stories of film stars. Baba reads film magazines at night in the convent dormitory; the height of flattery is to tell Cait she is 'like Rita Hayworth.' Films determine their understanding of romance:

> 'But we want young men. Romance. Love and things', I said, despondently. I thought of standing under a street light in the rain with my hair falling crazily about, my lips poised for the miracle of a kiss. A kiss. Nothing more. My imagination did not go beyond that.[69]

'Love and things': the grammatical equivalence between romance and objects of desire is telling. In the modernising discourses of marriage and self-fulfilment, romantic fantasies were combined with aspirations towards greater affluence; romance was linked to consumption through new forms of domestic and intimate space, filled with commercial goods such as TVs and washing machines, and new forms of leisure including going to the cinema and eating out. Dating was an activity that had to do with spending as much as amorousness and intimacy.

As O'Brien argues in *Mother Ireland*, romance was handed round in dog-eared copies of *East Lynne*, but it also came in the guise of the

---

[67] O'Brien, *Country Girls*, p. 155.
[68] Ibid., p. 37.
[69] Ibid., p. 186.

saccharine stories published in Irish women's magazines such as *Model Housekeeping* and *Women's Life*. These magazines traded on images of motherhood and domesticity (including home baking) but also ran fashion pages and stories based on romance matches. This was also true of *Ireland's Own*, which had the largest circulation within rural Ireland of material aimed at female consumption, though always within a broadly Catholic moral framework.[70]

Film magazines and both Irish and English women's weeklies could be bought in country newsagents of course, but they were also freely available in the larger towns at the professional hairdressers. M. J. Molloy was not alone in associating hairdressing with extravagance and even 'abroad.' In Elizabeth Bowen's 1955 novel *A World of Love,* the locus of feminine fulfilment in the provincial town of Clonmore is Miss Francie's salon, a 'magic oasis of tinted mirror, enamel and bakelite', which alone possesses 'the art of reviving the life-illusion.' It is in the salon that Lilia suddenly decides, in the middle of having her hair cut, that she should go to London. It's not just Miss Francie's scissors which have – halfway through the cut – already made her feel 'half-different' and able to extricate herself from the oppressive atmosphere at home in Montefort, but the alternatives to life at home which are on display. The glossy magazines resting on the gilded table in Miss Francie's salon are precisely the type of literature frowned on by the more conservative members of the Commission on Emigration. 'Prototype Woman' stares out at Lilia from the cover of her magazine, and she would undoubtedly be blamed for creating unrealistic expectations of life among local girls.[71]

This was despite the fact that the Irish women's magazines tended to work hard to bolster a broadly nationalist sense of women's commercial duties, featuring female cottage industries, the modernisation of farm work, and in the mid-'60s the 'Buy Irish' campaign, as alternatives to the scourge of emigration. The two most popular Irish magazines in the '50s were the fortnightly *Women's Life*, and the weekly *Woman's View* (amalgamated with *Model Housekeeping*) and boasting of itself as 'Ireland's Leading Woman's Magazine.' Advertisements and features in both magazines favoured Irish enterprises, with plugs for Amicardo Sherry and Enameline Stove Polish, for example, alongside editorials focusing on Irish enterprises

---

[70] Caitriona Clear's analysis of 1950s newspaper women's pages and women's magazines emphasises their urban bias, and 'staggering' ignorance of rural and farming women. She notes the similarity between Irish publications and those produced in 'very different industrial societies, and the almost complete lack of engagement with the realities of Irish women's lives', *Women of the House*, p. 93.

[71] Elizabeth Bowen, *A World of Love* (London: Cape, 1955).

headed up by women. Winter 1958 issues of *Woman's Life* extolled the hard work of Mrs Eileen Gallagher of Tallaght Enterprises, which started out as a jam- and chocolate-making concern in Donegal, and followed up with articles on how Donegal Cottage Industries and Irish lace-makers were helping to solve the problem of emigration, and on Cordon Bleu cookery courses as one way for women to contribute to the economy. A further article condemned the 'defeatism' of those who were emigrating, arguing that if people had sufficient recognition of their national duty they would stay to help rebuild the country.

Woman's View took a decidedly more modern line on women's economic potential and catered for a more urban (and younger) readership. Nonetheless the stories and features were careful not to stray too far from 'traditional' values. Tag lines for short stories were cautious with their priorities: 'Sally was a career girl, but it took a country lass to show her where happiness lay' (where Sally receives the helpful advice that 'a man's got to feel he's the boss'); 'Interlude of a Ballerina' warned, 'Dancing was Ann's life. To Michael it seemed greater than her love for him'; or 'They all saw her as a crisp, successful career girl – no-one knew her secret' (that she was in love). In the early '60s there were two new magazine ventures, both of them associated with the entrepreneur Sean O'Sullivan: *Woman's Way* started up as a fortnightly in April 1963, with Maura Laverty on the letters page, Clodagh, the 1960s design guru, on fashion and home furnishings, and Frank Hall interviewing the stars. The magazine was self-consciously youthful, devoting a page each week to news of the Show Bands, and self-consciously urban. One of the first articles dealt with young women's worries about how to behave on their first date in a smart restaurant – sadly too late for Caithleen Brady.

Woman's Way offered a form of interior design pornography, with features on electric ovens, refrigerators and built-in furniture which were out of reach for many readers.[72] Sean O'Sullivan's other venture, in collaboration with June Levine, was the *Irish Women's Journal*, which began in 1965

---

[72] In 1967 Clodagh was to move to *Young Woman*, a short-lived, determinedly hip fortnightly which featured articles on illegitimacy, the pill and sex education, alongside pieces urging consumerist patriotism and features on fashion, including lots of interviews with male actors. The articles on how to do up a bedsit, or what to expect on your honeymoon give a clear sense of its audience, as does the style: 'Hi, I'm Adam Flint. I work on a magazine and drive an old M. G. with a pad in Ballsbridge. It's not a flash place, mind you. A bit grotty really, but there you are. The walls are decorated in posters that Kim – he's a friend in San Francisco – sent me. They advertise groups like the Grateful Dead and Jefferson Airplane. All this psychedelick kick y'know.' The managing editor of the magazine was Norman Barry, and it included regular features by Helen Staunton, Clare Boylan and Terry Wogan, writing from London.

and advertised itself as 'the journal for the thinking woman.' Alongside short stories, fashion features and a regular Irish language slot, the magazine offered articles on contemporary issues such as teenagers, mods, beat clubs and, inevitably, emigration.

> Factories are closing down; Irish men and women are leaving once again. We must pull up our belts a notch while we get on with the talks for a free trade area with our great industrial neighbours. Our boys and men can always dig ditches in Birmingham, or pick spuds – in season of course – in Scotland.... If the shelves of our shops bulge with foreign merchandise, the shopkeepers will have to wake up and stop importing, stop stocking foreign goods. It's up to the thinking woman, who buys most of the goods, to keep her sons, her husbands, her brothers and uncles employed at home.[73]

The injunction to Buy Irish was an attempt to formulate a protectionist response to Ireland's subordinate place in an increasingly globalised economy, while embracing the benefits of capitalist modernity. Refusing to sell Irish labour power in England required an alternative form of investment, in Irish goods and services. None of this entailed a turn against luxury, however – far from it. The middle-class readers of the urban magazines were encouraged to support the transformation of traditional Irish domestic products – from jam to wool – into industrial and even luxury items. The requirement to resist foreign merchandise could, in this interpretation, coexist quite happily with the reputation of Dublin as site of luxury and specialist shopping. Middle- and upper-middle-class fashion habits could merge with the movement for Irish-made clothing and country life style.

What is noticeable in all these magazines is the striking level of support for a broadly traditionalist agenda – but one in which tradition was to be consumed, whether as folk practices, Donegal knitwear, old-style recipes, or cottages renovated as holiday homes. Arguably there was little else to be done with the dying culture of remote areas of the western seaboard but try to sell it, but there was a certain irony in the attempt to save a way of life which had developed in a subsistence economy by turning it into cash. One article, by Jean Sheridan in the *Irish Women's Journal*, described the bleak future for young women in Dunmanus Bay, County Cork, where 'in one parish seven homes have been deserted: at First Holy Communion last month there were only seven children from an out-parish of 360.' The thrust of the article was the duty of the well-educated urban middle class

[73] Editorial, *Irish Women's Journal*, December 1965.

to take their holidays in Ireland, turning the empty houses of the emigrants into holiday cottages, in order to save the 'the real, genuine people' who were still left.

> Nothing, no figures, no sociology lectures can bring home the facts of life on the Western seaboard as much as the physical evidence of them. There are people who complain that the Bishop of Cork, Dr Lucey, is monotonous in his exhortation to save what is left, to keep the people of these places from exile. He is in a position to see what is happening; the evidence is there on every Confirmation list, in a Sunday church door collection of twenty-five shillings. He would be a poor Bishop and a poorer sociologist if he was not affected by that evidence.... This is a place worth saving, this is where the real, genuine people are. They are a great people and in them one senses a deep Christian gratitude for what the good God has given them and which is not valued by the rest of us.[74]

In *Girl with Green Eyes* O'Brien draws an analogy between this kind of rhetoric and pornography. Cait and Baba gate-crash a 'private showing' of a travel film of Ireland: 'All lies, about dark-haired girls roaming around Connemara in red petticoats. No wonder they had to show it in private.' What was so shocking about *The Country Girls* was O'Brien's insistence that the real, genuine people had been buying and selling each other for years, had no deeper values than anyone else.

***

There is obviously nothing 'typical' about Elizabeth Bowen's Lilia (who is English and from London). Cait and Baba were not the types of girls most often discussed in 1950s debates on emigration, which focused instead on the dangers of losing too many marriageable girls in poor farming areas, and the need to provide factory jobs and places in cottage industries to keep them at home. Yet these novels do register the impact of consumerism and fashion on rural Irish women, and some of the ways in which that impact was interpreted. In O'Brien's case they also register the growth of a new female subjectivity which was to become the basis of a distinctive sixties feminism. O'Brien's characters are on the threshold of a new understanding of themselves; Cait's deceptively straightforward first-person narrative revels in the minutiae of her inner life, focused almost exclusively (like other early feminist works such as Doris Lessing's *The Golden Notebook*) on her relationships with men. Indeed, what both Lessing and

[74] Jean Sheridan, 'A Place in My Mind: Dunmanus Bay, Cork', *Irish Women's Journal*, July 1966.

O'Brien share in these early works is a sense that women's consciousness is mysterious, and mysterious even to themselves.[75]

The feminine mystique was partly a pose (Cait and Baba practice it in the mirror before going out at night) and partly a requirement of true romance, in its Hollywood, fictional or even real-life guises. What is revolutionary about *The Country Girls* is the way that the girls model themselves on and play with the array of types that are on offer in post-war Irish society. They appear to be no more defined by blood than they are by the images of women in the cinema and the magazines. They try them all on in a series of masquerades.[76] As I discuss in the next chapter, however, O'Brien's work, like that of her fellow post-war realists, is invested in a form of fatalism not so far from the impasse uncovered in neo-revivalist texts. In the end there is no way out for Cait or Baba.

I have suggested that the post-war rhetoric associating Irish women with consumer goods, luxury and modern forms of leisure expressed anxieties about the economy rather than about the women themselves. Women's changing relationship with money – earning and spending it – was a handy way of figuring the decadence which appeared to be infiltrating rural areas. The Catholic, community-oriented ideology of rural Ireland perceived urbanisation as a threat to its social programme, but as I have suggested, it was precisely because the materialist objects desired by Irish women were reasonable demands in the context of changing lifestyles that they appeared so ominous. Moralistic concern over the increasing reliance on shop-bought 'luxuries' disclosed people's powerlessness in the face of the inevitability of capitalist modernity as it encroached on rural areas, their sense that modernisation, while it brought benefits (such as plumbing and electric light) also entailed decline and degeneration: the loss of traditional communities, the ever-increasing rates of emigration,

---

75 See the interviews gathered in Dunn, *Talking to Women*. O'Brien's extraordinary interview in this volume touches on the realm of fantasy in the creative work of the writer, and the difficulty of combining writing with bringing up children. But its main focus is O'Brien's exploration of her own consciousness through her relationships. It includes a neat version of an emigrant, lapsed Catholic's view on austerity, restraint and indulgence, all of which are interpreted entirely in terms of her individual consciousness: she would like, she says, 'if I loved someone to be able to approach his mouth and then draw back. However, as I say this, I recognize that restraint can be another form of indulgence. I think balance is what counts' (p. 105). For a reading of the work of O'Brien, Nell Dunn and Lynne Reid Banks in relation to an emerging feminist consciousness, see chapter 2 of John Muckle, *Little White Bull: British Fiction in the Fifties and Sixties* (Bristol: Shearsman Books, 2014).

76 This is emphasised in the 1964 film version, with the opening sequences focusing on the female rituals of makeup and masquerade. *Girl with Green Eyes,* directed by Desmond Davis, Woodfall Films, 1964.

the disappearance of the rural labourer, the failure of smallholdings, the decimation of the small towns. Shopping required money, and that was one problem. But it brought others in its wake, such as the way it allowed women to cross boundaries of class and social status, and revealed the ambiguities at the heart of descriptions of them as good and poor types. Yet it is not possible to draw a simple distinction between concern about the economy, and concern about women's behaviour, as Edna O'Brien's heroines know all too well. Women could stand in for the failure of republican austerity precisely because they were women. As self-sacrificing mothers or dutiful, dowry-bearing daughters they had long been associated with all that the republic stood for, and as shoppers and emigrants they could as easily be associated with all that the republic feared.

rarewaves

Thank you for your purchase!

Rarewaves
Belkin House (Unit 2 Door No. 2)
Shipton Way, Express Business Park,
Northamptonshire, Rushden
NN10 6GL,United Kingdom
sales@rarewaves.com
www.rarewaves.com

Deliver To:

Christopher Bell
4 Summerswood Close
ebay2dlbfx7
Kenley
Surrey CR8 5EY

South America No:
ORDER No: EB25-12378-76798

Qty	Description	Price
1	WILLS, CLAIR THE BEST ARE LEAVING BOOK	18.42

Multiple orders may be sent seperately.
Shipping costs may be separately invoiced.
Vat No: 85415481

Sub Total: 18.42
Shipping : 0.00
Total : 18.42

Order Num: EB25-12378-76798 Marketplace:eBay UK

Reason For Return (Please complete so we can process your return

[ ] Damaged/Defective/Faulty   [ ] Incorrect Item Received
[ ] Unwanted/Changed Mind   [ ] Other Reason (State)

Do you require a Replacement/Refund/Exchange?
[ ] Replacement
[ ] Refund
[ ] Exchange(Different Item)

27486597

**For further information on our returns policies
please refer to the website where you placed
your order or contact our customer service
team on returns@rarewaves.com.**

PART II

Immigrants

CHAPTER 3

British Paddies
Realism and the Irish Immigrant

As I went to sleep tonight, the silence was broken with shouting and screaming, dreadful cursing and the noise of heavy blows. It was the Connemara men and the people from Dublin. They've been fighting this many a day.

Murphy and I went off to Mass together. I was astonished at the sermon that was preached – all about the lads fighting in the pubs and dance halls. The priest came out very strongly against them, saying they were nothing but ignorant beasts that let down their country and their Faith. There's no denying that this sort of thing is necessary for the devil has seized hold of enough Irishmen here in London.

Donall Mac Amhlaigh[1]

In the mad floodtide of those years there was no distinction between 'townie' and 'rager sham' from 'up the country.' McAlpine's Fusiliers took them all as they came, put shovels in their hands and let them get on with it.

John Healy[2]

For all its bravura wit *The Country Girls* is a story of masochistic repetition and failure. The trilogy opens with the death of Caithleen's mother by drowning, an event which is described as 'the last day of her childhood' for Caithleen – and closes with her own suicide by drowning twenty-five years later. In Tom Murphy's *A Whistle in the Dark,* Michael Carney, the upwardly mobile eldest son of the Carney family, who has emigrated from Mayo to Coventry in hopes of escaping from a brutalising social and familial environment, is pulled back into a cycle of violence. He re-engages in a battle with his father in which he accidentally kills his youngest brother. More than a cyclical plot, we could call this a downward spiral. The antithesis of progress structures numerous Irish novels from this period – Brian Moore's *The Lonely Passion of Judith Hearne,* and *The Feast of Lupercal,*

---

[1] Mac Amhlaigh, *An Irish Navvy*, pp. 73–74.
[2] Healy, *The Death of an Irish Town*, p. 24.

Maurice Leitch's *Poor Lazarus*. In John McGahern's work the cyclical form is not limited to one novel but stretches over his oeuvre as a whole. The loss of the mother and brutalising effects of the father figure explored in the '60s novels *The Barracks* and *The Dark* are revisited in his 1990 novel *Amongst Women* – emphasising again the frustration and deprivation of Irish society which cannot be escaped even if – like O'Brien's Caithleen and Murphy's Michael Carney – characters leave Ireland behind. This emphasis on the determinism of the past is of course a feature of the naturalist novel from Zola onwards, with naturalism understood in the Darwinian sense as an investigation of the fundamental 'laws' governing society and its evolution. But where British and French naturalism focuses above all on class as a determinant of social behaviour and social stagnation, the targets of Irish naturalism are somewhat different.[3]

This body of literature identifies a common core of affliction in Irish society, as it excavates the traumas of family violence, sexual abuse, clerical repression, and the patriarchal authoritarianism of rural Catholic Ireland in mid-century. Both McGahern and O'Brien, for example, focus on a tyrannical father, who becomes a figure for the repressiveness of Irish society in general. Their protagonists are would-be modern young men and women, who are beset by the anachronism or the belatedness of post-war Irish society – it is as though the impulse to move into a newer, more modern phase of civilisation is continually dragged backwards, or not allowed to develop in the first place. The wounds carried within Irish society are nearly always figured as self-inflicted in the literature of post-independence Ireland. But by the post-war period the blame for Ireland's inability to recover from its past, to move on into 'civilised modernity', is blamed on a violent, repressive and authoritarian older generation. The powerful grip of cruel, atavistic or tragic parental figures leaves youth floundering, hauled back by a violent history, caught in a repetitive cycle. The paradigmatic example of this literary formation is 'The Great Hunger', in which Patrick Maguire is denied generation and a future other than that bound by the natural agricultural cycle. 'He would have changed the circle if he could', warns Kavanagh, but Maguire is one of the defeated for whom 'there is no tomorrow, but only time stretched for the saving of the hay.'[4]

[3] Murphy, *A Whistle in the Dark*; Brian Moore, *The Feast of Lupercal* (Boston, MA: Little, Brown, 1957); Brian Moore, *Lonely Passion of Judith Hearne* (Boston, MA: Little, Brown, 1955); Maurice Leitch, *Poor Lazarus* (London: Panther, 1970); John McGahern, *The Barracks* (London: Panther, 1966); John McGahern, *The Dark* (London: Panther, 1967); John McGahern, *Amongst Women* (London: Faber, 1991).

[4] Kavanagh, 'The Great Hunger', in Quinn (ed.), *Collected Poems*.

The circling, repetitive structure of 'The Great Hunger', with its insistent use of full rhyme and echo ('Is there no escape/no escape') casts a long shadow over post-war Irish fiction, which figures entrapment within an anachronistic historical moment, the inability of Irish history to advance, through circular and iterative forms. Formally, the plot mechanism which reveals the crisis at the heart of Irish society turns on the unsuccessful *Bildungsroman*. Caithleen Brady, Michael Carney, John McGahern's young Mahoney are all characters whose classic narrative of personal development and the consequent renewal of Irish society is thwarted in some way (again, much like Paddy Maguire). These cyclical narratives are probably the least 'realistic' elements of the realist novels. Most lives, after all, are not plotted in a circular fashion. The melodramatic aspects of these plots are a useful reminder that the novels are shaped by a form of naturalist determinism which has its roots in styles of anthropology and sociology, which look to expose the sordid reality at the heart of the rural world, or occasionally, as in Brian Moore's *The Feast of Lupercal*, the social forces that constrict and constrain the growing adolescent in the urban world of Belfast.

The anthropological aspect of these novels points us towards a further shared characteristic – a focus on poverty and limitations. Dearth and scarcity are recurring features of the social background in many of these fictions – the struggling farms in *The Country Girls* and *The Dark*, for example – but they also shape the cultural background, as characters battle with the poverty of imaginative resources. The Church and religion on the one hand, and the natural world on the other, are often the only outlets for creative or imaginative thought on the part of the protagonists – noticeably, unlike Joyce's Stephen, none of the post-war protagonists is a young artist. Their lives are determined by lack.[5]

For all these reasons, Irish realism of the 1960s has been interpreted as an extension of the tradition of Irish naturalism, which had its genesis in Joyce's *Dubliners* and the novels of George Moore, and developed strongly in the 1920s and '30s amongst writers concerned to undermine the perceived romanticism of revivalist myths in post-independence Ireland.

---

[5] Flann O'Brien's *The Third Policeman* (London: Pan Books, 1974) can be read as the exception which proves the rule, a satire on naturalism. The plot is a cyclical narrative gone mad, as the unnamed narrator is destined to repeat his encounters with a series of inscrutable policemen until the end of time, learning nothing in the process. It is also a brilliant parody of the 'lack' to be found in the heart of rural Ireland. As the sun shines on the bright green fields throughout the novel we discover that the pastoral idyll contains absolutely nothing except a miserly old man, a bunch of policemen, a crowd of one-legged outlaws, and our narrator, a murderer.

Indeed the '60s realists have been criticised for their 'belated naturalism.' It is true that a style privileging 'sordidness', coded as naturalist manner and prized for 'objectivity', does get a repeated showing in this fiction. Patrick Rafroidi notes that Brian Moore's early novels are characterised by 'a downright ugliness of places and people alike, a dreary atmosphere, and mediocre destinies.'[6] Closed and unforgiving environments form the backdrop to bankrupt love affairs and seedy sexual encounters. Maurice Leitch's 1969 novel *Poor Lazarus* repeatedly returns to flecks of spit, mottled skin, and the coincidence of dirt and sexuality, as though to prove its realism. Arguably these texts do recycle the images of corrupt sexuality to which the censors objected in the work of Sean O'Faolain and Frank O'Connor.

But to characterise these fictions as 'belated naturalism' is to ignore the pressures of alternative modes of realism on these works, particularly the influence of sociological and ethnographic writing on class and community, and the strategies of documentary realism. While the tradition of Irish realist social critique was indeed an important strand in the fiction of the 1960s, and in particular in the work of John McGahern, it was cross-fertilised by other realist narrative modes. As Joe Cleary argues, the concerns of English post-war literary fiction lay heavily on Irish post-war writers, including 'issues such as the class structure of the education system or the travails of the talented, upwardly mobile but deracinated "scholarship" boy or girl.'[7] These new class-based narratives entailed not merely a change of subject but a change of narrative mode.

Certain aspects of English working-class fiction could be accommodated relatively easily in Irish naturalist prose writing, and vice versa. The story of thwarted ambition is as central to British realist writing as it is to the inheritors of O'Faolain and O'Connor. In Alan Sillitoe's *Saturday Night, Sunday Morning*, or Sheila Delaney's *A Taste of Honey*, the action turns on a character attempting to free himself or herself from the bonds of community – think of Arthur Seaton in *Saturday Night, Sunday Morning*: 'What I'm out for is a good time. All the rest is propaganda!' Nevertheless, by the end of the novel he has been domesticated by the community, safely paired up with Doreen and looking forward to a life at home and at work much like his father's. What is noticeable, however, is

---

[6] Patrick Rafroidi, 'The Great Brian Moore Collection', in Patrick Rafroidi and Maurice Harmen (eds.), *The Irish Novel in Our Time* (Villeneuve-d'Ascq: Publications de l'Université de Lille III, 1976), pp. 221–236.

[7] Joe Cleary, 'This Thing of Darkness: Conjectures on Irish Naturalism', in *Outrageous Fortune: Capital and Culture in Modern Ireland* (Dublin: Field Day Publications, 2007), p. 157.

that the cyclical plots in English working-class realism are far more benign than the Irish stories I have mentioned. Concern over the alienation of manual labour is tempered by a nostalgia for older working-class communities so that, in general, there is less of the violence and darkness associated with Irish '60s realism – the physical beatings, the sexual violence, the suicides. Moreover, English post-war fiction still cleaves to romance and the construction of new family units as plot resolution. Iconic British realist novels and films of the early 1960s all portray social enculturation, or its failure, through male-female relationships and marriage.

But for writers seeking to represent the experience of Irish migrants in Britain, romance proved a dead end. The rural matchmaker plots of M. J. Molloy or John B. Keane were clearly unable to address the experience of emigration or of country men and women transplanted to urban working-class communities. Romance had long been targeted as a dangerous chimera amongst the anti-revivalists, and this tradition was extended in the work of post-war novelists, such as O'Brien, Moore and Leitch. But the turn away from marriage and the family was most marked amongst Irish writers seeking to respond to the migrant experience in Britain. In this chapter, I explore the development of Irish realism by writers focusing on the world of the migrant labourer, who was cut off from family by the milieu in which he lived and worked. Memoirs and ethnographies, such as those by Irish-language writers Donall Mac Amhlaigh and Richard Power, shared a common focus with post-war Irish realism set in Britain, such as the work of Tom Murphy. Both forms of writing attempted to express the experience of the newly migrant Irish within an urban working-class community, which was not yet bounded by ties of family and marriage. In so doing they encountered the limits of both rural and urban realist forms. Irish migrant realism remained caught between contrasting versions of class and community and of the relationship of individuals to their social milieu.

The development of new forms of realism in the 1950s and '60s in Britain, including the working-class novel, documentary, and sociological ethnographic texts, opened up a space where new types of experience including migration and labour could begin to be addressed. They enabled a shift from a focus on the emigrant to the immigrant in the new society, and from family and farm to other types of community. The resulting tensions appear in Irish ethnographic texts of migration and labour, such as works by Mac Amhlaigh and Power. These texts were partly modelled on an earlier west of Ireland ethnography, derived from the work of J. M. Synge in the Aran islands, and the Blasket Island autobiographies, but also from a large corpus of ethnographic and anthropological studies of family and community in rural Ireland. However, the transplanted urban communities Mac Amhlaigh and Power explored differed in fundamental respects from the familial communities analysed in classic Irish ethnographic studies, since migrant documentary writing dealt primarily with homosocial worlds (and specifically male gang labour) rather than with the farm family and the wider intergenerational community. Representations of the labouring experience – whether in memoir, documentary, folklore or realist drama – reveal tensions within and between what could be termed 'neo-revivalist' and 'neo-realist' attitudes to class and community, as the new communities created by the migrants cut across 'traditional' and modern working-class boundaries.

It is not that documentary strategies were alien to Irish realism before the influence of British working-class fiction. I have written elsewhere of the relationship between the documentary modes characteristic of Irish wartime realism, and the social and political project of neutrality and wartime centralisation.[8] Nor did the influence of class-based sociological thinking radically alter the disillusioned tone of post-war Irish fiction. The shift from rural to an urban setting, often paralleled by a shift from an insular Irish to an immigrant British locale, may not have offered an alternative to the disenchantment characteristic of twentieth-century Irish realism. But in a manner typical of the history of naturalism it did allow new areas of social experience to be explored. In particular, the focus on a (usually male) labouring community offered a way of sidestepping the family-based plots which were a mainstay not only of the realist writers but of folk drama. So many of the fictional explorations of rural insularity utilise a basic *Bildungsroman* plot to highlight the struggle between the younger generation and family or parental authority, the youthful rejection of a grownup world which has failed. In the folk drama, the older generation is often criticised for its unyielding authority, viewed as a cause of emigration and rural collapse, but the drama itself turns on romance and marriage of the young as the solution to social malaise. Migrant realism on the other hand deals primarily with homosocial worlds, and with a horizontal rather than vertical axis of community.

Furthermore, as I have suggested, this emphasis on (usually but not exclusively) male communities sets it apart not only from Irish realism set in Ireland but also from British working-class realism, which tends to narrate social mobility, often through a romance plot. In the films of the

---

[8] See chapter 5 of Wills, *That Neutral Island: A History of Ireland during the Second World War* (London: Faber, 2007).

British New Wave, the pull of individualist social advancement against the constraints of working-class community is often imaged in terms of housing and against the backdrop of the modernising post-war city. However, in both documentary and realist Irish migrant texts of the 1960s, the link between home, family, and social mobility is consistently broken. The uncertain place of Irish migrants in the fictional world of the British working class reflects their peripheral status as labourers in, but not of, the social fabric of urban Britain. The 'community' in Irish migrant texts typically lacks homes, parents, and the basic ingredient of the couple. Thus, while Irish immigrant narrative mirrored some aspects of British working-class realist fiction and the New Wave films of the early '60s (particularly in its focus on labour), the rejection of a marriage and family plot was one crucial difference. Although there were many thousands of young, single Irish men and women in British cities by the mid-1950s who in reality paired up, couples did not become part of the written narrative, which focused instead on milieu. For male migrants in particular, building work and the landscape of reconstruction were not the background to personal stories, but the fabric of their lives. Construction sites were at once their workplace and one of the locations of their community. Thus, the Irish New Wave differs in important respects from its British counterpart. Irish fiction registers the ambiguous class position of the Irish in Britain, and narrative strategies common to working-class realist texts such as the delineation of the relationship between place and community and the tracking of social mobility proved inadequate as a means of articulating lives lived within the Irish community in Britain.

Ethnography and the Irish Male Immigrant

The combined influence of sociological writing and documentary film on British realism of the 1950s and '60s (the British New Wave) has been well documented. Similarly, new forms of sociological and documentary narrative modes influenced Irish writing, particularly the work of writers who migrated to Britain during the 1960s.[9] Representations of Irish migrants

---

[9] McGahern, O'Brien, Murphy and Leitch all spent time in London during the 1960s, as did a number of other writers less clearly associated with the realist renaissance in Irish writing, including Patrick Kavanagh, Anthony Cronin, John B. Keane and Brendan Behan. It is noticeable that documentary film makers figure relatively highly in Irish '60s fiction. Not only is O'Brien's Eugene Galliard a documentary maker, but the narrator of Leitch's *Poor Lazarus* is an emigrant film maker sent back to Ireland to discover a subject, and the narrative is told through his notes for the documentary.

drew on forms of racial and sub-racial categorisation which were embedded in Irish discourses of emigration, yet the following analysis emphasises the role of new forms of class analysis in the representation of the fundamental struggle between traditional and modern. The Irish community in post-war Britain, most visibly represented by the Irish labourer, was not merely composed of figures transplanted from rural Ireland, but was also formed by British discourses of class and race, which were themselves developing new methods of representation under the influence of sociology.

In the early '50s in Britain, a new type of sociological inquiry, principally centred at the London School of Economics and later in Birmingham, pioneered innovative forms of research and particularly of survey analysis, aiming to head off the influence of social Darwinism and to disentangle hereditarian discourse from social analysis through theoretically informed empirical observation.[10] One of the principal research agendas was an analysis of working-class life under the impact of social mobility, affluence, mass culture and changing conceptions of leisure. Some of the most widely read and discussed books of the period included sociological ethnographies such as Wilmott and Young, *Family and Kinship in East London* (1957) and Abel-Smith and Townsend, *The Poor and the Poorest* (1965). The publication of Richard Hoggart's *The Uses of Literacy* (1957) and Raymond Williams's *Culture and Society* (1958) cemented the popularity of sociology as an academic subject for a generation, and crystallised the idea that a loss of community was an inevitable consequence of the transformations of working-class life: the paradox of material improvement gained at the expense of cultural loss.

This surge in social research both fed off and fed into a broader ethnographic climate in Britain. The vogue for documentary writing and film in the late '50s coincided with sociology's rise to academic and popular respectability. Documentary films made by the Free Cinema collective in the 1950s, described by Lindsay Anderson as concerned with reflecting 'the stimulus of contemporary life',[11] influenced the British New Wave. Many of the directors – Anderson, Tony Richardson, Karel Reisz – were central to both movements. The rejection of Grierson-type documentary techniques also had an effect on the more politicised, social policy–driven, British television documentaries which came to the fore in the mid-'60s,

[10] See A. H. Halsey, *A History of Sociology in Britain* (Oxford: Oxford University Press, 2004).
[11] See Stuart Laing, *Representations of Working-Class Life* (Basingstoke: Palgrave Macmillan, 1986), p. 114.

notably Ken Loach's *Up the Junction* (1965) and *Cathy Come Home* (1966). Simultaneously, the novelists Colin MacInnes, Keith Waterhouse and Doris Lessing all began to describe their works as documentaries, associating them with popular film genres and focusing on community and place as an end in itself (and most usually for the benefit of outsiders to that community), rather than as a vehicle for the exploration of subjectivity.[12] These works on the borderline between documentary and fiction form my context for situating ethnographic writings by and about Irish migrants in Britain, which reveal the limits both of homegrown Irish representations of emigrants and of British representations of the socially mobile working class.

I have discussed the influence of Catholic social thought on attitudes towards emigration in previous chapters. Until the late '50s the empirical element of Irish sociology was written within an anthropological paradigm stemming primarily from outside Ireland (most notably the work of Arensberg and Kimball),[13] which relied heavily on an opposition between modernity and tradition and which therefore sat quite easily with the ethically normative framework of social policy deriving from conservative Catholicism. From the 1920s onward, Catholic influence on the discipline of sociology was designed to head off the ideological challenge to the church's teaching from unfettered capitalism, socialism and communism. Yet developments within Irish sociological research and community studies were beginning to offer a rather different perspective on emigration. And strands of Catholic social thought were also open to the empirical currents in sociology and Irish social science.

The 1964 Limerick Rural Survey is one example of the intersection between Catholic sociology and empiricism and of the attempt to move away from morally normative descriptions of Irish social life.[14] The survey was sponsored by the Catholic corporatist organisation Muintir na

---

[12] For an analysis of the divisions between 'literary' and 'documentary' fiction in the period, see Timothy Alan Bell, 'Envisioning the Working Class in British Fiction, 1957–1967', PhD dissertation, Queen Mary University of London, 2012. As Bell argues, literary reviews tended to criticize the documentary aspects in the work of popular regional writers such as Alan Sillitoe and John Braine, arguing that the works were 'sub-literary', or 'social problem literature', with the use of pejoratives such as 'flat' and 'grey' implying analogies with black-and-white documentary film.

[13] See Conrad Arensberg and Solon Kimball, *Family and Community in Ireland* (Cambridge: Harvard University Press, 1940).

[14] See Newman (ed.), *Limerick Rural Survey*; for comparable studies with a more clearly defined sociological methodology, see Jackson, *Report on the Skibbereen Social Survey* and Humphreys, *New Dubliners*. The Irish Agricultural Institute's *West Cork Resource Survey*, though primarily quantitative in approach, does include some sociological discussion of demographics particularly in section C, 'Economic Aspects of the Survey Area.'

Tíre, which looked for regeneration of the Irish countryside. But Jeremiah Newman, architect of the survey, also requested input from the school of sociology at the University of Chicago, and arranged for the principal young researcher, Peter McNabb, to study methods of scientific survey in the Netherlands. Thomas Wilson has argued that right up until the 1970s Irish ethnographers were held back by the influence of Arensberg and Kimball's work of the 1930s, unable to think outside their unit of analysis (the community), their focus for the analysis of social life (kinship and social structure), and their theoretical model of local society (structural functionalism).[15] The influence of Arensberg and Kimball on the Limerick social survey is unmistakeable – indeed one of the investigators, P. J. Meghan, had worked with Arensberg as a young man. Nonetheless, Peter McNabb's sections on demography and social structure reveal traces of alternative models, and certainly different emphases. McNabb accepted the farm family as his central unit of analysis, and the categories into which he divided his discussion reflected the priorities of previous studies – the nature of marriage, the role of the father, the characteristics of the bachelor group, the type and function of leisure. But he subjected the farm community to an explicit class analysis. He argued that 'The most striking phenomenon in the rural regions of County Limerick is a change in class structure; from being a stable and closed community, having a rigid class structure assented to by all its members, it has become unstable and open.' He put this change down to what he called the 'revolt' of the farm worker, arguing that the typical rural labourer of the early '60s refused to accept the low social status accorded to him in Ireland and went to where he knew he would gain 'more respect', in England. Rather than blame the farm worker for his greed or moral weakness, McNabb placed responsibility with the community which 'is not prepared to meet the social and economic aspirations of the farm worker.' He saw the tensions within rural society as economically driven: 'With the emancipation of the working class and the change-over to the wage system, farmers' sons remaining at home are finding it difficult to maintain their social standing.'[16]

Quite apart from the sudden appearance of phrases such as 'the emancipation of the working class' in a study of rural Ireland, this section of the survey is notable for McNabb's reliance on informed respondents rather than knowledgeable experts. In the late '40s the Emigration Commission

[15] See Thomas M. Wilson, 'From Clare to the Common Market: Perspectives in Irish Ethnography', *Anthropological Quarterly*, 57:1 (January 1984), pp. 1–15.
[16] See Patrick McNabb, 'Demography', and 'Social Structure', in Newman (ed.), *Limerick Rural Survey*, esp. pp. 193, 209, 218.

had conducted a survey of intending emigrants which relied very heavily on local authority figures (priests, guards, officials in the employment exchanges) for information, many of whom had no qualms about dividing migrants into 'good types', 'poor types', 'inferior types', and so on.[17] This style of classification was in part a euphemism for class but it also signalled a belief in observable natural types. By contrast, though McNabb carried out lengthy individual and group interviews with different sections of the community, at no point does the language of types or stock appear in an explanatory guise. Indeed at one point he defines 'good stock' economically, as meaning a prosperous farmer.[18]

It is tempting to argue that this more economically informed analysis allowed a more complex evaluation of the relationship between nature and environment, and a more variegated examination of emigrant choices. What registers in McNabb's work, and other social surveys of the time, such as John Jackson's *Report on the Skibbereen Social Survey* (1964), is a moment when pressure was being put on traditional definitions of the Irish community. That pressure came from several different directions. Jackson, for example, argued that the local community extended to those who had already emigrated, and as part of his analysis he interviewed the sons and daughters of small farmers and shopkeepers who were living in England, where they formed part of the industrial working class. The tensions between class and traditional community as ways of interpreting Irish emigrant experience are clearly marked not only in the sociology but also in ethnographic and fictional texts by and about Irish migrants in Britain.

One of the best-known accounts of Irish labourers in Britain, Donall Mac Amhlaigh's *Dialann Deoraí* (*An Irish Navvy: Diary of an Exile*), was published in Irish in 1960 and in an English translation by Valentin Iremonger in 1964. Mac Amhlaigh left Kilkenny for Britain in 1951, first to work as a hospital orderly and later as a labourer at various sites in England, particularly around Northampton, where he eventually settled. *Diary of an Exile* is the story of his first seven years in England. When Mac Amhlaigh's narrative begins he is twenty-two years old and has been unemployed for three months, after his discharge from an Irish-speaking

---

[17] See the 'Rural Surveys' conducted by Commissioners, held in the Arnold Marsh Papers, Trinity College, Dublin, which I discuss in Chapter 1, TCDMSS 8306.

[18] McNabb's sociological contribution was marginalized when the Report was published. See Peter Murray and Maria Feeney, *The Market for Sociological Ideas in Early 1960s Ireland: Civil Service Departments and the Limerick Rural Survey, 1961–1964* (Dublin: National Institute for Regional and Spatial Analysis, 2010), Working Paper Series No. 53. Murray and Feeney argue that the government was not ready to entertain his more economically informed analysis, which argued for a more complex understanding of the relationship between nature and the social environment.

battalion of the army. Living with his parents in Kilkenny, he gets twenty-two shillings and sixpence from the Labour Exchange, which, he explains, '[isn't] enough to keep anybody.'[19] His introduction to 'going foreign' is a textbook example of the process which exasperated M. J. Molloy. He responds to an advertisement, to which he is alerted by his mother, for a job as a stoker in a hospital near Northampton. The news that he has secured the post is celebrated with a shop-bought cake. Most of all, Mac Amhlaigh's narrative appears to underwrite the claim that Irish urbanisation furthers rather than forestalls migration. Though Mac Amhlaigh identifies throughout his memoir with Connemara, 'where my people came from', and considers Connemara people 'the finest men' and 'the most beautiful women', his narrative continually returns to the fact that he has already lost contact with the west. His family's move to Kilkenny features as a staging post in the migrant journey, a decline from the true 'manliness' of Connemara to the more comfortable world of shops and pubs in the town. The city certainly fails to offer a livelihood or stave off emigration, and by the close of the memoir, in 1957, all Mac Amhlaigh's siblings have moved to England: 'Kevin is in Daventry, Noel in Hampshire, Brian in Sussex and Dympna, our only sister, in London. It's the same story in many houses here and, indeed, all over Ireland.'[20]

Although Mac Amhlaigh stresses his pragmatic, and economic, reasons for leaving home, his rhetoric also chimes with neo-revivalist ideas about the dangers of the city to rural life. He meets a man from County Galway who 'would never go back to Lettermullen for love or money for he's ruined by city life';[21] he strolls through Piccadilly at night and muses that 'It's the bright lights and not so much lack of work that entice the Irish over here away from their own country.'[22] The memoir bears many of the marks of an older Irish anthropological and ethnographic style, heavily invested in the idea of traditional communities becoming lost to the onward march of modernity – even to the extent of including phrases that had already been made the butt of anti-primitivist jokes in Flann O'Brien's *An Béal Bocht*. Talking with older men from the Gaeltacht MacAmhlaigh cites Tomas O'Crohan's 1929 autobiographical ethnography of the Great Blasket:

> I like to hear them talking about home for just like the Islandman, God be with him, we'll never look upon their likes again. Connemara is

[19] Mac Amhlaigh, *An Irish Navvy*, p. 3.
[20] Ibid., p. 178.
[21] Ibid., p. 52.
[22] Ibid., p. 125.

changing and a new generation will spring up there that won't have the same attributes the present one has. Maybe the young won't have the same vices; but they won't have the same virtues either. All these characters are like the sailing boat and the spinning wheel, on their way out; the young get all their opinions and habits from outside.[23]

The diary is full of little homilies on the behaviour of Irish women and of Irish speakers, which fit comfortably within a broadly conservative moral framework. He has what one contemporary reviewer termed a 'County obsession,' which allows him to describe the conduct of different groups of Irish migrants with reference to their origins: Connemara men are fine physical specimens, full of camaraderie, and they know how to talk; Dubliners are small, lazy, liable to cheat, and interested only in money. He is prone to spouting the populist line on the dangers of emigration and the destruction of family life in Britain (such that in the drive to afford luxuries such as TV sets, women are encouraged to work rather than look after children). He laments the loss of Irish distinctiveness as 'Ireland of the jukebox: Ireland the imitator' passively apes British 'progress.'[24]

Mac Amhlaigh's invocation of *The Islandman* is of a piece with his ambition to write an 'insider's' narrative of an Irish, and Irish-speaking, community – albeit one which has become scattered throughout Britain. To that end he repeatedly emphasises the traditional qualities of the 'finest' Irish men with whom he works, lives and socialises (and he contrasts them with the absence of those qualities in the metropolitan Irish – men from Dublin and its environs). Given that everyday rural life has been completely disrupted by the move to industrial Britain, he seeks the signs of traditional custom and behaviour in language: unadulterated Irish, lively conversation, storytelling and repartee, much of which happens in the pub. The real Irish are defined by talk, and the finest communicate in the finest Irish. They are therefore as easily to be found in London or Derby as in the Gaeltacht, since so many of these men have emigrated. Alongside the narrative of loss caused by emigration, Mac Amhlaigh describes emigrant life as enabling continuity with traditional culture, as Irish-speaking men (and occasionally women) are brought together by Britain's industrial boom. Communities are recreated in digs, in camps, on the sites,

---

[23] Ibid., p. 94. See, for example, the closing passage of *The Islandman*: 'I have written minutely of much that we did, for it was my wish that somewhere there should be a memorial of it all, and I have done my best to set down the character of the people about me so that some record of us might live after us, for the like of us will never be again.' Tomas O'Crohan, *The Islandman*, trans. Robin Flower (Oxford: Oxford University Press, 1977 [1929]).

[24] Mac Amhlaigh, *An Irish Navvy*, p. 163.

and in the pubs and dancehalls. In March 1957, Mac Amhlaigh spends an evening listening to traditional musicians playing together in the Bedford Arms in Camden: 'This town is, in many ways, more Irish than a lot of the towns at home. More Irish is spoken here and much more Irish music is played here.'[25]

The tension between the maintenance and the loss of traditional culture powers much of Mac Amhlaigh's narrative. Against the camaraderie and 'good talk' of his compatriots, Mac Amhlaigh lines up the effects of waged labour in the industrial city, which undermines the old values: 'Drink, squabbling and big pay – that's all they want and the devil take anything else.' 'The Irish at home, so far as I know, haven't got this ugly habit – always talking about work and money – but they get as materialistic as the rest when they have been here awhile.'[26] Yet work and money, rather than the rhythms of traditional community life, are the focus of much of his own narrative, as he describes the daily routine of the labouring emigrant.

In a manner similar to McNabb's analysis, Mac Amhlaigh's traditionalist framework on emigration is undercut by an empirical, economically informed approach to the working lives of the migrants. English working and social life is documented from an 'outsider' perspective, in loosely ethnographic style:

> The Smokers is a pub frequented by dealers in 'scrap', tramps of one kind or another from didicoys (English tinkers), to Irish workers and ordinary navvies. It is on Mayorhold Square, a very old, very poor quarter ... [27]

The use of explanatory parentheses is prevalent, as Mac Amhlaigh translates English labour for his Irish readers – for example, in describing work in a foundry: 'On overhead rails, there are wheels that carry around the casks (or skips, as they are called) with the skips hanging by chains from the wheels.'[28]

This impulse to inform the reader about English work and leisure also dictates the style used to describe the Irish in Britain to the Irish who have remained at home. Life in a post-war labourers' camp at Stanford-in-the-Vale would have been as unfamiliar to Irish readers as any more well-established aspect of English society:

---

[25] Ibid., p. 112.
[26] Ibid., pp. 57, 160. As an emigrant youth interviewed for Philip Donnellan's film *The Irishmen: An Impression of Exile* (BBC, 1965) puts it, 'The only thing you have in mind is money, like.'
[27] Ibid., p. 82.
[28] Ibid., p. 80.

The camp is not any way expensive. Seven and six is charged for the bed (stopped from your pay) and meals, which you pay for yourself, are to be had in the canteen. You can live easily on fifty bob a week, and even including the other charges, we're a damned sight better off here than we'd be in 'digs' in some towns.[29]

Passages such as these are remarkably similar in tone to the documentary style of popular sociological texts of the 1950s, such as the work of Ferdynand Zweig, devoted to analysing changing attitudes to work and leisure amongst the British working classes. Zweig's description of an Irishman working in a factory in Luton mixes reportage and free indirect discourse, striving to articulate not only the conditions in which he lives, but also his attitude towards them:

He lives in a furnished room, sharing it with his 'pal', and they each
pay 11s. His rations cost him 10s. a week but he eats his
breakfast, dinner, tea and supper in workmen's cafés, which costs
him about 6s. per day.... He spends 25s. a week on
drink, having about five or six pints a day, at least four times a
week.... He doesn't save anything and he doesn't believe in saving. When
he has no money his pal or some other friend will give him a pound or treat
him to drinks. He would do the same for them. But on the whole he loses
on friendship.[30]

Mac Amhlaigh's narrative resituates a west-of-Ireland ethnographic discourse in an urban industrial environment. The language of the Islandman is redeployed in an analysis of waged labour, and the experience of living under the welfare state (in encounters with the National Health Service, for example). It is moulded to the 'materialist' concerns which Mac Amhlaigh would like to believe are alien to the finest men from the Gaeltacht. That tension between rural tradition and urban modernity is addressed explicitly in the narrative. Yet, as Zweig's description of the Irishman in Luton suggests, a more fundamental difficulty for the revivalist model was that the contours of the community being described had entirely altered. The community was no longer made up of a network of extended familial relationships, but of isolated individuals grouped together by nationality, friendship and – most noticeably – gender. These were men sharing digs, working together, and drinking together. Mac Amhlaigh's narrative is punctuated by admiring comments about the women from the west of Ireland and derogatory comments about anglicised Irishwomen who

[29] Ibid., p. 48.
[30] Ferdynand Zweig, *The British Worker* (Harmonsworth: Penguin, 1952), p. 135.

imitate the English in figures of speech and modes of dress, yet the over-whelming focus of his interest is on male relationships. This absence of family life sets the men adrift from the rural farm-based community at home, but it also marks out their difference from the working-class community in England.

Mac Amhlaigh's text reads as an anthropological study of an emigrant community by a native informant, interpreting the experience of exile for the benefit of natives who have stayed at home. Yet Mac Amhlaigh was already at one remove from the Gaeltacht culture he wrote of and for. The mobility of his point of view, and his ability to inhabit the role of go-between amongst Gaeltacht, Dubliner, and English groups, occurs in another, comparable, Irish text, Richard Power's *Úll i mBárr an Ghéagáin* (*Apple on a Treetop*), published in 1958.[31] Power, like Mac Amhlaigh, was a non-native-Irish speaker who chose to write in Irish, and both their works reflect on the relationship between a West-of-Ireland and a British plane of experience. And like Mac Amhlaigh, Power explicitly references his ethnographic model in the book. Allusions to Synge pepper the text, which he presents as the record of a year spent living in the Aran islands, a Syngean experiment fifty years on.

The entire narrative turns on who is inside and who is outside certain groups, and what defines the limits of a group. Power's own status as an outsider is constantly shifting. When he arrives on the island he discovers that Inishmore is already packed with foreigners – he meets a Dutchman on the boat; in the house where he lodges there's a new Zealander, an English couple and a Dubliner. When talking to the Dutch or the English he feels one with the islanders, but when talking to the islanders he is not so sure. To make matters worse, Power keeps running into other ethnographers or would-be ethnographers. The English couple who share his lodging are engaged in their own material gathering and writing assignment. The couple appear to be veiled portraits of documentary makers Nell Dunn and Jeremy Sandford, who are witheringly described as a pair of Chelsea artists, worried that their dining room furniture is just a little bit 'festival of Britainish.'[32] Power enjoys telling stories about them which reveal their failure to properly gauge the nature of the community they are living in – on one occasion, because they are finding it difficult to get the young people to talk to them, they buy a couple of barrels of beer in order

[31] Richard Power, *Apple on a Treetop*, translated from *Úll i mBárr an Ghéagáin* (1958) by Victor Power (Dublin: Poolbeg Press, 1980).

[32] Ibid., p. 46. Dunn was later famous for *Up the Junction* (1963) and *Poor Cow* (1967), and Sandford for *Cathy Come Home* (1966).

to hold a party and thereby 'gather material.' Power records the host's anger over this manipulation of the islanders, but the irony is inescapable, since he too is engaged in gathering ethnographic material.

If half of Europe and the New World is tramping about the Aran islands, at the same time the 'locals' themselves are far flung. Josie, a central character in the island household Power describes, in fact works as a masseuse in Springfield, Massachusetts, and is only home on holidays. Most of the men at the party held by the English couple are returning to Birmingham in the morning. When a fisherman leaves for England, Power has to learn to row so that he can take his place in the boat. All of this makes the study of the relationship between community and place a little more difficult – what are the geographical boundaries of the group, even, or more than anywhere, on an island?

About two-thirds of the way through the book, Power too decides to leave the island, not because the year is over, or because he has had enough of island life, or gathered sufficient ethnographic material, but because he is lonely once the others have gone. Again and again in emigrant stories and memoirs, a desperate feeling of having been abandoned is the spur to leaving. It is as though this trope directs Power's thinking, causing an odd moment in the text when he appears to experience himself as one of the islanders:

> I had to leave. Every time I went past Cóilín's house, the old door locked up, the stain of dust on the windows, my optimism faltered. Dara Pheig was gone. The girls who once danced by my side, they were gone. The young strangers who used to amble along the roads at night, swimming in the sun and enjoying themselves on the beach, they were gone. In the place where they played handball, pools of water gathered and green moss grew.[33]

Rather than return to Trinity College, Power follows Cóilín into what he calls 'my exile' in London, and later Birmingham. At this point in the narrative he really does become one with his community, that of male labourers, living in digs and working on building sites. Undoubtedly, from the point of view of English observers of the Irish labourers, he is the same as the rest. Yet it is at this point that the term 'they', used of the Irish, begins to occur with greater frequency. 'They', referring to Irish men in Britain, punctuates Mac Amhlaigh's narrative too, as he moves between different roles, from participant observer to journalist or ethnographer commenting on the behaviour of the men with whom he lodges and works.

---

[33] Ibid., p. 151.

Such shifts in point of view indicate structural changes occurring in these works, particularly shifts in the understanding of the nature of the Irish community. They reveal Irish labourers as both part of and separate from white working-class culture. Stylistic parallels suggest a source in contemporary sociology for the more ethnographic passages in Mac Amhlaigh's and Power's texts. Yet Zweig's description of the economic life of an Irish worker was relatively unusual for the period, and where analysis of the Irish does appear, their problematic status as members of the working-class community is repeatedly stressed. Even though the Irish were the largest minority in Britain in the 1950s, and the numbers of newly migrating Irish far exceeded other nationalities, there were almost no sociological studies devoted to them. In the early '50s British sociology focused on class and social mobility, and the effects of affluence and mass culture on traditional working-class communities. Analysis of Irish workers appears by chance – for example, where studies were conducted in areas with a high concentration of Irish migrants, such as Luton. (The rare exceptions include two articles on Irish navvies by A. J. Sykes, and a series of short pieces on Irish migrant labourers in the journal *New Society*.) By the early '60s, the focus of British sociology had shifted to colour and the assimilation of black migrants into British cities. However, analysis of Irish communities in Birmingham and Croydon forms one strand of the well-known comparative studies by John Rex and Robert Moore, *Race, Community and Conflict: A Study of Sparkbook*, analysing racial tensions and housing in Birmingham, and Sheila Patterson, *Immigrants in Industry*, exploring attitudes towards assimilation of immigrants in the workplace.[34]

All these studies discuss Irish migrants broadly in terms of the extent to which they conform, or fail to conform, to the working and social lives of the British working class. Zweig, for example, investigated the Irish factory workers in Luton as part of his general inquiry into British workers. Similarly, several employers interviewed by Sheila Patterson in Croydon were unable to quote the numbers of Irish workers in their firms because they did not count them as 'other.'

Nonetheless, commentators on the Irish community repeatedly acknowledged the ambiguous status of the Irish as a group, as their class

---

[34] A. J. Sykes, 'Navvies: Their Social Relations', *Sociology*, 3:2 (1969), pp. 157–172, and 'Navvies: Their Work Attitudes', *Sociology* 3:1 (1969), pp. 21–34; Terry Coleman, 'The Elite Inside the Tunnel', *New Society*, 6 January 1966, pp. 6–8; Jeremy Bugler, 'Ireland in London', *New Society*, 14 March 1968, pp. 369–371; John Gretton, 'The Lump', *New Society*, 18 March 1970, pp. 469–470; John Rex and Robert Moore, *Race, Community and Conflict: A Study of Sparkbook* (Oxford: Oxford University Press, 1967); Sheila Patterson, *Immigrants in Industry* (Oxford: Oxford University Press, 1968).

identity was cut across by a 'racial' or tribal identification, particularly in the case of Irish men. It is no surprise that commentators on the Irish in Britain began to think of the labourers as a class and as a community in and of themselves. In the early '50s they were an easily identifiable group, working and living together. But precisely for that reason their differences from the British working class were as noticeable as their similarities. Both sociological and literary texts continually draw attention to the uncertain position of the Irish migrant within the British working-class community, with 'No Coloureds, No Irish' appearing in advertisements for accommodation, and employment notices announcing that 'No Irish Need Apply.' Rex and Moore note that the Irish were in several respects the most accepted group of post-war migrants (by the late '60s they had taken over some local Labour Party groups, for example). But they were also regularly described as 'the worst' group – Patterson quotes several employers who preferred 'coloured' migrants 'to the Southern Irish, whom we find too mobile and won't employ.'[35] Alternatively, they were called 'as bad' as Caribbean migrants, for example, by a manager of a factory employing Irish women: 'the Irish are as bad as Jamaicans in the toilet anyway.'[36] In an earlier study focused on the 'respectable' areas of Brixton, Patterson noted that in terms of conformity to the ways of the street, standards of cleanliness, quietness, privacy, and propriety, both West Indian and Irish migrants fell short:

> No immigrant group has in the mass so signally failed to conform to these expectations as have the West Indians. . . . Southern Irish migrants are often said to be 'as bad as the darkies'; but they are not so easily identifiable, and the criticisms are therefore not so sharply focused. In the case of the Southern Irish and the West Indians, of course, the differences and frictions are intensified by the fact that these are lower-class migrants moving into a highly status-conscious, upper-lower or lower-middle-class local society.[37]

Patterson here gropes towards an analytical framework which could account for both the class and racial identification of Irish (and West Indian) migrants, but she overlooks the social exclusion of large numbers of migrant men, who lived and worked in marginal areas of the urban environment: building sites, lodging houses and pubs. The term 'lower-class' cannot account for the large groups of single labourers employed in construction who were least well fitted into post-war English society, as

[35] Sheila Patterson, *Dark Strangers: A Sociological Study of the Absorption of a Recent West Indian Migrant Group in Brixton, South London* (London: Tavistock, 1963), p. 112.
[36] Patterson, *Immigrants in Industry*, p. 217.
[37] Patterson, *Dark Strangers*, p. 179.

their reputation for dirt, drunkenness and brawling attests. Indeed Irish factory workers were a problem insofar as their behaviour mirrored that of the 'mobile' casual labourer.

The memoirs and ethnographic studies leave no doubt about the causes of their reputation as anti-social and unreliable. 'I suppose, it must be a terrible scourge for a little place like this to have so many wild people on their door-step', says Mac Amhlaigh, reflecting on the habit of drinking and fighting which seemed to be hardwired into the Irish labourers.[38] He tries to discourage a young man at the hospital where he works who 'thinks because he's Irish he has to be always challenging people.'[39] He notes how dances are not for dancing but excuses for getting involved in fights and for gambling, opportunities for the display of a reckless attitude to money and personal safety. He enjoys recounting a tale of getting the better of a gang of Teddy boys on the Seven Sisters Road; he describes an almost tribal battle between a man from Meath and a man from Leitrim, which seems to have no other rationale than the need to fight.

In a similar manner, Richard Power tried to analyse what lay at the heart of the drinking and scrapping. As he points out, the English youth are always fighting too; it is what young people do. But for the Irish, he argues, fighting is not about their role in a larger social organisation, but about their lack of a role.

> The Irish troublemakers were not quite the same, however. They were not adolescents. They were not contestants in a jousting tournament, nor did they get much pleasure out of fisticuffs.... It was some unspoken pact between the members of each clan, a tribal loyalty that was responsible for it. That and the restless, unsettling way of life that they engaged in, without any definite goal, without household, without authority, without having to answer to their family, to the state, to anyone at all.[40]

A key phrase in Power's description of the labouring Irish is "without household." Unlike British labourers, Irish migrants employed in unskilled gang labour were resistant to the organisational structures of capitalist industry.

[38]   Mac Amhlaigh, *An Irish Navvy*, p. 62.
[39]   Ibid., p. 21. See also Keane, *Self Portrait* on Irish labourers 'boasting of great feats of tunnel-digging, block-laying and masonry', and of fights which take on mythic connotations: 'It reminded me of Cuchullain breaking his bonds' (pp. 64, 82). For representative English newspaper coverage of Irish fights, see 'Mad Orgy by Irish Drunks', *Birmingham Mail,* 16 May 1956. For a discussion of the trope of the Celtic hero, and the Cuchulain figure in particular, see 'Navvy Narratives' in Tony Murray, *London Irish Fictions*, pp. 42–54.
[40]   Power, *Apple on a Treetop*, p. 195. This attitude is corroborated by several interviewees in Philip Donnellan's *The Irishmen*: 'We're dependant on nobody. We have to fight to exist', says one emigrant. An observer explains, 'They're over here. Their father and mother aren't here and they can do what they blooming well like, more or less. Nobody can say a word to them.'

The crew culture of these mobile male work gangs was not so different from that of groups of peasant men forced off the land in Britain through previous centuries, who found work as agricultural labourers, sailors and navvies. The gang labourer mentality was about endurance and pride in physical feats, from digging the deepest ditch to consuming the largest quantity of alcohol. There are plenty of stories of men suffering accidents with laughter or refusing to abide by safety guidelines. Profligacy, binge-ing, gambling, excessive consumption, conspicuous generosity in the pub all took the place of saving and planning, which tended to be regarded as mean and cautious behaviour.[41] Arguably the behaviour of the 'gang' was a consequence of their displaced relationship with household and home, their failure to conform less a sign of the tribal nature of the 'traditional communities' from which they came than a result of their uneasy place within the very different society in which they found themselves.

The Irish in post-war Britain were not just mainly working class, they were mainly young and single, taken out of the vertical axis of their com-munity and suddenly freed from tutelage and from generational struggle. The displays of 'excessive' masculinity, including heroic feats of physical strength in the workplace, as well as ritualistic fighting and drinking, set Irish labourers apart from the classic protagonists of British working-class realism, which focuses on social constraints experienced by individual young men (and occasionally women, as in Sheila Delaney's *A Taste of Honey*). The pattern of intertribal rivalry is worlds away from the forms of rebellion practised by youths such as Arthur in *Saturday Night, Sunday Morning*, or Billy in *Billy Liar*, where the struggle is against the author-ity (and lack of imagination) of the older generation, set alongside the more subtle demands made by the women who want their men to settle down. The wildness of the wild men described by Mac Amhlaigh stands in stark opposition to that narrative of domestication. Those whom Power describes as the 'Irish troublemakers' refuse to conform to the pattern of the socially mobile working-class male, just as they fail to be contained by stories of domestication and increasing affluence which form the core of many of the British new wave narratives. For this reason, as I will discuss in the next chapter, the wild Irish were a source of envy as much as fear.

---

[41] For a discussion of links between masculine violence, binge consumption and gang labour, see R. Wilk, 'Loggers, Miners, Cowboys, and Grab Fishermen: Masculine Work Culture and Binge Consumption', in R. Oka and I. Kuijt (eds.), *Social Economies of Greed and Excess: Lessons from Recessions, Past and Present* (New York: Altamira Press, forthcoming). On the culture of Irish labourers in Britain more generally, see Cowley, *Men Who Built Britain*.

The sociology which fed into British working-class realism and documentary in the 1950s and '60s displayed a sympathetic interest in working-class communities, combined with unease about the quality of life, and particularly the changing patterns of consumption and new forms of leisure in urban society, a process Orwell had previously described as the upward and downward extension of the values of the middle class.[42] Richard Hoggart's *The Uses of Literacy* lamented a decline under the influence of mass culture, a waning of the values of resilience and solidarity forged out of material hardship. These values appeared to have been eroded by the new forms of leisure and consumption (a cultural shift mirrored in the general move away from heavy manual labour to light industries). With its anxiety over the influence of mass culture, Hoggart's nostalgic portrait echoed aspects of Irish neo-revivalist fears about the modern city, despite the urban industrial setting in which working-class values had been forged. Moreover, in the novels and films of the British New Wave, the degeneration of traditional working-class virtues was associated with the consumerist desires of upwardly mobile women, again echoing Irish discourses. As Terry Lovell argues of New Wave films, especially *Saturday Night, Sunday Morning* and *A Kind of Loving*, 'this cycle of films persistently portrays the status-conscious woman as the vulnerable point of entry for seductions which might betray a class and its culture.'[43] But rural Irish labourers were, for the most part, excluded from the shift away from heavy manual work. Precisely because they continued to be relied on for their physical strength and engaged in labour which was little altered from that of the nineteenth-century navvy, they existed on the margins of postwar working-class culture. Their habits of over-consumption were a kind of regressive, self-destructive parody of the flashy new forms of consumerism which worried those who feared the death of the traditional working-class community: an absolute refusal of domestication and the affluent society. While, as we have seen, women migrants' inordinate desires were associated with aspiration, male excess was its polar opposite, the demolition of respectability. The paradox for these unmodified working men was that, insofar as they were able to recreate partial copies of their traditional communities on the sites, in the pubs, and in their lodging houses, it was

---

[42] Orwell, 'the rich and poor read the same books, and they also see the same films, and listen to the same radio programmes.' On deproletarianization, see Laing, *Representations of Working-Class Life*, p. 13.

[43] Terry Lovell, 'Landscapes and Stories in 1960s British Realism', in Andrew Higson (ed.), *Dissolving Views: Key Writings on British Cinema* (London: Cassell, 1996), p. 167.

precisely because they lacked the family context in which those communities had originally developed.

Turning a Shade Darker

The ambiguous position of Irish migrants in post-war British society is evidenced in the sociological, ethnographic and documentary texts in a number of ways: the shifting between categories of race (and sub-racial types) and of class; the uncertain location of migrant labourers within urban geographical space, and particularly in relation to domestic spaces; the absence of inter-generational relations; the lack of male-female relationships. All the representations I have focused on are of men only – and men in their sphere of labour. In fact, Mac Amhlaigh married in the 1950s, but the narrative of courtship is absent from his text. Arguably, by excising any representation of himself as part of a couple, Mac Amhlaigh was able to avoid the conventions of the marriage or domestic plot, which had become a dead end for writers looking to respond to the labouring world of the Irish immigrant. M. J. Molloy and John B. Keane were inheritors of the role of writer as critic of the national narrative which derived from the revivalist period. This role had taken a peculiar turn during the Second World War, partly through the prominence of journals such as *The Bell*, which brought together a realist impulse with the stance of the liberal critic of the status quo. Both writers framed their critique of the culture of emigration as stemming from an 'authentic' Ireland, but one revivified by sexuality and romance. In doing so, they remained trapped within a discourse of sexuality and reproduction on and for the land.

It is of course not surprising that work is so little present in Irish-based narratives of emigration – people were leaving because there wasn't any. But labour was also not part of the public discourse around going to England, which focused instead on money, the need for it and the dangers of having too much; faith or the lack of it; entertainment and the perils of that too; community and the difficulty of maintaining it. However much individual emigrants might have thought about the work they were going to do, in the broader discussion around emigration, work was incidental.

By contrast, in ethnographic accounts of migrant experience (Mac Amhlaigh, Power) and in sociological and documentary work on Irish migrants (Zweig, Patterson and the New Society articles) the focus is on communities of men working and living together. This is a feature too of the realist drama and fiction focused on migration. Indeed, an early and uncharacteristic play by John B. Keane, *Hut 42* (first performed in 1962), is set within the male world of a labour camp and focuses on the friendship between an English and an Irish labourer who are looking out for each other.[44] Keane's play reveals the tragedy for the migrants dislocated from family and home and is in that sense of a piece with his focus in Irish-based plays on the need to staunch the emigrant flow by repairing and renewing the rural family. Yet despite the overall tragic narrative mode, the energy and drive of the play rests with the young male 'couple.' Homosocial, rather than heterosexual, relationships carry the possibilities of dynamism and change in the play and suggest new alliances across race, language and class.

This interpretation of 1960s migrant realism suggests that an older homosocial narrative, derived from tales of heroic Celtic masculinity, was redesigned post-war for the emigrant experience, while the heterosexual narrative was repeatedly pulled back by associations of women and reproduction with the body of the nation, and could not free itself from discourses of breed, stock and race, even if its language was that of romance. (Though I have been focusing on male labour I do not mean to suggest that it was only the relationship between men that could carry this radical charge – one example of intimacy between women substituting for fulfilled romance is the relationship between Cait and Baba in Edna O'Brien's *The Country Girls Trilogy*.) In arguing for the realist depiction of male labour as 'progressive' in relation to earlier, family-based treatments of the emigrant narrative, however, it is important to acknowledge the overall tragic mode into which these depictions are inserted. As Richard Power noted of Irish gang fights, they were goal-less, full of venom and strife. They revealed the labourers' lack of agency and the impossibility of combating the natural and socio-economic laws which had positioned them at the bottom of the pile.

One of the most celebrated realist treatments of migrant experience is Tom Murphy's 1961 play, *A Whistle in the Dark*, which dramatises the conflicts within an Irish family transplanted from Mayo to Coventry. The play explicitly opposes the English New Wave narrative of working-class affluence, signified by women and domesticity, with one of violent, 'tribal' and Irish masculinity. As Joe Cleary has argued, the play can be read as a development of Irish naturalism, revealing the entrapment of the migrants in a cycle of violence, as it charts the failed attempts of the ambitious brother Michael to gain a degree of respectability within English

---

[44] Keane, *Hut 42*.

working-class society.[45] Michael, the upwardly mobile eldest son who has married an Englishwoman, is taunted by the other members of his family for lacking 'pride' and for wanting to be 'a British Paddy.' The battle within the family takes place on a horizontal plane, as Michael is pitched against his brothers, who conform to the stereotype of drunken, brawling Irish and who are egged on rather than restrained by the father in their rejection of 'anglicised' social mobility.

In a similar spirit to Cleary, Fintan O'Toole has argued that, despite its naturalistic staging, the play should be understood as a tragedy exploring the fatal clash between a repressive Irish rural community and a new urbanising modern society, represented in the play in the story of the County Mayo road-sweeper whose son has become an engineer in Ireland. '*A Whistle in the Dark* dramatises the tensions of a society on the brink of industrialisation, about to become belatedly "civilised". It is 'not a play about emigration.'[46] In O'Toole's reading the struggle is between past and future, both defined as Irish. He argues, for example, of the culture of fighting within the family (which eventually precipitates the tragedy), that 'the roots of this tribal pride are historical, and Dada's appeal to it brings the play back again to Ireland's dark past.'[47] That the tragedy reveals a group imprisoned within class and racial categories which ultimately destroy them is certainly true. But in the play those categories, far from simply being inherited from rural Ireland, are also created within British urban working-class culture. The excessive masculine display ritualistically indulged in by the Carney brothers, who engage in fighting with other Irish 'tribal' families, is described as, in part, a hangover from their need to fight or prove themselves against their association with the most socially excluded groups in County Mayo – several of the brothers recall being taunted as 'tinkers.' But the tribalism of the group is not just an eruption of 'old' repressive Ireland within the new forward-looking Irish society of the 1960s. It is also an expression of the association of the migrant Irish with socially excluded and racially 'other' labour, contrasted with the

---

[45] Cleary, *Outrageous Fortune*, pp. 168–173.

[46] Fintan O'Toole, *Tom Murphy: The Politics of Magic* (Dublin: New Island Books, 1994), pp. 58, 59.

[47] Ibid., p. 65. See also Aidan Arrowsmith, 'Gender, Violence and Identity in *A Whistle in the Dark*', in Christopher Murray (ed.), *Alive in Time: The Enduring Drama of Tom Murphy* (Dublin: Carysfort Press, 2012), pp. 221–238, where Arrowsmith argues that Michael's bid to escape his past 'parallels the attempt by post-Whitaker Ireland to move into capitalist modernity, an era whose rationalism contrasts sharply with the violence and tribalism symbolised by Dada' (p. 224); Liam Harte, '"You want to be a British Paddy?": The Anxiety of Identity in Post-war Irish Migrant Writing', in Keogh, O'Shea and Carmel Quinlan (eds.), *Ireland in the 1950s: The Lost Decade* (Cork: Mercier Press, 2004), pp. 233–251.

socially mobile white working class. 'You suck up to them, I fight them. Who do they think most of, me or you?' Harry asks Michael. It is important to recognise that there is nothing romantic or epic about these fights, which are presented as mean, crude and desperate, with weapons such as broken glass and chains ('Your man's face after the chain'). The fights are of a piece with the amorality of the Carneys' way of life. Harry and Iggy make their money from pimping and running a racket taking bribes from black migrants to find them work.

The Irish migrants have failed to adapt themselves properly to the milieu of the respectable working class, and particularly the female-dominated domestic scene which is key to the presentation of post-war affluence. They turn Michael's house into overcrowded lodgings and eventually eject Michael's wife ('Bitchey! Polly! English trash! Whore!'). Moreover they have failed to prove themselves fully white. As Harry Carney insists, the racialisation of the Irish places them in an ambiguous position on a spectrum somewhere between white and black:

> But I still like them. Respect them. Blacks. Muslims. They stick together, their families and all. And if they weren't here, like, our Irish blue blood would turn a shade darker, wouldn't it? (*To* MICHAEL.) Hah? And then some people'd want our cocks chopped off too.[48]

Recent scholarship focusing on African Caribbean and South Asian migrants in post-war Britain has emphasised the extent to which black migrants were, largely, excluded from the more obvious markers of the growing 'affluence' commonly held to characterise British society in the 1950s – the narrowing of the gap between working and middle classes though the transformation of the workplace, the impact of the welfare state, the changing dynamic of leisure and consumption, suburbanisation, home ownership and increased social mobility. With black migrants typically marginalised in low-status jobs and with poor provision for their housing needs, critics such as Wendy Webster have argued that racial divisions not only marked the landscape of British cities but in part enabled their transformation, not least through the impact of migrant labour on the relationship between public and private spheres.[49] Webster's focus is

[48] Murphy, *Whistle in the Dark*, p. 50. Murphy has said that when he was in Birmingham he heard stories of an extended Pakistani family who ran a number of brothels, and he decided to transpose this family onto his Irish tribe in Coventry, who make their money from pimping in the play. The shadow of the Pakistani enterprise is registered in the play as the presence of Muslims in Coventry, who help to keep the Irish somewhat white. I discuss the ambiguous racialization of the Irish in Britain in more detail in Chapter 4.

[49] Wendy Webster, *Imagining Home: Gender, 'Race' and National Identity, 1945–64* (London: UCL Press, 1998).

on the ways in which the role of 'indigenous' women as primarily wives and mothers was facilitated by the recruitment of migrant women to Britain as workers, but it could be extended to encompass the manner in which migrant workers of both sexes underpinned the productive economy of post-war Britain. In the case of the Irish male migrants I have been discussing, that input included the building of motorways and houses, as well as the manufacture of cars, upon which suburbanisation depended.

My analysis has suggested the need for a more nuanced perspective on the racialisation of migrant labour in post-war Britain, allowing for the existence of 'peripheral' groups such as the Irish (and, though this is beyond the scope of this chapter, the Maltese, Cypriot and European 'Displaced Persons'), who belonged neither to the white working class nor its black 'other.' I have discussed a range of strategies through which policymakers and creative writers attempted to represent these migrants, moving from the morally inflected discourse of racial 'loss' through emigration stemming from the perceived population crisis in post-war Ireland, to realist representations informed by the economies of class and social milieu. Though focused on the male migrant, both modes reproduced anxieties about the 'feminisation' of modern, affluent society which were not purely Irish in origin. Indeed Irish discourses on the population crisis which associated female emigration with an individualistic, acquisitive worldview, alien to the frugal world of rural Ireland, were in part a reflection of Anglo-American associations of the affluent society with forms of 'feminine' consumption focused on the home. Similarly, the realist rejection of romance plots, noticeable in Mac Amhlaigh and Murphy, shared some of the tropes of British New Wave narratives of regional working-class masculinity, particularly the fear of emasculation in the upwardly mobile home. Yet they were plotted in a milieu entirely alien to working-class fiction and film of the period – in the peripheral spaces of the city: lodging houses, camps and building sites.

The mass emigration of the Irish in the 1950s and early '60s proved a challenge to established Irish conceptions of community, based on family and farm. In the long run, the need to account for migration and the effects of urbanisation was to transform Irish sociology. But Irish labour also challenged British discourses of class and community. Not quite alien but not quite white either, the Irish exposed the benefits but also the limits of British social democracy. The move to industrial Britain liberated the 'poor types', those described as 'physically and morally inferior' in Irish official discourse, into the ranks of the working class. Yet they remained peripheral to the urban working-class communities they helped build. As

I have proposed, male gang labour was the point where Irish migrants proved least amenable to the narratives of class developed within British sociology of the 1960s and to realist documentary strategies, dependent in turn on a sociologically informed analysis of the relationship between physical place and the nature of the community, and on the representation of social mobility through changing milieu.

The cyclical plots characteristic of Irish post-war realism emphasised characters' entrapment within an anachronistic historical moment. The pull of a deterministic past – Cait's repetition of her mother's death by drowning in *The Country Girls Trilogy*, or Michael Carney's reenactment of familial violence in *A Whistle in the Dark* – signalled the inability of Irish society to develop or progress into modernity in ways which might be seen as typical of the western European nation-state. But the fault did not lie only at home. While the migrant texts discussed here attributed the benighted state of Ireland and the failure to move into 'civilised' modernity in part to the burden of a violent and repressive older generation (the brutal father figures in O'Brien and McGahern, for example), the shift from repression to a narrative of social and economic aspiration was far from simple. The language of typology which I discussed in the first chapter both depended on and purveyed an ethically normative determinism which positioned individuals as good or bad types, according to a hierarchy of 'Irish' qualities. It was a language which was internally articulated, superficially directed towards elucidating local conceptions of status, class and respectability in a period of immense change in the rural economy, though in fact it functioned as a way of masking class distinctions. Transferred to a British social milieu those typologies became fixed as aspects of an ethnic stereotype which functioned in a very different manner: not to position the rural poor in relation to their more respectable provincial neighbours, or their urban counterparts, but to position Irish immigrants as a whole in relation to their British working-class others. The Carney brothers destroy Michael's dream of social mobility, not because they have been conditioned by atavistic social processes back in Ireland, but because they know that the alliance between social and racial prejudice in Britain is just as pernicious as that at home.

CHAPTER 4

The Vanishing Irish
Assimilation, Ethnicisation and Literary Caricature

They're worse than any other immigrants. We've had a fair number, possibly because this is a strong Catholic area, but their turnover is very high and few even stay as long as two years. A handful do settle in low category jobs but they never get to the point when they can be given responsibility. They're slow and want driving. They're also unintelligent but have a certain cunning and they certainly stick together. We nearly had trouble with them once. A ringleader got hold of them and they were 'going to show the English something.' We haven't got any of them here at present.

Personnel Manager, Heavy Engineering, quoted in Sheila Patterson[1]

We held all the key positions now, I thought: the pubs, the buses, the garages and the building-lots. We might well take over in the end.

Michael Campbell[2]

My own belief is that there is nothing but good in the English Health Service. Go into any doctor here. You find yourself in a nice warm room awaiting your turn. When you get in to the doctor, he treats you pleasantly even though he may be busy enough. He'll give you to understand that you are a person and not a beggar; and he'll give you a prescription to take to the chemist where the best drugs and medicines are given to you with a heart and a half.

Donall Mac Amhlaigh[3]

Writing in the *Irish Press* in 1954 of a late-night encounter in Waterloo with a group of Teddy Boys hanging around a jellied eel stall, Brendan Behan records his nervousness on being accosted by one of the group with the question, 'Yew Ahrish?' He admits that he is:

> He turned to his friends, and said: 'Vere. Woh eye sye?'
> He smiled at me, and said: 'These geezers contradicted me, I knew you was Ahrish w'en I 'eard your browgue. We're all Ahrish 'ere.'

---

[1] Patterson, *Immigrants in Industry*, p. 78.
[2] Michael Campbell, *O Mary, This London* (London: Heinemann, 1959), p. 47.
[3] Mac Amhlaigh, *An Irish Navvy*, p. 65.

> Proudly he pointed out his friends: "'e's Mac Carfy, en 'e's O'Leary, en 'Ealy,
> en 'Ogan, en Kelly, en my name is – give a guess.'
> 'Murphy.'[4]

Which turns out to be right. Although Britain has played host to waves of Irish immigrants since the early nineteenth century, and despite their large numbers, it is noticeable that many post-war representations (literary, documentary, or sociological) conjure an image of young people emigrating on their own, to places that need to be newly made Irish-friendly, as though each wave of migrants constitutes a fresh wave of pioneers. This is partly because post-war Irish settled in different areas to their nineteenth and early twentieth century forebears (less Manchester and Liverpool than London and the Midlands). But it also reflects the fact that 'lost' generations of previous immigrants seemed to have merged with the urban English, their children indistinguishable from English youths, even down to their preference for jellied eels.

Yet as Behan's interlocutor makes clear, though the assimilated, second- and third-generation Irish might be entirely comfortable in their modern, urban skins, they are nonetheless conscious of their Irishness. In the aftermath of the Notting Hill riots four years later, a BBC radio interviewer unearthed a similar attitude amongst youths asked for their opinions on the causes of the street violence. Much of the debate following the September 1958 riots focused on anger amongst local white youths over West Indian men taking their jobs, their unemployment benefits and their women. The BBC interview records the conversation of a group of young men from a nearby estate in White City, where seven of the nine rioters convicted of racially aggravated violence lived. The conversation certainly reveals a good deal of insecurity amongst the youths, as it keeps circling around the issue of black men going with white girls, and Jamaican migrants getting more money and better treatment at the dole office. The group interview is full of openly racist comment: the youths admit that some of them were involved in the attacks, that they would get involved again, and so on. The following passage ensues from a discussion of the need to stop West Indians from entering the country:

2ND VOICE: Who is a British subject? Is a darkie a British subject, correct, an Irishman isn't, right? Now who would you sooner have in your country an Irishman or a darkie?
VOICES: An Irishman definitely.
INTERVIEWER: An Irishman definitely, why?

---

4 Brendan Behan, *The Dubbalin Man* (Dublin: A & A Farmer, 1997), p. 53.

VOICE: Me old man's Irish isn't he?

2ND VOICE: Well, OK, why would you prefer an Irishman in your country, because, not because your old man's Irish, but why would you prefer an Irishman in your country to a darkie?

VOICE: Why because they're not so much scandal are they?

2ND VOICE: Not so much scandal? Well, I'll contradict you there, an Irishman can be the worst man out.... He can drink (yes), fight (yes), he can run brothels, same as the darkie (yes). He can do anything.

VOICE: But they're not so bad as the darkies are they? Are you running your own country down?

2ND VOICE: No I'm not running my own country down, no no, but I've seen myself in Shepherd's Bush, in Acton, in Camden Town, in numerous parts of London, I've seen Irishmen in trouble.

VOICE: So you condemn all the blacks.

2ND VOICE: No, no, I'm not condemning the Irish or the black men. But I do believe this, I've met Englishmen that condemned the Irishmen. My name is Danny and they condemn me because I am Irish. They know my name is Danny but they won't call me Danny, they call me Pat, but when they meet a darkie they call him by his name.[5]

The passage is fascinating because of the way the young Irish man articulates more than he understands. His main point seems to be that it's not fair that the Irish are treated badly since they are better than West Indians, as everybody knows. But he argues this by claiming that the Irish are really just as 'bad' – 'the worst man out.' Then there's that slippage between the Irish who cause trouble, and the Irish who are in trouble. The young man's confusion about where to place himself isn't edifying – what he wants is to be the same as his white mates, including in their racism, but what he articulates is his own uncertain racial designation, neither one thing nor the other.[6] It is exactly this formation that Tom Murphy explores through the character of Harry Carney.

There is a considerable body of work on the processes through which Irish immigrants to the United States became enfolded into a majority

---

[5] Ruth Glass, *Newcomers: The West Indians in London* (London: Allen and Unwin, 1960), pp. 265–266.

[6] The interview as a whole targets immigrants rather than solely black people as benefit cheats, pimps and troublemakers. It ends in general agreement that the Jamaicans and the Maltese are the problem, picking up stereotypes of the Maltese derived from the case of the Messina Brothers. For coverage of Irish benefit scroungers, see, for example, *The People*, October 1955, which argues that the Irish use false names at the labour exchange, and pretend they have wives and children at home in Ireland in order to cut down their rates of income tax. Stories of tax evasion, if not benefit scrounging, are broadly corroborated by Richard Power and Donall Mac Amhlaigh. On arrival in Birmingham, Power and a friend are asked, 'How many children do you have – I mean – for the income taxes, like' (*Apple on a Treetop*, p. 165). Mac Amhaligh reports the opinion of a Glasgow tax inspector. 'There must be more than ten million people living in the Irish Republic because, according to the forms I have here, nearly every person of the age of eighteen upwards or so has over five of a family at home.' (*An Irish Navvy*, p. 151). On tax evasion, see also Cowley, *The Men Who Built Britain*, pp. 160–161.

'white' ethnic identity, including significant interventions by Noel Ignatiev, David Roediger, Matthew Frye Jacobson and others. Arguments range from Ignatiev's contention that the Irish skillfully engineered their social place in ante- and post-bellum America ('To enter the white race was a strategy to secure an advantage in a competitive society') to broader historical claims. These interpret the gradual acceptance of a number of 'probationary' white races as part of a shift away from biological theories of race, towards theories of ethnicity, as a way of describing cultural difference. So, for example, Frye Jacobson maintains that from the 1920s onwards the category 'Caucasian' increasingly embraced not only Anglo-Saxons, but also Celts, Teutons and Slavs. Where once Mediterraneans, Hebrews, Celts and Slavs had formed part of a hinterland of 'inconclusive' whiteness, a shift from biological understandings of race towards cultural designations of ethnicity enabled a new paradigm of assimilation and mobility, setting the stage for a celebration of cultural diversity against which black racialised identity was found wanting. 'As if by collective fiat, race was willfully erased among the so-called divisions of humanity; the culture-based notion of "ethnicity" was urgently and decisively proposed in its place; and the racial characteristics of Jewishness or Irishness or Greekness were emphatically revised away as a matter of sober, war-chastened "tolerance."'[7]

That shift from Irishness as a racial cue to an 'invisible' cultural trait is encapsulated in Behan's Waterloo encounter – the youths can recognise Behan as an Irishman because he sounds (and possibly looks) like an Irishman; their own Irishness lingers in their names and their identifications, but it is otherwise impossible to read. Yet the history of vanishing Irishness in Britain differs substantially from the U.S. history of ethnicisation. There is broad agreement among sociologists of race that 'a dichotomous model of race dividing the population into the extremely broad racialised groupings of white or black has predominated both in academic and policy circles in Britain since the post-war period.'[8] As Chris Waters has argued, in a much-cited article critiquing race-relations theorists of the 1950s, the dominance of this paradigm stems from the reconfiguration of the nation as white and homogeneous in the 1950s and 1960s, in the

---

[7] Noel Ignatiev, *How the Irish Became White* (London: Routledge, 1995), p. 2; Matthew Frye Jacobson, 'Becoming Caucasian', in *Whiteness of a Different Colour: European Immigrants and the Alchemy of Race* (Boston: Harvard University Press, 1998), p. 96. See also David Roediger, *The Wages of Whiteness: Race and the Making of the American Working Class* (London: Verso, 1991); Kevin Kenny, *The American Irish: A History* (Ann Arbor: University of Michigan Press, 2000).

[8] Mary Hickman, 'Diaspora Space and National (Re)Formations', *Éire-Ireland*, 47:1&2 (2012), p. 28.

context of historic immigrations from the Caribbean and the Indian sub-continent. While United States race relations discourse was formulated in the context of debates around segregation and desegregation, the emphasis among race relations sociologists in Britain was on migration and the behavioural norms of host and stranger communities – the basic model was of xenophobia and the need to combat it through good communication, which would lead to cultural accommodation on both sides of the host/stranger divide. Yet by positing, or seeming to describe, relationships between relatively homogeneous communities, the paradigm employed by the sociologists tended to imply that 'races' existed as more or less 'natural' socially defined groups. Waters argues, 'These race relations experts consistently narrated the migrant other as a "stranger" to assumed norms of what it meant to be British, or at least English' – and in doing so helped define apparently commonsense notions of race, and the post-war boundaries of national belonging.[9]

Waters makes a strong case for the particular anxieties engendered by 'dark' strangers. Where nominally white Irish (and Jewish, Cypriot, Maltese, Italian, Polish or Ukrainian) post-war migrants fit into this paradigm is harder to see. Research on the ambiguous 'whiteness' of the Irish in Britain is cast primarily in sociological rather than historical terms, and has been spearheaded by sociologist Mary Hickman and geographer Bronwen Walter in particular. Building on work on the racialisation of national belonging in post-war Britain, Hickman and Walter both highlight the occlusion of the impact of previous immigrations on British society and outline the processes by which the migrant Irish were 'included' in the majority white ethnicity. The conflation of issues of race and nation with skin colour, especially in the context of the end of Empire and the arrival in Britain of Commonwealth and colonial migrants, created a situation in which white people were perceived as part of the indigenous majority and black people members of an immigrant population, whatever their origins. Whiteness allowed Irish migrants to position themselves as part of the majority, but as Hickman argues, it also masked the subtleties of the existing processes of racialisation: 'In the black-white dichotomy that was installed, whiteness masked suppressed ethnicities, hidden racializations and preexisting hierarchies.'[10] She revisits the exclusion of the Irish from the terms of the 1962 Commonwealth Immigrants Act, which has often been interpreted as the critical moment when the black/white binary was explicitly invoked to deny citizenship to Commonwealth migrants but sanction the white Irish, despite the fact that Irish citizens born after 1922 could lay no legal claim to British citizenship. Hickman acknowledges the racialising intentions underlying the Act, but argues that it masked rather than undid bigotry and intolerance towards the Irish:

> The 'whiteness' of the Irish therefore facilitated both continued access to their manual labor power for British employers and served to render them invisible within a reformulated claim about white cultural homogeneity. One consequence of the changes in official discourses was that a veil was drawn over the hostility and discrimination Irish migrants of this period experienced.[11]

Although the historical situations differ, these arguments are similar in kind to those of Frye Jacobson, placing the emphasis on political and strategic impetuses for redrawing boundaries of race, rather than on the behaviour of the migrant group. Both Hickman and Walter insist on the post-war moment as key to this process and on the 'construction of the racialised binary' as 'a binding together of "indigenous" people as white', rather than simply an exclusion of those defined as black.[12] One concern is about the impact of the new 'invisibility' of the Irish on social policy in Britain and particularly its concealment of continuing discrimination against them. The targets here are assumptions of the successful assimilation of the Irish into white working-class culture, and of the dilution of anti-Irish prejudice. Yet the particular processes by which the working-class Catholic Irish may have been 'absorbed' into white ethnic groupings undoubtedly had consequences at the level of historical representations too. For example, Walter examines the work of two post-war sociologists of English 'outcast' life, Betty Spinley and Madeleine Kerr, and notes how both writers failed to recognise that the communities they observed were not only the 'deprived' but were also Irish.[13] So while both writers mention the Irish background of their subjects, neither acknowledges that the immigrant status of the Irish families living in their target 'slum' areas of London and Liverpool contributed to their poor housing conditions – they were last in the queue for rehousing. Indeed Kerr remarks of her Ship Street residents,

---

11 Ibid.
12 Bronwen Walter, 'Whiteness and Diasporic Irishness: Nation, Gender and Class', *Journal of Ethnic and Migration Studies*, 37:9 (2011), p. 1302.
13 B. Spinley, *The Deprived and the Privileged* (London: Routledge and Kegan Paul, 1953); Madeleine Kerr, *The People of Ship Street* (London: Routledge and Kegan Paul: 1958).

The people we worked with form a residual core of families for whom the life of the street is the only one they know, and the only one they want to know. Although surrounded by immigrants, near the brothel area of the town, and with their derelict houses gradually being superseded by Corporation flats, they still preserve a pattern of living specific in many ways to themselves.[14]

'Immigrants' here clearly means colonial migrants, although Kerr acknowledges that her study group are mainly third-generation Irish. In fact, there are numerous other markers of Irish ethnicity and Catholic background that the sociologists miss, or perhaps misinterpret. Kerr acknowledges the group's 'isolation from the more general ideas and ways of the town' as connected in a vague sense with their Catholicism; her critical analysis of the figure of the Catholic matriarch ('Quite a number of old ladies have what they call "bachelor sons" living with them. These men say they will never marry so long as their mother is alive') might have been rendered more nuanced, if perhaps no less negative, by a comparison with the work of Arensberg and Kimball on the farm family.[15] As Walter contends:

Contrary to popular belief, the racialisation of the Irish in England did not fade away at the end of the nineteenth century but became transmuted into new forms which have continued to place the 'white' Irish outside the boundaries of the English nation. These have been strangely ignored by social scientists, who conflate Irishness and working-class identities in England without acknowledging the distinctive contribution of Irish backgrounds to constructions of class difference.[16]

Thus, the settled working-class Irish seem to have disappeared, but Irish traits, aspects of an Irish stereotype, have become generalised to the white underclass by the 1950s. There are two related threads to Walter's argument: first, that the underclass is marginal to whiteness (and she argues that this is a thread which links the experience of the Irish diaspora in the United States and in Britain); and second, that the marginality of the underclass derives from unacknowledged colonial understandings of the Irish. Irishness has become coded in class terms (tainted with the forms of excess that are habitually associated with the undisciplined other: excessive fertility, conviviality, binge culture, lack of propriety). Arguably this process might best be understood as a further twist in the long history of the

---

[14] Kerr, *The People of Ship Street*, p. 4.
[15] Ibid., pp. 29, 44.
[16] Walter, 'Whiteness and Diasporic Irishness', p. 1295.

representation of the lower classes in racial terms, as the well-known met-
aphors of penetrating the dark continent of the Victorian slums remind
us. As we have seen, the fears of degeneracy associated with the Victorian
Irish, designated as uncivilised or primitive on the evolutionary scale, were
one impetus for Irish counter-arguments about the purity of the Gaelic
race. These fears of degeneracy did not disappear as ideas of national
belonging absorbed new racial formations in the post-war period but were
shifted onto the white underclass, which continues to carry unacknowledged colonial racial markers.

Walter's concern is with the ways in which sociological and historical
research is blind to the Irish heritage of those read as typical of Britain's
underclass. It is a policy concern focusing on the fact that these groups
cannot access the sorts of funding and social help that would be available
to them if they were seen as a disadvantaged ethnic group. For our purposes, such images of doubtful or invisible Irishness are helpful reminders
of how Irishness might appear, or rather disappear, in various traces, how
it may be coded not as ethnicity but as class (or alternatively religion), and
how, as with Behan's 'velvety' Teddy Boys, the Irish can become invisible
even to the Irish. When they vanish from the historical record they may
do so for a number of reasons, including having become assimilated into
English working- and middle-class life, or alternatively having slipped
into outcast territory.

Yet alongside the disappearance of the Irish, their intractable visibility
persisted during the post-war period. In a double-sided process the settled Irish assimilated, or were designated an indigenous underclass (failing to penetrate the ranks of the respectable working class), but the new
Irish continued to be read 'ethnically', and often in negative terms, as we
have seen in the last chapter. Indeed, part of the reason that the settled
Irish may have appeared to have become 'invisible' was that the stereotype of the feckless Irish was transferred to the new, more easily identified,
migrants (although the testimony of Danny, the young second-generation
Irishman from White City, suggests that there was a great deal of slippage
between settled and new Irish when it came to stereotyping). To put this
another way, the reason that the Irish cultural stereotype could persist was
because the ground was continually being cleared. As the migrant Irish
appeared to assimilate, they disappeared as 'Irish', allowing the negative
stereotype to remain unchallenged.

Yet, as with the enduring opposition between wholesome ruralism
and decadent urbanisation, discussed in Part 1 of this book, it is necessary to account for both the persistence and the historicity of the idea

of Irishness. While the ethnic stereotype may have appeared as a simple repetition of negative attitudes towards the Irish reaching back to the nineteenth century, it functioned differently in the social climate of 1950s Britain, and specifically in the context of the welfare state. The caricature of the nineteenth-century Irish immigrant as dirty, shiftless, belligerent and drunk may appear almost identical to the caricature of the post-war Irish labourer in London, but the economic conditions in which the latter operated were vastly different, and therefore too its function in the post-war reconfiguration of national identity.

Moreover, if we acknowledge that stereotypes do historical work, then we also have to acknowledge their function in shaping our access to the historical moment. The stereotype is not merely a screen behind which lies the real experience of the immigrant, in some kind of pure state. Rather, it helps shape that experience and thus also what we can know of it. In addition, outside of the stereotype, the immigrant, at least the white immigrant, becomes invisible in the literature, or coded as something else. The assimilated Irish, for want of a better word, are only visible as Irish when some aspect of their experience or behaviour resonates with the stereotype, so that ethnic or racial caricaturing acts as a kind of limit or bound to experience even for those who may appear to have escaped the caricature. Thus the task is to find a way to revisit the history of immigration which both acknowledges and resists this form of typology, which both reads and reads through stereotypical representation.

Analyses of the transformation of post-war national belonging typically highlight the impact of the end of Empire, ironically signalled for most Britons by the arrival of Commonwealth and post-colonial migrants, and by the decline in Britain's prestige during the Cold War. Economic conditions, including the need for vast pools of labour to power post-war economic recovery, and the growth of the welfare state, are understood as the background to the 1950s crisis of 'race relations.' Marxist theorists of race and racism, for example, argue that migrants constituted the 'reserve army of labour' necessary to fill the jobs abandoned by the indigenous working class as post-war production was reorganised.[17] A related form of economic causation has been outlined by historians such as Alistair Bonnett, who argues for the determining conditions of welfarism as key to the reorganisation of the post-war boundaries of whiteness. White identity, Bonnett

---

[17] See, for example, Robert Miles, *Racism and Migrant Labour* (London: Routledge, 1982); Stephen Castles and Godula Kosack, *Immigrant Workers and Class Structures in Western Europe* (Oxford: Oxford University press, 1973).

suggests, from being incorporated into the reproduction of Victorian laissez-faire capitalism in the nineteenth century, became integrated into consensus-oriented, state-managed capitalism in the latter half of the twentieth. Arguing that the British working class themselves were not securely understood as 'white' until the 1950s, when their incorporation formed part of a process of national community building around the concepts of the 'ordinary' and the populist nation, Bonnett maintains that it is not enough to see working-class white identification as a rearticulation of the colonial imagination in a 'newly multi-racial' society (i.e., as a response to black migration and the end of empire). 'The reformation of the symbolic economies of race and class cannot be abstracted from the reformation of British capitalism.'[18] The transition from liberal to welfare capitalism entailed the formation of a popular 'national community' through an interventionist, consensus-oriented form of economic management. So, for example, the benefits of welfare were articulated through a discourse of the nation – the need to look after the people's health, housing and education in order to ensure the country's future strength and prosperity – and developed in tandem with a populist nationalism. The denunciation of sponging and scrounging and the stress on the need to conserve resources in order to look after 'our own people', with which we have become so familiar in recent years, were thus born with the welfare state itself. 'Welfare came wrapped in the Union Jack.'[19] As Ross McKibbin has argued, the seeds of this recreated working-class identity, forged by social welfare and nationalisation, were sown during the Second World War. The economy of conflict restored full employment as it helped to revivify the political culture of the declining North and to foreground social democracy over what he calls 'individualist' democratic principles. 'When in the 1950s or 1960s people spoke of the "traditional" working class, they were speaking of a class which was re-created in the 1940s, just as the "traditional" matrilocal working-class household was in part created in the 1940s.'[20]

[18] Alistair Bonnett, *White Identities: Historical and International Perspectives* (Harlow: Pearson Education, 2000), p. 38. See Walter, 'Whiteness and Diasporic Irishness', for an in-depth discussion of Bonnett's argument in relation to the ambiguous construction of the post-war Irish as white.

[19] Ibid., p. 39. See also Virginia Noble, *Inside the Welfare State: Foundations of Policy and Practice in Post-war Britain* (London: Routledge, 2009); E. J. B. Rose et al., *Colour and Citizenship: A Report on British Race Relations* (London: Institute of Race Relations, 1969), pp. 551–604.

[20] Ross McKibbin, *Class and Cultures: England 1918–1951* (Oxford: Oxford University Press, 2000), p. 536. For a different perspective on the importance of the war in reconfiguring the sense of British national identity, see Tony Kushner's work on anti-alienism in the 1940s. See, for example, Kushner, *We Europeans? Mass Observation, 'Race' and British Identity in the Twentieth Century* (Aldershot: Ashgate, 2005); 'Anti-Semitism and Austerity: The August 1947 Riots in Britain', in Panikos Panayi (ed.), *Racial Violence in Britain, 1840–1950* (Leicester: Leicester University Press, 1993), pp. 149–168.

Understood in this context, the post-war Irish stereotype was one of several whose function was in part to police the boundary of a newly 'ordinary' British national community. The Irish were not simply *on* the margins of English working-class culture, they *were* the margin, though they were not the only one. It is this understanding that Danny from White City articulates by means of, rather than in spite of, his confusion. Much of the debate recorded by the interviewer in the wake of the Notting Hill riots focused on Jamaican migrants' preferential treatment by officials at the Labour Exchange and dole office, and their supposed ability to fiddle the welfare system. Danny's uncertainty about his acceptance by the English is expressed in the context of welfare, and of an emphasis on the ordinariness of being 'a British subject', as opposed to the exoticism of black identity. He articulates the ambiguity over the Irish which will be revealed in the 1962 Immigration Act. Part of the white majority but at the same time 'the worst man out' – he knows exactly who he is.

The Deserving and the Undeserving Poor

Towards the end of *The Life of Riley*, Anthony Cronin's comic narrative of a downwardly mobile Irish grocer's assistant cum literary editor, the hero moves to London where he gets a room in the Rowton House in Camden Town, one of a string of hostels built by a Victorian philanthropist to provide cheap and clean lodgings for working men. It is a period of economic slump. Riley's fortunes have been steadily declining – he has recently fallen out of favour with a group of Irish writers employed in the features department of the BBC, who hang out at the pub. (The pub is named the Stork, but was based on the George, on Great Portland Street, where Irish writers and broadcasters such as Reggie Smith, Louis MacNeice and W. R. Rodgers drank after work – all of whom appear lightly disguised in the novel). Riley fails to rise to the level of Celticism required of him by the Irish literary set, and by this point in the novel his ambitions are focused on a nice warm job shouting 'Mind the Doors' on the London underground. He be-takes himself to the local Labour Exchange:

> a tastefully appointed building in Camden Town, looking like something left over from the Festival of Britain which had been spat on too often and could never be cleanly swept out. There were long queues, appearing to consist of three main classes of persons. There were the gloomy, intent and resentful representatives of the English working classes, the rightful heirs and beneficiaries of this whole set-up. There were the darkies, Maltese,

Cypriots and Irish, all in fine fettle, exchanging salutations and jokes in a variety of languages and dialects. And there was a third element, nattily dressed, many of them in blazers and silk scarves, occasionally consulting gold watches impatiently when the queue dragged, conversing intently in their own particular argot. Long experience of the Stork and the sight of one or two vaguely familiar faces enabled me to identify these latter as actors.[21]

The actors' insouciance derives from their part-time relationship with welfare: they draw their money when temporarily unemployed, or 'resting.' At the other end of the scale the members of the English working classes appear to search, desperately and resentfully, for work. Between these two groups are the immigrants:

They had landed on these hospitable shores in full expectation of being allowed to put their hands to the plough. Finding no work available they traversed the hospitable road from the labour exchange to the National Assistance Board. In the first they were solemnly assured that there was in fact nothing at the moment; in the second they collected their money, after which they retired, the Irish to the Rowton and the adjacent pubs, there to continue their temporarily interrupted quarrels; the Cypriots to the room over the caff; the Maltese to check the girls' earnings; the West Indians to the fug of crowded, happy rooms in Notting Hill Gate where the smoke of reefers mingled with the soft sing-song of another clime and the memories of perennial sunshine.[22]

If readers were for a moment tempted to take these stereotypes at face value, that reference to the 'happy rooms in Notting Hill Gate' is a clear warning, given that the novel was written in the years following the anti-black riots in Notting Hill in 1958, and the separate racist murder of a West Indian, Kelso Cochrane, in the same area, in 1959.

So what, beyond the comedy of familiarity, is the function of these stereotypes, and how should they be read? Cronin's novel has similarities with the '50s social comedy and ethnography of Sam Selvon, or Colin MacInnes, which also dramatise racial and ethnic preconceptions. But in Cronin's satire, rather like that of Flann O'Brien, the narrator is both subject and object of radical parody. By this point in the novel the reader has become accustomed to an array of satirically drawn stereotypes, as Paddy Riley (his name not only a popular trope for easy living, but also an echo of the emigrant 'Paddy Reilly' in a Percy French song from the turn of the twentieth century) recounts the fortunes of a number of post-war Irish

[21] Anthony Cronin, *The Life of Riley* (Dublin: New Island, 2010 [1964]), pp. 142–143.
[22] Ibid., pp. 143–144.

'types' in both Ireland and England. These include Dublin shopkeepers, eccentric big house grandees, good Catholic girls, immigrant labourers and so on. He also offers a portrait of post-war Irish literary society, including fictionalised portraits of Peadar O'Donnell, Louis MacNeice and W. R. Rodgers, who collectively create a stereotype of the Irish writer in London, trading on Celtic charm. But Riley himself also inhabits various Irish clichés through the course of the novel, as his fortunes fail and he progresses from bohemian intellectual, to Irish writer in London, to navvy, and finally to homeless vagrant.

Several features of these stereotypes have a long historical reach: the characteristics of drunkenness, belligerence, semi-vagrancy and unreliability were commonly associated with the Irish from the early nineteenth century (and indeed earlier). In the passage quoted previously, Cronin situates them alongside various 'new' post-war ethnic stereotypes: the Greek entrepreneurial café owner, the Maltese pimp (fixed in the imagination of '50s Londoners after the notorious case of the 'white-slaving' Messina Brothers) or the most visible new arrivals, the West Indians. All these groups share a colonial history. Though in private (after they 'retire' from the bureaucratic space of the dole office) their behaviours conform to individualised national and ethnic stereotypes, in public they represent the generalised 'other' to Englishness. They are loud, lively, talkative and pleasure seeking, in contrast to the 'gloomy, intent and resentful' English. Cronin traces the confirmation not of whiteness but of Englishness as an identity, in opposition to the variegated identities of the migrants. The 'rightful heirs' of the benefit system, indeed of the welfare state as a whole, are solid, respectable and 'ordinary', in contrast to the varieties of excess characteristic of the migrants: unbridled consumption, sexual indulgence, noise.

The English are also powerless. Indeed they are gloomy, intent and resentful precisely because they are powerless in the face of the inclusivity of the welfare state's definition of the nation's working class, to which 'foreigners' and even actors are allowed access. What the welfare state enables, in this formulation, is the inclusion of the excessive other within the bureaucratic boundaries of the nation. 'Sponging' is made possible, and even acceptable, though not, apparently, to the English, who are presented as work hungry rather than work shy.

The former colonials, whether nominally white or not, all inhabit the same role vis-à-vis the 'ordinary' English, that of chancers who abuse the hospitality of the state. Yet the characterisation of the Irish is unusual in that it both reprises nineteenth-century racialised stereotypes and resituates them in the context of post-war decline and the welfare state. In fact, the new welfare bureaucracy offers a different context for the Irish stereotype, which therefore shifts in meaning from vagrant to scrounger. So far from being merely a social problem (vagrancy, drinking, fighting) the Irish migrants can now be represented, alongside other post-war migrants, as an economic problem (parasitic, taking benefits which are not due to them, lessening the resources available to the 'ordinary' working class). Indeed, if we accept that the post-war settlement helped engender new definitions of national character, then we should expect to see a shift in the placing of the Irish as members of the residuum, the undeserving poor, under Victorian laissez-faire capitalism – to a new class positioning of Irish ethnicity in the welfare context.

After all, in the mid-nineteenth century the Irish stereotype helped distinguish what was different and dangerous about the Irish (and the working class in general) for the industrial, entrepreneurial English middle classes; one hundred years later the migrant Irish, like other migrants, were perceived as a threat to the 'ordinary' English.

Cronin is clearly interested in the manner in which racial and ethnic stereotypes become displaced and layered over one another in time. As Paddy Riley's fortunes fail, it proves impossible for him to inhabit any role other than one of a series of ethnic 'jokes' which slowly recede further in historical time so that he passes from down-and-out, to navvy, to slave, and finally homeless and filthy vagrant. Each of these stages fall as a consequence of Riley's inability adequately to perform the various roles assigned to him as post-war immigrant Irishman. Following his hopeful registration for employment in the Labour Exchange, Riley visits the National Assistance Board, where, true to his failure to manage any of the moves required of him by the bureaucratic state, and despite the fact that he is destitute, he finds himself ineligible for any sort of financial assistance. The problem turns out to be that he is technically homeless – he has a daily rather than weekly ticket for the Rowton hostel – and therefore he can't apply for help with rent and food. He is told that all he is entitled to is a bed in a Salvation Army hostel and 5 shillings towards his dinner, rather than a weekly payout to cover his expenses: 'This was a bit of a facer. I had not the slightest doubt that my commonwealth cousins did better than this for themselves.'[23]

'Tell me', he asks an elderly man in the pub who has also been refused by the National Assistance Board (NAB), 'tell me, I hear stories of blokes

[23] Ibid., p. 149.

getting five or six quid a week out of them, chaps just off the boat and what not.' The problem, as explained to him, is that claimants require a fixed address for any payments to be made. This is an interesting moment in the novel, when the stereotype of the immigrant scrounger merges with that of the respectable, or deserving poor. Riley's initial approach to the labour exchange had been prompted by an ironic reading of adverse publicity: 'The Tory newspapers had been full of reports about the vast sums which the welfare state was disbursing to the undeserving poor.' As he discovers, however,

> The Tory papers were quite wrong. Far more than private Victorian charity it [the welfare state] favoured only the deserving poor.... It was designed for the respectable proletariat, who would never fall below that fatal first step, and though thieves and chancers from Ireland and the West Indies could avail themselves of it, that was because they stepped ashore on the first step. They had organization and backing, which I had not. They were orthodox, that is to say, respectable.[24]

Certain passages in Donall Mac Amhlaigh's *Diary of an Exile* corroborate Cronin's picture of a capacious welfare state bureaucracy, which allows the migrants to inhabit both the stereotype of 'thieves and chancers' and the respectable working class at the same time, whether the English like it or not. In a passage reflecting on the democratising role of the National Health Service, through which Irish immigrants were eligible for free treatment, Mac Amhlaigh compares the experience of trying to access healthcare in Ireland. Of an English doctor, he says, "He'll give you to understand that you are a person and not a beggar."[25] For Mac Amhlaigh, the explicit class structure into which the Irishman was inducted in Britain reflected negatively on the implicit and hidden class structure back home. He goes as far as to claim that all the Irish in England are 'working-class', compared to the way there are 'all sorts' in Ireland. This was obviously not true – not all the Irish in England were working class – but a mixture of English prejudice, and the jobs available to Irish migrants, encouraged the merging of a national and a class identification, and importantly this was understood in part as liberating.[26] According to Mac Amhlaigh's account,

---

[24] Ibid., pp. 152, 153–154.

[25] Mac Amhlaigh, *An Irish Navvy*, p. 65.

[26] Mac Amhlaigh's perspective has been skewed by the vanishing of the Irish into various 'un-marked' class fractions, discussed earlier. The dominant stereotype of the working- or lower-middle-class Irish man and woman in post-war Britain not only distorts the picture for the historical researcher but for contemporary commentators such as Mac Amhlaigh. He sees the Irish who are marked out as Irish and not the others, or, more properly, the others cannot be understood as Irish

the Irish became working class and persons at the same time. The equivalence is perhaps understandable, given that this was the moment when many of them first became waged.

Cronin's narrator, however, signally fails to hold on to the bureaucratically created identity of working-class personhood. The narrative ends as Riley slips irrevocably from what he calls the 'law of the first step', the niche inhabited by the new welfare state immigrant, into a much older category, that of the vagrant, 'reduced to daily slavery.' The plot is complicated, but through a series of introductions he meets the very rich Amelia, who has the status of a colonial overlord – her money comes from a plantation in Sierra Leone (just newly independent when Cronin was writing).[27] Taking on the role of Victorian philanthropist, Amelia decides Riley needs 'improving.' In a perfect satire on the idea that charity should be dependent on redundant public works (as during the famine) she manufactures a job digging a hole in her back garden with a pick and shovel. For this she pays him a few shillings a day in order to teach him the value of work.

The inscrutable tone of Cronin's novel renders almost any attempt at interpretation, let alone politicised interpretation, hopelessly in excess of the comic plot. As much as anything Cronin's distinction between the welfare state immigrant and the undeserving poor is a plot device propelling the innocent foil to the satire. Yet it is hard to ignore the superimposition of the economies of slavery, Victorian laissez-faire and consensus-oriented post-war corporate capitalism. Each depends on the deployment of racialised categories, which appear to be unchanging, but which position the Irishman each time as a different form of outsider. Riley himself is unable to resist the power of the cultural stereotype – 'we become what we pretend to be' he explains – and in this he resembles all the other Irish characters in the novel.[28]

We become what we pretend to be: it is perhaps not surprising to find the excessive performance of an Irish caricature in comic texts of the 1950s. Yet this performance was equally central to autobiographical and even documentary works, as well as representations of the emigrant 'tragedy.' Donall Mac Amhlaigh's memoir recounts story after story of men outdoing one another in drinking, fighting and feats of physical prowess such

in the same way. The disappearance or unreadability of alternative versions of Irishness is a prerequisite for the reproducibility of the stereotype.

[27] The character of Amelia was apparently based on Margaret Gardiner. See Antoinette Quinn, *Patrick Kavanagh*, p. 305.

[28] Cronin, *The Life of Riley*, p. 166.

as digging the deepest ditch or shifting the largest iron girder, alongside tales of a binge culture, a refusal to save and become 'respectable', which was also a consequence of being on the social margins, where respectability would always remain out of reach. In Murphy's *A Whistle in the Dark*, Harry Carney performs a grotesque version of the stereotype of the drinking and fighting Irishmen. His brother Michael believes in a narrative of social mobility but Harry's mode of 'escape' from the stereotype is to emphasise it. As he says, 'I wouldn't want to disappoint them.'[29] These texts imply that for Irish migrants there was no option but to inhabit the stereotype, and that there was a fine line between its comic and tragic manifestations.

The Bucklep

Riley's hopeless descent from respectable grocer's assistant to caricature down-and-out stems in large part from his failure to capitalise on the one bankable characteristic of the Irish in Britain: their charm. Cronin's portraits of the Irish clique at the BBC (Rodgers, MacNeice and H. A. L. Craig) suggest talent ruined by the performance of Irishness, the only thing for which it appears they reliably get paid. Writers and producers exaggerate the Celtic note in order to ensure repeats of their programmes, but to make their productions 'authentic' they need to perform Irishness outside of work too.[30] 'In the circle in which I moved an unmistakeable Celticism of word and spirit was demanded. One was required to subscribe to the tweedy view, at least in theory, as an aesthetic and a way of life.' Cronin's portrait of W. R. Rodgers (Billy Boddells) is of a man destroyed by his relentless performance of Irishry, a cautionary example of Riley's adage that 'we become what we pretend to be.'

> He was the most extreme. He spoke in gnomic pseudo-proverbs, indecipherable to the rational mind, indeed probably meaningless. What he

[29] Ironically, the responses to Murphy's play in 1961 reveal the grip of the stereotype. As Fintan O'Toole has argued, the play was lambasted for its hyper-realism, basically for letting the Irishmen on stage: 'The only thing that separates his characters from a bunch of wild gorillas is their ability to speak with an Irish accent'; 'a spew of stewed Irish that fouled the London stage'; 'Thomas Murphy is the kind of playwright one would hate to meet in a dark theatre'. See O'Toole, *The Politics of Magic*, pp. 9–10. This appears to be an instance of Murphy the writer becoming what his characters pretended to be.

[30] This suggests another possible reading for the trope of the 'repeat' in Louis MacNeice's 1953 poem 'Autumn Sequel.' For a discussion of 'diasporic performance' in Cronin's novel, see Murray, *London Irish Fictions*, p. 78.

intended to convey I imagine was a sort of dark peasant wisdom, something from the deep and mysterious consciousness of the race, the knowledge of centuries gnarled and knotted and knuckled, knobbly and knotted as the hands of an old knaught man.... But I am talking like Boddells himself.

MacNeice had recruited Sam Hanna Bell and W. R. Rodgers as BBC producers, and while both worked on the Third Programme, the BBC's classical music and high-culture radio station,[31] Rodgers came to be known specifically as a Third Programme producer, since much of his work was broadcast on the network.[32] The listings of 'Irish-themed' cultural programmes on the BBC during the 1950s do suggest a narrow 'Emerald Isle'-type interest, suggesting that despite the high-brow aims of the Third Programme (and some noticeable Irish successes such as Beckett's 'All That Fall'), in order to make money, in other words to ensure repeats, feature writers needed to buy into tourism, folklore and traditional culture.[33] Much of the programming peddled an idea of Ireland as home to a romantic, mythical and fading civilisation. So the aspiring writer Riley is assured by Coosins (H. A. L. Craig),

> 'Ashtowk Paddy it is not trash you'll be writing for the Home Service or any other service. It is for the third programme that you'll be making the randy words tumble each other like rabbitts in the morning sun. Ay', he concluded in a voice genuinely hoarse with emotion, 'and if there was a fourth programme aself, it is you that would be on it.'

Irish writers associated with the Third Programme included MacNeice, Denis Johnston, Sean O'Faolain, Elizabeth Bowen, Frank O'Connor, James Stephens and later the director of the Irish Folklore Commission, J. H. Delargy. The first programme in Rodgers's series *The Irish Storyteller* was subtitled 'picture of a vanishing world':

> On the western fringe of Europe are fast vanishing evidences of a civilisation that once covered the whole Atlantic area. Its literature was oral; and the storyteller with his sagas and wonder-tales was the book, the newspaper, and the film of his society. This programme presents the fading picture

---

[31] Barbara Coulton, *Louis MacNeice in the BBC* (London: Faber and Faber, 1980), pp. 78–79.

[32] Kate Whitehead, *The Third Programme: A Literary History* (Oxford: Clarendon Press, 1989), p. 35. I am indebted here to Elizabeth Robertson, particularly 'Broadcasting Ireland: The BBC Third Programme and the Cult of Nostalgia', MA research essay, Queen Mary University of London, 2008.

[33] The playwright and balladeer Dominic Behan also wrote for the Third Programme from 1955 onwards, but the folk imperatives stretched beyond the Third. Between 1952 and 1958 the musician and collector Seamus Ennis curated a long-running folk music programme on the BBC Home Service, *As I Roved Out*, which featured Irish traditional music alongside English folk.

of storytelling today. The Gaelic recordings were made by a BBC recording unit in the course of a recent Irish journey.[34]

As one of the Irish storytellers featured in the series, Bryan McMahon, acknowledged, the world was vanishing in part because of the radio. Youth, the radio, cinema and the printed page were all at fault for bringing to an end 'an ancient world', but the medium was also a tool for preservation: 'In the past ten years the Irish Folklore Commission under Dr. Delargy has, with meagre means, done remarkable work in collecting over a thousand volumes of oral tradition and stories.'[35] Delargy would later present a series of *The Irish Storyteller*, in which over six parts, a traditional Irish story was told in English.

If *The Irish Storyteller* skirted close to offering a nostalgic version of Irish culture to English listeners, Rodgers's other series, *Irish Literary Portraits* which ran until 1966, was savagely criticised for its stage Irishry by Patrick Kavanagh, in a manner which seems to have paved the way for Cronin's portrayal of the confused and confusing Boydells. The literary portraits were billed as 'a symposium of voices', and Rodgers himself was proud of what he claimed was a new technique of splicing together excerpts from interviews so it would appear that interviewees were discussing with one another.[36] The emphasis was on lively and 'authentic' voices, but Kavanagh was scathing:

> How did you bury Joyce?
> In a broadcast symposium.
> That's how we buried Joyce
> To a tuneful encomium.
>
> Who carried the coffin out?
> Six Dublin Codgers
> Led into Langham Place
> By W. R. Rodgers.[37]

He accused Rodgers of peddling a folksy image of literary Irishness ('buck-leppin', in the epithet he coined himself) with the emphasis on the colourful anecdote and engaging note of 'genuine' Irishry:

> The centenary of the birth of George Moore was celebrated this year and to honour the occasion W. R. Rodgers, who has introduced the bucklep to

---

[34] 'The Irish Storyteller', *Radio Times*, 13–19 June 1948, p. 9.
[35] W. R. Rodgers, 'Tales from "Hidden Ireland"', in Harden Jay (ed.), *Irish Literary Portraits* (London: BBC, 1971).
[36] Rodgers, *Irish Literary Portraits*.
[37] Kavanagh, 'Who Killed James Joyce?' *Envoy* 5:17 (1951), p. 62.

London literary society, where they think it wonderful, held the usual symposium on the radio.[38]

The value of the 'bucklep' lay not only in the reproduction of 'peasant' quality (after all the literary portraits steered away from oral tradition and rural life), but in the reproduction of an Irish sound.[39] The 1950s saw the beginning of the long heyday of Irish entertainers on British popular radio and TV, including Eamonn Andrews, and – slightly later – Terry Wogan, Dave Allen and Val Doonican, all of whom offered variations on caustic, kitsch and sentimental, but most of all soft-voiced and articulate, versions of Irishness. As Brendan Behan discovered after his drunken appearance on Panorama (in a 1956 interview with Malcolm Muggeridge about *The Quare Fellow*, which had recently opened at Stratford East), incoherence was no barrier to popularity. What English audiences found themselves warming to in Behan's performance were the same qualities to which they objected in Irish immigrant labourers en masse: drunkenness, irreverence, lack of inhibition (he sang a song from the play on air), the refusal to be tamed by the expectations of polite society.[40]

The caricature of emotional, truth-telling, spiritual, earthy Irishness, the type Cronin suggests was being peddled on the Third Programme, has just as long a history as the violent, cunning, drunken type. Running right through the image of Irish migrants as stupid, dirty, feckless, unreliable and dangerous lies a seam of 'more natural', untamed, convivial qualities not so far from those associated with the 'real, genuine people' of the western seaboard by city-dwellers, especially Dubliners, now cut off from their rural pasts. It is not simply that they are positive and negative sides of the one coin. Rather they should be understood as the same side of the coin – Irishness as code for forms of pre-modern conviviality that were both desired and feared by the 'ordinary' English.[41]

---

[38] Patrick Kavanagh, 'Sex and Christianity', *Kavanagh's Weekly*, 24 May 1952, pp. 7–8.

[39] Cronin describes a successful Boddells (W. R. Rodgers) programme: 'like most of what they admired, it was Celtic, loquacious, adjectival, metaphorical, alliterative, bouncing, lyrical and largely meaningless.' Cronin, *Life of Riley*, p. 171.

[40] Behan was being watched by MI5 because of his IRA and communist activities. A report dated 11 June 1956 concludes that 'as an individual he is too unstable and too drunken to be particularly dangerous.' *Brendan Francis BEHAN: Irish.* NA KV 2/3181. On Behan, see John Brannigan, *Brendan Behan: Cultural Nationalism and the Revisionist Writer* (Dublin: Four Courts Press, 2002); *Irish University Review: A Journal of Irish Studies*, Special Issue on Brendan Behan, 44:1 (2014).

[41] As Homi Bhabha argues, the stereotype names something apparently obvious, something known, but which nevertheless has to be anxiously repeated. Understood psycho-analytically it is a fetish, a locus of ambivalence, which masks desire. See Bhabha, 'The Other Question – the Stereotype and Colonial Discourse', *Screen*, 24:6 (1983), pp. 18–36.

As I have suggested, 'ordinary' Englishness was a quality still under construction in post-war Britain, and much British literature and film of the 1950s was invested in exploring its character. In northern working-class fiction, in the plays and novels produced by the 'angry young men', and in middle-class novels of discovery, characters rail against the stultifying effects of both middle- and working-class commodified culture, consensus politics and the assumption that everyone wants to become more bourgeois. Just as Irish immigrants represented something slightly new in the context of the welfare state, so this literary milieu offered an alternative post-war complexion for Celtic charm. In London-based novels of the late fifties, such as Colin MacInnes's London trilogy and Lynne Reid-Banks, *The L-Shaped Room*, middle class mores are set into relief by a gallery of urban types in which the immigrant newcomer looms large. The Irish appear, along with West Indian migrants, Jewish characters and members of the white underclass (particularly prostitutes) as figures for the warm and genuine 'other' of post-war middle-class respectability and reserve in a good deal of post-war British fiction. Correspondingly, in Irish journalist Michael Campbell's 1959 comic novel, *O Mary, This London*, the main character and his friend themselves provide the Celtic yardstick against which a gallery of English 'types' are found wanting.

Campbell's novel traces the fortunes of Peter Gavin and his friend from Trinity College, Charles Ferguson, who have moved to London in their early twenties to 'seek enlightenment and escape provincialism.' Instead, with few exceptions, they encounter dullness, lack of ambition, and an empty performance of civility. The middle-class English are 'dull, stupid, unread and devoted to their work'; the party set communicate with one another in redundant, dead phrases, such as 'how perfectly beastly', and 'sort of' ('Topsy's in a sort of *state*. I can only sort of *linger* a moment. I've had to sort of *edge* myself out.'); the angry young men, bookshelves stocked with Sartre and Camus, thrive on a similar species of repetition: 'There's nothing left but copulation.... It's boredom. It's anaemia. It's boredom, boredom, boredom.' But perhaps the working class has reached the acme of non-communication:

> This was a typical London pub: an anonymous place, set between one thing and the other, where people's brains have dried up and there is just the staring and waiting. The ageless barman was wiping the inside of a glass with a grey dishcloth. Separated from him by a plastic cover with two stiff-looking sandwiches under it, a man sat on a stool smoking a pipe. They were not speaking. The Test Matches were over long ago. Two others sat elbow to elbow at a table just inside the door.... The two beers on the table in front

of them were untouched. They too were silent. It was the spirit that had refused to panic throughout the bombing of London.[42]

The two Irish men pitch themselves into this unforgiving environment, searching for authentic communication, intellectual companionship and, most of all, 'la fantaisie'. True to Irish novelistic reality, France is the true home of the soul, of self-expression, imagination and 'panache.' At moments of crisis the friends lapse into their student French, and one of their few moments of meaningful contact in London is with an elderly French prostitute, who recognises both the need for imagination to live, and the lack of it in the English.

The principal complaints of the Irish seekers-after-truth is that the English don't know how to talk, for in the art of conversation lies the art of being human. And as Peter Gavin explores the city, he discovers that it is not only the college-educated Irish who feel cheated by the social opportunities on offer. As the domestic help, a girl from Bantry, puts it: 'There's no go in them. To tell the honest-to-God truth, I don't care for them at all. They're not human reely. I mean, when you're among an Irish crowd you can count on a bit o' sport, d'yeh know what I mean?'[43]

The idea of the Irish as more vital, more spontaneous and less philistine than their English counterparts has a long history. As we have seen, it colours accounts of emigrant culture as well as immigrant memoirs, such as Donall Mac Amhlaigh's narrative; indeed, however ironically, Campbell underwrites a broad narrative of loss not so far from that found in Mac Amhlaigh. Peter Gavin's statement that 'we Irish have a capacity for not growing up' is meant as a compliment. His portrait of a provincial Irish town is of highly stratified social relationships, where the Protestant minority retain much of the financial power, but it compares favourably to the artificial life of the metropolis: 'at home we met and lived and loved and had our beings *together*. We formed some sort of human entity.'[44]

The tragedy is that these quasi-rural communities do not thrive. In the corrugated iron barn serving as the 'Mayfair Ballroom', 'seven girls danced with fourteen young men, practicing their steps for the Tottenham Court Road.' Through the Victorian red-brick station, '*emigrés* came back home for fortnightly holidays and others set forth with wet eyes but swelling hearts'. And at the other end of the journey, in grimy Euston they gathered:

---

[42] Campbell, *O Mary, This London*, pp. 131, 37, 107, 153.
[43] Ibid. p. 28.
[44] Ibid., p. 175.

a crowd of us there, all of unmistakable nationality: red-faced men in baggy suits, pretty women all dressed up in bows and pleats with little blue hats and veils, and older mothers, presumably of the men, dressed in black with yellow wrinkled faces, the peasantry come to live in London, uncomfortably equipped with shiny black handbags.[45]

The country in the city. The visibility of the Irish here is put down to their clothing, smart but out of fashion, which identifies them unmistakably as rural types, 'uncomfortable' in the big city. There is, of course, no natural association between non-metropolitan migrants and unfashionable dress – West Indian newcomers had a reputation for particularly sharp dressing. But in a 1970s article Mac Amhlaigh noted the preference among Irish labourers for a conservative style dating from the 1940s, including starched detachable collars, which long outlasted the disappearance of the fashion in Ireland itself:

> Suits would be neatly pressed for the most part, and if your trouser leg was any narrower than twenty-two inches the effect was considered rather shabby.[46]

The idea of the Irishman in Britain as a kind of throwback, an unchanged element of rural reality, isolated from both British and Irish society and therefore uncorrupted, lies behind much of the ethnographic writing on Irish migrants from the 1950s. Both Mac Amhlaigh and Richard Power imply that the 'real' Irish (and therefore the best ones) were to be found in the industrial cities of Britain, though Power was typically suspicious of his own motivations in following the Aran Islanders to Birmingham.[47] It is precisely this form of 'peasant' romanticism that Cronin satirises in *The Life of Riley*. Riley's journey to London has been prompted by Prunshios McGonaghey (Peadar O'Donnell), who advises him, 'Go to England and live in a doss-house. The present dialectical situation con only be understood in the doss houses of London.'[48] What Riley discovers is that the 'real' Irish workers in the Camden doss house (throbbing with 'the pulse of the people', according to Prunshios), are indistinguishable from the hyper-Celticised intellectuals at the BBC who ape them. The idea of rural authenticity has overtaken reality.

---

[45] Ibid. pp. 172, 51.
[46] Mac Amhlaigh, 'The Celt and His Clothes', *Ireland's Own,* 30 October 1971, p. 14.
[47] See Chapter 3.
[48] McGonaghey is introduced as editor and Riley's boss at 'The Trumpet', a reference to the journal *The Bell*, edited by O'Donnell from 1946 to 1954, where Cronin worked for a time in the early fifties.

'An Indefinably Natural Quality'

In terms of the late revivalist debate discussed in the first chapter, the 'real, genuine' Irish who stood in opposition to the artifice and anonymity of the industrial city figured as a surviving remnant of a rural Ireland becoming lost to the march of modernity. There was considerable irony in the fact that by the early '60s the emigrants who had been castigated for their 'national defeatism' in leaving rural Ireland in the immediate post-war years were being held up as examples of incorruptibility. Left behind by English urban modernisation, and cut off from Irish social developments, these surviving countrymen in the city became the focus for sentiment, nostalgia and, later, guilt for the manner in which their limbo existence was both pitied and ignored. As early as 1956, in *The Bachelor's Daughter*, M. J. Molloy had seen the parallel between the harshly treated Irish immigrant 'bulldozing his way through the London blitz' and the qualities deemed necessary for the frugal and back-breaking conditions of unmechanised small-farm life. But neither Irish men nor Irish women were prepared to pay that price in order to ensure the survival of a traditional way of life. As electricity, running water, farm mechanisation, television, secondary education and small measures of industrialisation all began to make inroads into rural Irish society, those who had been cut off from home in the 1950s were the ones who appeared to hold the past most dear.

The image of the emigrant faced in two directions. On the one hand emigrants carried with them the taint of abroad – their subtle alienness was always about to be betrayed by their attitude to money, their clothing, their accent or a turn of phrase. At the same time they were stuck in the past, embarrassing (or worthy) representatives of an outmoded way of life. But seen through the lens of a British debate about culture, they were also a distinctly post-war phenomenon. All the novels I have discussed in this chapter describe Irishness as an element in excess of post-war British attitudes and modes of behaviour. In so doing they echo contemporary debates about traditional and mass culture, particularly those popularised by Richard Hoggart in his 1957 lament for the loss of close-knit urban communities, *The Uses of Literacy*.[49] Hoggart's analysis of the effect of consumerism on working-class culture is primarily elegiac. His scrutiny of Hollywood cinema, advertising, popular fiction, magazines and newspapers argues that industrial communities have been increasingly

---

[49] Richard Hoggart, *The Uses of Literacy* (London: Penguin, 2009).

hollowed out by manufactured mass culture, the everyday cultural life of the working class rendered increasingly atomised and anonymous. Hoggart's influence on 1960s British fiction has been well documented, but it also colours portraits of the Irish as more vital figures in the urban English landscape. In *O Mary, This London*, the Irish 'come from the fields and the good healthy air and the neighbourliness' to a world of 'artificial phrases, clothes and houses.' Echoing Hoggart's concern over the commercialisation of sex in pseudo-American 'spicy mazagines' and 'gangster-novelettes', Michael Campbell's description of the cultural desiccation of the city focuses on the titillating coverage of sex crimes in the tabloids, and advertisements for tawdry erotic attractions. Real prostitutes are fine, indeed earthy. It is the mass production of erotic excitement that appalls (both Campbell and Cronin link the sexualisation of popular culture to child rape and murder). Paying obvious homage to Hoggart's invented catalogue of titles for what he calls 'the newer novelettes' ('Sweetie, Take It Hot'; 'Death-Cab for Cutie'; 'No Talk from Tombstones'),[50] Campbell runs with a list of shows playing at the London theatre, including *Murder at Little Mitcham* "Her greatest yet"; *No Beds without Breakfast* "My sides ached"; *A Corpse in Colchester* "She's done it again"; *The Doting Debutante* "I found it quite delicious"; *No Darts for Sid* "I didn't 'arf larf."[51] While English culture is apparently reduced to advertising, cheap entertainment and a supine worship of the television, the Irish seek for genuine imaginative experience. Cronin's distinction between the Irish and the English working class ultimately comes down to the fact that the Irish make their own entertainment. The corridors of the Rowton 'resounded by night and day with shouts of "Ashtowk Paddy!", "I'll shplit the bashtard", "Come up, Mick!", "By Jasus I'll ate 'im", "I'm after buryin' the mother", "Puck him, Christy" and other such pleasantries', while the English watch the television in silence.[52]

Many of the literary examples offered here suggest that the visibility of the post-war Irish in Britain was actually experienced as their audibility. The Irish were identifiable by their brogue, their loudness, their curses, their Celticisms, their singing – in short, their lack of auditory propriety, all of which was made worse by drink. But they were also visible in public as Catholics. The crowds outside Sunday mass in areas of high Irish concentration, the paraphernalia of feast days and holy days, the dressing up

---

[50] Hoggart, *Uses of Literacy*, p. 231.
[51] Campbell, *O Mary, This London*, p. 177.
[52] Cronin, *Life of Riley*, p. 125.

for First Communions, Corpus Christi processions, Confirmations – all marked Irish Catholics out as belonging to an alternative community.[53]

In David Lodge's first novel, *The Picturegoers* (1960), it is the Catholicism of the Irish which enables them to resist, and provide an alternative to, post-war commodified mass culture. Lodge has stated that he wrote the novel having been influenced by Hoggart's *The Uses of Literacy*,

> which I read shortly after it was published in 1957. Hoggart's examination, critical without being condescending, of the connections and contradictions between the often tawdry and trivial products of popular literature and journalism, and the real lives of the people who consume them, encouraged me to think about the role of the cinema in society in a similar spirit. Much of the material discussed by Richard Hoggart belonged to the pre-war era, and was being supplanted by brasher, slicker publications. By the late Fifties, cinema-going was also in decline, under the impact of television and other developments in popular culture, and I made this a theme of my novel, giving it a slightly elegiac note which also resonates in parts of *The Uses of Literacy*.[54]

The sociological concerns of the novel are immediately evident, as the central character, Mark Underwood, escapes from the dullness and respectability of his middle-class home-counties family (his father goes to Masonic dinners, his mother watches the television), to the teeming and apparently disorganised life of a large Catholic family in south London, who take in lodgers. The reader encounters the various denizens of Brickley (Bromley) as they respond to the films put on at the local picturehouse, from the frustrated Teddy Boy, to the local priest, the young man on National Service, the usherette, the recent Irish emigrant, and the established, seemingly assimilated Irish family, the Mallorys. Mark's quest is both cultural and spiritual, and the Mallorys represent an 'everyday' Catholic alternative to the life of a student of English literature, which Mark finds increasingly hollow. The novel offers one example of the development of Catholic fiction in post-war Britain. While in the work of writers such as Evelyn Waugh or Graham Greene, plots revolve around matters of conscience (whether comically portrayed or not), the emphasis of post-war writers is less on questions of conscience and truth than on modes of behaviour. It is the ordinary world of lower-middle-class and middle-class Catholics, and

---

[53] See, for example, the testimony in M. Lennon, M. McAdam and J. O'Brien, *Across the Water: Irish Women's Lives in Britain* (London: Virago: 1988), p. 220: 'I think at one stage we were the only Irish family living in our street – so that set us apart a bit. We all went to Catechism on a Saturday and Mass on a Sunday as a family. It was obvious where we were going and with things like my brother's First Communion and my First Communion, I mean, you couldn't miss us.'

[54] David Lodge, 'Introduction', in *The Picturegoers* (London: Penguin, 1992), p. xi.

particularly their means of squaring religious belief with everyday encounters in the modern urban environment, which is the subject of writers as various as Lodge, Muriel Spark and John Braine.[55]

Unlike the Irish labourers discussed elsewhere in this book, Lodge's suburban, home-owning Irish family is 'invisible' in the public arena. The children study hard at their grammar schools, the father is in regular employment, all the members of the family enjoy the offerings at the local cinema, even the risqué exploits of 'Amber Lush' in a film about an extra-marital affair. Yet they are emphatically not the same as their English neighbours. They are semi-detached from contemporary urban culture because of their Catholicism, identified as different by their devotional practice, by the sentimental religious tat with which their home is decorated (photographs of First Communicants and the Sacred Heart), and by turns of phrase ('offering up' vexations to Our Blessed Lord, for example). Mark is initially unnerved by the communal prayers and the domestic trappings of religion: 'the plastic holy water stoup askew on the wall, the withered holy Palm, stuck behind a picture of the Sacred Heart which resembled an illustration in a medical textbook, and the statue of St Patrick enthroned upon the dresser.' Mrs Mallory has no illusions about the impact of Catholic conduct – far more than Catholic faith – on her English neighbours:

> It's not that we have anything against non-Catholics, in fact I've far more against some Catholics I could name – no, it's just that it could be uncomfortable and awkward for a non-Catholic living with us – no meat on Fridays, everybody rushing about like mad things on Sunday mornings, and so on.[56]

Yet Mark's 'bourgeois upbringing' and 'superficial sophistication' give way to an admiration for the vitality of the family, which, in keeping with the novel's Hoggartian perspective, prizes community over respectability. 'In the Mallorys he felt he had rediscovered the people', reads one telling sentence. Culturally and spiritually alive without being pious, the Mallorys offer an image of embourgeoisement without loss of contact with 'folk' culture – as opposed to the 'passive' consumption of culture which is

---

[55] See, for example, David Lodge's novel, *How Far Can You Go?* (London: Secker & Warburg, 1980), which explicitly turns on the difference between conscience and behaviour in relation to sex. In *The Picturegoers* the orphan Bridget has been brought up by nuns in Ireland and is now working in a café in London. She says her nightly prayers but does not go to church. In Muriel Spark's *The Bachelors* (London: Macmillan, 1960), Irish Catholic Matthew Finch has a bad conscience about sex, but this is presented as a problem of conduct rather than a source of inner conflict.

[56] Lodge, *The Picturegoers*, p. 46.

hallmark of the working and middle classes in 1950s novels. They refuse to throw anything away – souvenirs, old magazines, the hook for the dog's lead, though the dog has long gone – so that the house becomes a shrine to the value of the ordinary. Their life has 'an indefinably natural quality. It was the kind of life one could live for years, he thought, without becoming bored or dulled by routine.'[57] Lodge's 'rediscovery of the people' suggests that Irish authenticity offers an alternative to both the dullness of English middle-class culture and the constrictions of English working-class life. We have seen how the whiteness of the migrant Irish might allow them to vanish into the 'outcast' territory of the deprived, or of 'failing' working-class culture. Lodge's formulation suggests another class position for the migrant Irish, neither middle nor working class but 'the people' – a classless formulation which in turn recycles revivalist idealisations of traditional rural communal bonds.

Irishness enters the fictional world of post-war Britain in a number of ways. It is, first of all, part of the 'real' world of 1950s London. For writers such as Lodge and Spark, location is important, whether it is Hampstead, Kensington or Bromley. Both these writers are also concerned with questions of faith, but their Irish characters offer not only images and narratives of religious devotion but an alternative to a stultifying 'bourgeois' version of Englishness. In this respect, their literary fictions echo aspects of the 'social exploration' narratives popular in the early 1960s, such as Doris Lessing's *In Pursuit of the English*, or the more straightforwardly fictionalised ethnographies of urban life by writers such as Colin MacInnes. As both Cronin and Campbell suggest, Irishness confers an aura of exoticism, whether it is through the rituals of going to mass, Corpus Christi processions, fish on Fridays, the genuine folk culture embodied in traditional music, or alternatively the physical sensuality of otherness – one character finds it hard to refrain from running his hand through Matthew Finch's black curls in Spark's *The Bachelors*. All these representations build on cultural stereotypes of the Celt which ultimately derive from Ernst Renan and Matthew Arnold. As Seamus Deane argues in *Celtic Revivals*, 'every virtue of the Celt was matched by a vice of the British bourgeois; everything the philistine middle classes of England needed, the Celt could supply.'[58] The lure of the charming, exotic, voluble Irishman may have been one way of domesticating the fear of the violent, primitive, taciturn one.

---

[57] Ibid, p. 47.
[58] Seamus Deane, *Celtic Revivals: Essays in Modern Irish Literature* (London: Faber and Faber, 1985), p. 25.

CHAPTER 5

Clay Is the Flesh
Looking at Manual Labour

They have no home life whatever, but at the same time, they are so free.

The Irishmen, Philip Donnellan[1]

One felt much closer to what was going on in the street, there wasn't any particular indoor life ... so this [the sites and the streets] was really the fabric of one's life.

Frank Auerbach[2]

A crowded public bar, navy blue suits, hard hands round pint glasses, oiled curly hair and red faces, the voices of Connemara and Mayo, the black beer gurgling down.... These men were "Tunnel Tigers" – a gang who took deep drainlaying on contract and did it against the clock. Dangerous work.... Men like these were the niggers of Britain for a century or more until blacks came to take their place in the public prejudice. They lived in ghettoes in the big cities or in nameless digs on the road somewhere and England was ignorant of the hard work they did, seeing them only as drunken, two-fisted, womanizing.... The description the gang gave of drainlaying; the golden payslips – these all suggested a powerful counterpoint of revelation against cliché. In my mind's eye I saw a sensational programme.

Philip Donnellan[3]

Philip Donnellan's recollection of the impetus behind his 1965 documentary, *The Irishmen*, touches on many of the issues discussed in these pages. The men encountered in the pub are obviously countrymen in the city, marked out by their voices, their old-fashioned clothes, their hardened physical appearance. Donnellan echoes the descriptions of

---

[1] *The Irishmen: An Impression of Exile.* Directed by Philip Donnellan. BBC, 1965. [Not broadcast].

[2] 'Podcast 1: London after the War', *The Courtauld Gallery Podcasts: Frank Auerbach, London Building Sites 1952–62.* http://www.courtauld.ac.uk/GALLERY/exhibitions/2009/auerbach/auerbachpodcasts.shtml.

[3] Philip Donnellan, 'We Were the BBC: An Alternative View of a Producer's Responsibility 1948–1984', unpublished typescript. Donnellan Archive, Birmingham Central Library, pp. 150–151. See also www.philipdonnelland.co.uk.

rural labourers stranded in an urban environment found in the autobiographies of John B. Keane and Donall Mac Amhlaigh, and explicitly targets the assumptions that the 'English' harbour about them: that they are violent, drunken and uncivilised. He implies that the 'revelation' he sought through making the documentary was to be found through an analysis of labour, focusing on the working rather than the drinking and fighting Irishman.[4] Yet a large part of what Donnellan calls the cliché of the Irishman in Britain turned on his ability and willingness to do hard physical work; above all, the sign that the Irishman was a countryman in the city was that he did the work of a rural labourer in an urban environment – digging London clay.

Donnellan's film should be interpreted in the context of the 1960s folk revival and particularly the popularisation of Irish traditional music by original songwriters such as Ewan McColl and Dominic Behan, both of whose songs feature in the documentary. The relationship between the recovery of traditional music and song by collectors such as Seamus Ennis (who promoted the music on the BBC during the 1950s) and urban-based folk groups such as The Clancy Brothers and The Dubliners is complex, and was partly mediated by balladeers such as McColl, Behan and Pete Seeger.[5] Alongside republican politics and the vicissitudes of love, many of the most popular 1960s ballads are working songs. They turn on the fact of labour, from the celebration of sheer physical strength to the alternately wry and angry accounting of the physical cost of using mere human bodies to undertake vast mechanised civil engineering projects, and for others' profit. Some of the most well known of these songs only lightly veil their socialist political intent: 'Building Up and Tearing England Down', a Dominic Behan song recorded by Christy Moore in 1968, 'McAlpine's Fusiliers' and 'Crooked Jack', both written by Behan for The Dubliners,

---

[4] For similar descriptions of west-of-Ireland gangs, see Mac Amhlaigh, *An Irish Navvy*: 'One gang of fifty men are working for Proctor of Manchester and every man jack of them, from the boss down to the cook, is from the Aran Islands. They work non-stop from Saturday night until Sunday afternoon and get a huge pay-packet' (p. 147). Ultan Cowley offers the best analysis and description of working on major civil engineering projects in the 1960s (see 'Public Works,' in Cowley, *The Men Who Built Britain*). For an analysis of tropes of idleness and hard work in Irish revivalist and modernist texts, see Gregory Dobbins, *Lazy Idle Schemers: Irish Modernism and the Politics of Idleness* (Dublin: Field Day Publications, 2010).

[5] A number of contemporary recordings reveal the connections between Irish traditional music, English folk, skiffle and American jazz during the period: *Irish Music in London Pubs*, recorded by Ralph Rinzler and Barry Murphy (Folkways Records, 1965); *Paddy in the Smoke*, Irish Dance Music from a London Pub (Topic Records, 1968); *The Singing Streets: Childhood Memories of Ireland and Scotland*, Ewan McColl and Dominic Behan (Folkways Records, 1958); *The Irish Rover*, Dominic Behan (Folklore Records, 1961). The Reg Hall Archive at the British Library is an unparalleled resource for the oral and musical history of Irish traditional music in England.

and McColl's 'The Tunnel Tigers', commissioned for *The Irishmen* itself, about the excavation of the Underground Victoria Line:

> The curragh rots on the Achill Island,
> Tourists walk on the Newport quay;
> The Mayo boys have all gone roving,
> Digging a tunnel through the London clay.

For the emigrants from small-farm Ireland, employment on ground works – digging out the foundations of large building sites, tunnelling through underground clay, excavating the footings for roads, digging the trenches for laying pipes and cables – offered both continuity with the work back home and estrangement from it. The physical tasks were similar but the environment, tempo and scale entirely different. Many of the representations of urban labouring or civil engineering works focus on the contradictions of scale – the body of the labourer which seems so large in the context of the pub is dwarfed by the massive earthworks, becoming part of an almost elemental battle between man and nature.

Urban construction sites were one place where this battle could be witnessed. In the mid-1950s, large civil engineering companies set up observation posts at major sites; while the draw was ostensibly the opportunity to see the erection of concrete and steel buildings through modern construction methods, nonetheless office and shop workers on their lunch breaks watched the labourers at work. By the early 1960s, these observation platforms even had closed-circuit TV.[6]

For men looking for work on the sites, whatever their nationality, their visual appearance as hardened to physical labour was both an asset and a liability. As a young man interviewed by Donnellan put it, 'You'd need your trousers dirty, or you're not wanted.' Michael Campbell described the lines of men queuing for building work on street corners as indisputably Irish: 'From their red faces, black hair and vaguely peasant appearance, I judged every one to be a fellow countryman.'[7] But the easy identification meant that those countrymen could also be discounted as wild and uncivilised. As a builder called John McHugh recalled, in an interview with Donnellan:

> I've heard English men to say, and English women, 'My God, are they not savage?' When they used to see the lads with their vests off, nothing on them but their trousers, but them lads couldn't help it, they were working hard.

---

[6] See, for example, the history of Taylor Woodrow, which includes images of 'Teleview' platforms where ongoing construction projects could be watched by the public. Alan Jenkins, *On Site 1921–1971* (1971).
[7] Campbell, *O Mary, This London*, p. 176.

In order to get work, Irish men had to look like labourers, but looking like a labourer cut the men off from other kinds of work and social interaction. And as many of the employers interviewed by sociologists such as Sheila Patterson in the early 1960s revealed, the cliché of the Irish labourer affected the ways in which other Irish workers, in factories, hospitals and hotels, were regarded.[8]

One individual who may have taken advantage of the on-site viewing platforms was the painter Frank Auerbach, who completed a series of paintings of London building sites between 1952 and 1962. These paintings signal an important moment both in Auerbach's own artistic development and the evolution of representational painting in post-war Britain. Auerbach had arrived in Britain in 1939, aged seven, sent by his parents from Berlin in a private arrangement associated with the Kindertransport scheme. From 1947 he lived in London, and from 1954 in Camden, while studying at St Martin's and the Royal College of Art, and taking classes with David Bomberg at Borough Polytechnic. The building site series was begun while he was still a student, and he has described the sensation of a 'breakthrough' while working on an early site painting: 'Suddenly I was conscious of something underneath it.'[9] That painting, *Summer Building Site, 1952*, is reproduced on the cover of this book. The labourers are visible in red, ladders picked out in yellow, against an abstract but highly coloured scene. Over the next ten years the colours of the building site paintings darkened, and the forms of labourers, earth shapes and equipment became more and more indistinct.[10]

As several critics have argued, the experiments of painters such as Auerbach, Leon Kossof and Francis Bacon in the 1950s, concerned with exploring the limits of representational meaning without abandoning it completely, constituted a break with the neo-Romanticism and symbolism of much war-time and post-war art.[11] In terms of subject matter, what was

---

[8] The Philip Donnellan Archive at Birmingham Central Library contains Charles Parker's taped interviews with Irish labourers, made during the research phase of the film. Many of the interviewees bitterly recount their anger against Irish 'gangermen' for forcing men to work in appalling conditions – for example, refusing to put canopies on the lorries and avoiding safety guidelines: 'You'd nearly cry, every morning in Camden town, the finest lads ... Archway, the Brecknock.... You won't get an English man working on Lowery's or Murphy's or R. S. Kennedy.' Philip Donnellan Archive, MS 4000/6/1/42/1/C.

[9] Frank Auerbach, 'Fragments from a Conversation', in David Wright and Patrick Swift (eds.), *X: A Quarterly Review* 1:1 (1959), p. 34. This issue of the journal also contains contributions by Samuel Beckett, Anthony Cronin and Patrick Kavanagh.

[10] For reproductions of the complete series, see Barnaby Wright (ed.), *Frank Auerbach: London Building Sites, 1952–62* (London: Courtauld Gallery, 2009).

[11] For example, Barnaby Wright notes the decisive break between the neo-Romantic paintings of bombed London by John Piper and Graham Sutherland, and Auerbach's interpretation of the

important about Auerbach's building site paintings was their shift from
the romanticism of the city's ruins to a sublime, and far more elemental
landscape, 'a marvelous landscape with precipice and mountain and crags,
full of drama formally.'[12] A recent curator of these works has argued, 'For
Auerbach, the building sites were a contemporary equivalent of a sublime
landscape – one that could inspire the fear, excitement and strangeness of
an uncharted mountain terrain.'[13]

As Barnaby Wright and others have noted, Auerbach was drawn
not to bomb sites and ruins (already inscribed within a neo-Romantic aesthetic) but to the construction sites which superseded them.
Significantly, however, he tended to draw and paint sites at an early
stage of development, so that his paintings focus less on height – the
massive steel constructions rising out of the earth – than on the earthworks themselves. Viewers find themselves confronted with huge piles
of sand, or vertiginously placed above massive excavations of mud and
clay. The dramatic landscape of the earthworks is represented as a form
of ordered chaos, with the straight lines and angles formed by cranes,
girders, planks, and so on, cutting across and therefore helping to order
the shapelessness of the sites.

Several contemporary reviewers noted the analogous positions of artist
and builder in these early works. In a review of Auerbach's 1959 Beaux Arts
exhibition, Neville Wallace argued of the painter that

> he [peers] down into the building craters ... and so bulldozes his thick,
> glutinous pigment across the canvas to convey an exact scene of the intrac-
> table mounds of clay, and the thrust and strain of tackle.[14]

Later commentators have rejected any simple parallel between artist and
excavator, arguing that the predominantly earth tones and thick impasto
of the paintings have less to do with a mimetic attempt to reproduce
the qualities of mud, sand and clay than the fact that Auerbach used a
great deal of paint, and earth tones were cheaper. There is certainly a case
for arguing, as Wright does, that the thickness of the paint was a 'by-
product' of Auerbach's habitual compositional method, whereby paint
accrued during multiple sessions of revision.[15] But such arguments are

---

building sites. See Wright, 'Creative Destruction: Frank Auerbach and the Rebuilding of London',
in Wright (ed.), *Frank Auerbach*, pp. 13–33.

[12] Ibid., p. 14.
[13] Ibid., p. 30.
[14] Quoted in Wright, 'Creative Destruction', pp. 22–23.
[15] The paint was also applied thickly on the portraits that Auerbach painted at around the
same time.

in danger of underestimating the importance of the focus on earth and clay (both heavy, inert matter, and the raw material for art). The sublime mountains and crags of Auerbach's landscapes are not soaring but rather plunging edifices, gaping holes in which artist, workman and viewer find themselves lost.

Clearly the formal drama of the sites, the huger the better, was important to Auerbach. As Wright argues, 'the areas of the construction site that most interested him were the excavated mountains and canyons of earth, whose broad expansiveness he played off against the linear forms of the crawler cranes and equipment: these offer a sense of only temporary structure and visual order amidst the otherwise incomprehensible muddy mass.'[16] Yet the paintings also capture stark contradictions of scale, as figures of labourers are positioned against the 'muddy mass', dwarfed or swallowed by the earth.

Auerbach's recollections of his sketching trips to the sites frequently mention the construction workers:

> I remember in those days going to places where I was scared to stand and drawing.... On these planks people wheeled wheelbarrows across totally confidently, I would sit down and edge my way along them in order to do my drawings....
>
> In my memory they were nothing like the way they are now, with hard hats and visible clothing and regulation boots. I seem to remember people in trousers and shirts and possibly peaked cap, wheeling wheelbarrows along planks to convey materials or cement.[17]

The presence of these figures was clearly significant. Nearly all the paintings of the building site series feature workmen, often tiny and hard to distinguish against the 'mountains and crags' of the earthworks, but central to the exploration of scale. The importance of the workmen is clear in the artist's work on his major Oxford Street Building site paintings (1958/59). After the site had moved on from the early stage at which he had sketched it, he realised that although he had depicted workmen he didn't have them in sufficient detail. He therefore asked an artist's model to pose as a labourer, both standing and bending to his work. That these figures are almost indistinguishable in the left-hand foreground of the final painting suggests that while the process of drawing from life was an important part

---

[16] Wright, 'Creative Destruction', p. 24.
[17] 'Podcast 3: The Earls Court Road' and 'Podcast 1: London after the War', *Courtauld Gallery Podcasts*.

of the compositional method, it had little to do with a straightforward mimetic or representational ambition on the part of the painter.

In 1961, the critic David Sylvester championed Auerbach by arguing that 'these forms have been arrived at empirically. These structures seem to be known from the inside, as if the painter had become each object, had become the light, and had painted them from the inside out.'[18] Following Sylvester's interpretation, the paintings are not merely witness to the formal drama of mountain and crag but are painted from inside the earth, from a position in parallel with the workmen who shift the earth.

Sylvester's review was one salvo in his ongoing battle over the nature of realism with the painter and art critic John Berger. Both critics were in favour of representational art in this period, but as James Hyman has argued they divided over the necessity for an identifiably social content to realist art. In 1952 Berger curated a group show devoted to realist painting at the Whitechapel gallery arguing that 'The importance of such painting … is that it is obviously an attempt on the part of painters, and particularly young ones, to re-enter the ordinary world, to participate in its activities and to communicate with their unselected neighbours.'[19] Sylvester was scathing about the exhibition, arguing that the pictures showed a 'social not a visual realism.' One of the problems he identified was a hangover from Soviet realist or New Deal representations of workers from the 1930s and '40s. Berger's own painting of the Festival of Britain site in 1950[20] does appear to echo aspects of state-sponsored art, while at the same time it recalls the vogue for aestheticised black and white photographs of construction workers. Several photographs of the Festival of Britain site offer austerity versions of grand-scale construction works, such as Charles C. Ebbets's celebrated 1932 image, *Lunch atop a Skyscraper*, of eleven construction workers sitting on a crossbeam picked out against the New York skyline.[21]

---

[18] David Sylvester, 'Nameless Structures', *New Statesman,* 21 April 1961.

[19] See James Hyman, *The Battle for Realism: Figurative Art in Britain during the Cold War 1945–1960* (New Haven, CT: Yale University Press, 2001), pp. 114–119.

[20] Berger's 'Scaffolding – Festival of Britain' focuses on the height of the construction works, against which tiny figures are visible top and bottom. The site operated from early 1950 to mid-1951 and employed 1,500 workers, more than half of whom were Irish. This site was well known for labour agitation, which was championed by the communist-leaning Connolly Association newspaper, *The Irish Democrat*. In 1951 the workers marched to Hyde Park calling for an extra sixpence: 'the Irish were there in strength, the soft brogue mixing with the metallic cockney twang shouting the slogan, "We want the tanner."' The march occasioned the story of the well-to-do lady on Oxford Street who was shocked they were making such a fuss over sixpence, and had to have it explained to her it was sixpence an hour they were after. *The Irish Democrat*, April 1951.

[21] A number of the workers on the girder on the New York skyline have recently been identified as Irish in *Men at Lunch*, dir. Seán Ó Cualáin (Sónta Films, 2012).

Spiderman: The Dome of Discovery under construction for the
Festival of Britain, on London's South Bank.

The figures are placed in these pictures in order to tell us something
about danger, but also about scale. The monumentality is focused not on
the worker, with his muscles and hammer, but on the works themselves.
After all, the Festival of Britain site was designed as a sign of Britain's new
Labour-led resurgence, and much of the art which responded to it echoes
rebirth and recovery.

In choosing to represent clay and earth, rather than soaring modern construction, Auerbach was perhaps registering an immigrant's discomfort with the idea that construction meant national resurgence. His
paintings began in sketches and drawings he made on the sites, but the
process of completing them was one of applying thickening paint over the
naturalist drawing. The dense impasto of the works refuses clear distinctions between clay and man, rather as the labourers described themselves
as dragged down by the clay. There may appear to be a contradiction
between Auerbach's draftsman's concern to get the construction workers 'right' and the scrubbed-out figures which suggest the disappearance
of the labourer in his labour, his invisibility as a person. Though these

Harry Kerr, *Building above London* (1956). A construction worker at work on the water storage of a building in Golden Lane, with St Paul's Cathedral in the background.

paintings may offer a truer representation of the feelings associated with being on and working on the sites, in the artist's attempt to disclose the phenomenology of labour, the individual disappears. Yet Auerbach's comments comparing himself to, or putting himself in the position of, the workers suggest another interpretation. For the majority population the labourer was a person to be watched or witnessed from afar, from a closed-circuit TV viewing platform or simply from the side of the road. Auerbach foregrounds instead the artist's identification with the labourer, their mutual experience of being inside the chasm. He attempts to look from inside out. Recalling the atmosphere of post-war London, when he was living in Camden Town, himself a recent immigrant among immigrants, Auerbach has described 'a curious feeling of camaraderie' among 'the survivors scurrying about the ruined city.'

> One felt much closer to what was going on in the street, there wasn't any particular indoor life ... so this [the sites and the streets] was the fabric of one's life ...[22]

Auerbach's comments, in the 1959 'Fragments from a Conversation' and more recent interviews, reveal him to have been acutely aware of his own viewing perspective, and the ambiguous relationship between the artist's body and that of the workers. There is both 'camaraderie', solidarity and recognition, and distance: Auerbach looks while they work. The creation of the paintings sets up a tension between artist and subject (and between viewer and subject) on one side and the inevitable complicity between artist and viewer gazing at the aestheticised scene, including the bodies of the labourers, on the other. Yet Auerbach's technique makes looking difficult. Distinguishing the bodies of the labourers, picking them out against the masses of mud, sand and clay, is part of the problem the paintings pose for the viewer. To that extent, aestheticisation is resisted. What is sought is not a reproduction or even a representation of the building site, and the labour of building, but an 'experience' of matter or 'actuality', discovered through the process of painting.[23] The aim is to reach towards a form of embodied perception, a looking beyond looking, partly captured in the density and tactility of the painting. Nonetheless, precisely by merging the labourer with his labour and rendering the distinction between flesh and clay obscure, the paintings draw close to suggesting a 'natural' identification between the two. The forms of industrialised labour depicted by Auerbach reach back to forms of rural labour which have often been associated with authenticity and instinct, with the rhythm of the seasons, and with a tempo which has little to do with clock-time and the dictates of the modern factory. Even as the paintings repudiate forms of romanticised realism in favour of a modernist emphasis on fracture and self-consciousness, arguably they still echo and depend for their effects on a pastoral ideal, the archetype of the countryman in the city. Auerbach himself has suggested that the building sites themselves offered a 'tiny echo of the creation', the raising of life out of mud, 'creating out of soil in the way that we are supposed to have been created.'[24]

---

[22] 'Podcast 1: London after the War.'
[23] See Paul Moorhouse, 'A Human Universe: Auerbach's Building-Site Paintings and Existentialism', in Wright (ed.), *Frank Auerbach*, pp. 57–69.
[24] 'Podcast 5: The Oxford Street Building Site Paintings', *Courtauld Gallery Podcasts*.

'You're Not Fully Alive if You Haven't Got Out'

The contradictions of an industrial pastoral – deriving from an idea of the Irish as 'modern nomads' – are central to Philip Donnellan's film *The Irishmen*, which is similarly dependent on the idea of the sites as 'the fabric of one's life.' As a voiced-over observer puts it in the film, 'They have no home life whatever, but at the same time, they're so free.' The emphasis of the documentary is on physical toil (Donnellan said he wanted to show '[t]he heat and dirt of the labour') and on two large-scale works in particular: the roadworks for the M1 motorway and the underground tunnelling for the Victoria Line. As in Auerbach's paintings, earth itself provides visual focus, in the piles of sand and gravel, the vast craters excavated for the motorway groundworks, the mounded lumps of clay. Pile drivers, cabling, shuttering, concrete foundations, drills – it is the hidden fabric of the urban environment, the drama of construction, that structures the narrative. But the bodies of the labourers also become part of that background environment, part of the raw material of building. Just as the camera focuses on the separated elements of cement, iron, glass, leather, mud, wood, and most of all, holes, so the film showcases displaced, distorted bodies, the human body in pieces. In a manner similar to Auerbach's paintings, the formal composition of the film undoes the distinction between workman and work. The visual narrative is one of equivalence between body

and material – and it may be for this reason that the BBC rejected the film as 'shapeless, pretentious and, to be frank, boring.'[25]

It is certainly true that scenes in the film come close to reproducing a 'muddy mass', as the camera focuses on 'shapeless' mounds of earth which dwarf and swallow the labourers. In certain shots, the analogy between industrial labour on the sites and the experience in First World War trenches is unmistakeable. Donnellan's visual references to the trenches recycle associations between industrial labour and warfare, such as the notion that the soldiers, including officers, had become like miners, with all the implications for class distinctions which that entailed. But they also create echoes for the viewer of images familiar from poetry and writing about life, and death, in the trenches: the experience of being sucked into the morass, the fear of the mud as a living creature, the anxiety of being swallowed by the mud as both a literal and an existential threat, the fragility of the human in the face of the non-human.[26] The Irish labourers provide the occasion for an aestheticised experience of or meditation on such existential anxieties, but at the same time Donnellan's film insists on the specific material conditions which give rise to this experience, by tracking through the film a narrative of Irish exile which 'punctuates' the shapeless masses.

Television documentary was a swiftly evolving medium in the early 1960s, with a number of related forms – the drama documentary, the actuality documentary, the story documentary – competing for airtime, and favour with the controllers at the BBC. While dramas such as *Cathy Come Home* used documentary visual techniques in order to heighten the naturalistic effect, actuality films often depended on film reconstructions and storylines to hold the viewer's interest, a practice that partly grew out of the creative combination of scripted material and actuality recordings made popular by the BBC Radio Features unit during the 1940s and early

---

[25] Donnellan, 'We Were the BBC', p. 153. See also Lance Pettit's 'Philip Donnellan, Ireland and Dissident Documentary', *Historical Journal of Film, Radio and Television*, 20:3 (2001), pp. 351–365 and *Screening Ireland: Film and Television Representation* (Manchester: Manchester University Press, 2000), pp. 85–88; Charlotte Brunsdon, '"A Fine and Private Place": The Cinematic Spaces of the London Underground', *Screen*, 47:1 (2006), pp. 1–17.

[26] For a discussion of mud and slime as existentialist threat, see Santanu Das, *Touch and Intimacy in First World War Literature* (Cambridge: Cambridge University Press, 2006). Parker's interviewees frequently mention the exhausting and dangerous work in the trenches: 'Men are dying in trenches – you might be down 12 maybe 13 feet, no timber there and anything can happen, I often saw a crack maybe four feet back. You say to the ganger man is there any timber here he'll just laugh at you.... Man lands here he might only have a pound, he might have nothing, ... he has no option, if he doesn't get down in that trench he has no food, he has no digs, he's lost.' (Philip Donnellan Archive, MS 4000/6/1/42/2/C).

'50s. Donnellan's film is indebted to the 'story' mode, as the film constructs a narrative thread from the journey of one young emigrant (Josie McDonagh) from Mason Island, Carna, an Irish-speaking area in County Galway, to London.

Donnellan's description of his research for the film, and the development of this particular story of 'exile', betrays a broadly romanticised view of Irish culture, and in particular corroborates aspects of Anthony Cronin's satirical view of a BBC clique obsessed with the 'authentic performance' of Celticism. Donnellan chose the musician Seamus Ennis as his guide to 'the heartland of Gaelic culture':

> We had first met in the Gluepot near Broadcasting House in 1949. Seamus and big Brian George, the Dubliner, just back from the ould sod recording singers. MacNeice was there, Dylan Thomas in the other corner of the bar and David Thomson in his thick glasses putting down the Bass. After that there were lots more times when amidst the beery uproar Seamus would suddenly murmur 'Ach now that puts me in mind, ... ' push his faded trilby back on his head, reach into an inside pocket for a fistful of penny whistles and choosing one, silence the bar with an instant rattling jig or delicately command consent with an exquisite slow air in which the notes would seem to hang upon the smoke.[27]

The narrative developed by Donnellan and Ennis was constructed as a forward projection of a nostalgic backward look, for which music provides the spine. The small farmstead at home, the simple but homely interior, peopled by loving parents, the beautiful but desolate landscape, the journey by train and by boat – all are presented through the lens of anticipatory loss, and juxtaposed with quick scene cuts to the labour of tunnelling, implying that a lost rural Ireland is being recalled by the labourers. As the scene cuts back and forth between McDonagh's fictional (or scripted) journey and actual industrial workplaces in England, the film clearly signals the costs both for individual emigrants and for the communities which they have left. But Donnellan also implies the inescapability of the emigrants' plight, the inevitability of the movement from home to labouring exile. Repeated images of four-square cells punctuate the narrative – the rocks in the Connemara landscape, doorways, holes, wooden frames, tunnels. These images draw attention to the filmic framing, the constructed nature of the narrative, even the squares of celluloid. But they also imply the fated and determined nature of the emigrant's story, for whom there is no alternative but to pass through the cell doors from one

[27] Donnellan, 'We Were the BBC', p. 151.

wild, inhospitable landscape to another. The cells conjure images of isolation and of the repetitive cycle of passing from country to city, from labour to leisure-time in the pub. The predestined nature of the emigrant journey is emphasised in voice-over snippets of interviews with the labourers, which focus on poverty and the pull of fate: 'There's something wrong with you if you haven't got out. The suction out of Ireland is tremendous.' 'You're not fully alive if you haven't got out.' 'Being young, in the west, you always have the feeling, why am I here? … Can I go on staying here? What's it to be, England or America?' The idea that there is 'something wrong with you' if you stay is, of course, a version of the notion that 'the best are leaving.'

This naturalistic narrative is akin to the deterministic visual backgrounds characteristic of British New Wave films – the looming presence of the factory as part of the landscape of the industrial city in *Saturday Night, Sunday Morning*, or the constricting environment of the back streets in *A Kind of Loving* (a film which was described as 'upholstered with documentary techniques', clearly derived from John Schlesinger's work as a TV documentarist).[28] Much like *A Kind of Loving*'s visual survey of the characteristic settings of Northern working-class life, Donnellan's film offers an inventory of the typical backdrops to – primarily male – Irish migrant life: the building site, the canteen, the pub, the Gaelic football ground. In these scenes the viewer appears to be brought inside the 'real' migrant milieu (although as we will see, several of them were staged). So much for the basic techniques of documentary; what is unusual about the film is that these scenes are rarely counterpointed with direct interviews with the emigrants themselves.

In his memoir Donnellan described the Irishmen he filmed as 'genetically programmed to suspicion of English television.' They were unwilling to allow the cameras into their homes (with the exception of one builder, Jim McHugh, who was interviewed surrounded by his wife and children in his flat in Holloway). Many of them were reluctant to speak to camera, though his colleague in Birmingham, Charlie Parker, did persuade them to accept the more 'anonymous' radio microphone. During background research for the film, in response to a query from Parker about the lack of upward mobility among Irish workers compared to the English ('The figure of the age at the moment in England is the working class boy making for the room at the top … the predominant image of our culture'), one interviewee insisted that by contrast 'the young worker in Ireland has no

---

[28] Laing, *Representations of Working-Class Life*, p. 34.

chance at all.' With no opportunities in Ireland the young move to building work in England, where 'they keep their heads low': 'the reason they
won't talk is 'cause they are ashamed ... this is why you don't get much
information from these boys on the tunnels.'[29]

Donnellan argued that the eventual documentary format of the film,
with intercutting of voice, visuals and musical soundtrack, developed in
response to what he described as the 'absence of direct visual evidence' –
the relative lack of talking heads.[30] Donnellan's account emphasises historical contingency, but the film's dynamic is also indebted to experiments
at the BBC with film documentaries designed as composite or collage-
like portraits, created by superimposing sound-radio material on pictures
filmed separately.[31] These formal experiments had parallels with the *Radio
Ballads* of Charles Parker and Ewan McColl, both of whom worked with
Donnellan on *The Irishmen*. The *Ballads* were innovative in their combination of field recordings (used as a direct element in the programmes,
rather than as the basis for scripted speech) and folk songs or newly commissioned songs which were derived from vernacular traditions, long a sta-
ple of BBC features programming. The second of the *Radio Ballads*, 'Song
of a Road', took the construction of the M1 as its subject, weaving together
actuality recordings made with the construction workers, many of whom
were Irish, and working songs which formed the narrative thread of the
programme.[32] It was an obvious model for Donnellan, who uses song as
a 'poetic' device in *The Irishmen*, charting a narrative of exile and labour
which both reinforces the deterministic naturalist narrative of the film as a
whole (and insists on work as the primary determinant of the lifestyle and
outlook of the Irishmen) and at the same time offers a further dimension
beyond the realist conventions of documentary form.

[29] Donnellan Archive, MS 4000/6/1/42/21: 'There's two types, the under dogs and the top dogs.
Young people never get the chance to get on [in Ireland], the man who has his own business,
his son is going to be marvelous, and he'll get on.' It is striking that a large amount of the taped
interview material used as research for the film focuses on anger against the class system and lack
of opportunities for working men in Ireland, and against the behaviour of Irish gangermen on construction sites in England. Neither of these issues is explicitly aired in the film.

[30] Comparison with Donnellan's 1964 documentary *The Colony* (BBC, 1964) may make the point
more clearly. *The Colony* deploys the 'story' mode in the narrative of a Jamaican railway signal-
man, but this is juxtaposed with face-to-face interviews with Caribbean migrants (both men and
women) in a variety of settings including in the market, in their homes and at work.

[31] On Denis Mitchell's use of the 'think-tape' method for *Night in the City* (1957) and *Morning in the
Streets* (1959), see Laing, *Representations of Working-Class Life*, pp. 161–162.

[32] 'Song of a Road', produced by Ewan McColl and Charles Parker (BBC Home Service, 5 November
1959). On Parker and the radio ballads, see Paul Long, 'British Radio and the Politics of Culture in
Post-War Britain: The Work of Charles Parker', *The Radio Journal: International Studies in Broadcast
and Audio Media*, 2:3 (2004), pp. 131–152.

The singer Joe Heaney's powerful rendition of 'The Rocks of Bawn' emphasises continuity between the work at home and in England, where the labourer's milieu is, equally, one of raw materials, unfashioned clay:

> Come all you loyal heroes wherever you may be
> Don't hire with any master till you know what your work may be
> Don't hire with any master from the clear daylight till the dawn
> For he'll want you rising early to plough the rocks of Bawn.

The film struggles with the tension between the 'actual' experience of the migrants and the 'folkloric' script, which also determines that experience. The viewer hears their reflections, caught in short snippets of interviews, on making money, and the possibility of marrying and settling down, for example – their personal forward-looking narratives. But these reflections are juxtaposed with, and indeed overwhelmed by, a nostalgic story of exile. Despite the snippets of interviews, throughout the film the Irishmen's thoughts about their situation are for the most part to be gleaned from their music, which is clearly intended to stand in for their inner feelings, represented as thoughts of exilic yearning for a way of life that is characterised by poverty and hardship, but also community. The labour is no less backbreaking and onerous at home than it is in industrial England, but at least it is at home. As I have argued, the bonds of community in rural Ireland were partly derived from values of austerity and self-sufficiency, and often appeared to be at odds with the affluence deemed central to post-war industrial society (whether it was achieved or not). Thus adversity was no barrier to nostalgia and may even have intensified it, with all the potential for romanticisation this implies. Poverty is mythologised in the film even as it is offered as a rational cause of emigration.

Alongside the experimental use of repeated four-square shapes in the film and the mirroring of Galway and London clay, insisting on the Irishmen as surviving countrymen in the city, the musical soundtrack shapes and carries 'excess' of meaning. As several contemporary critics noted of the New Wave films, visual portraits of Northern working-class towns provided a form of spectacle which was often unmotivated by plot. Alongside the factory, the locus of British post-war realism was the home, sociologically designated according to the established hierarchy of urban geography (the terrace, the suburban house, the '60s high-rise). Some of the most iconic scenes in the British New Wave films of the early 1960s frame the narrative against a backdrop of housing (rows of terraces and back-to-backs) and factories (chimney stacks against the skyline). Critics such as Andrew Higson and John Hill have analyzed the documentary aspects of the New Wave and Higson in particular has taken issue with the manner in which the industrial background is used as a shorthand for the relationship between character and milieu.[33] He argues that the views of northern industrial landscapes ('That Long Shot of Our Town from That Hill') function as spectacle, shots which are aesthetically satisfying in themselves and are often not sufficiently integrated into the narratives to be justified. Landscape functions differently in *The Irishmen*: although the shots of rural Connemara and urban London clay are 'spectacular', they are also strongly narrativised, through visual correspondences and through music. Nonetheless, while the landscape of bare Connemara rocks and ruined houses is brought into the narrative of exile and work in industrial England through traditional ballad and song, in the process music itself takes on a role in excess of 'plot', in a manner which draws close to Higson's theory of the spectacle in New Wave films. Much as Higson targets the framing shots of industrial towns for being insufficiently integrated into the narrative of British New Wave films, music aestheticises the faltering narrative point of view in Donnellan's film. In one awkward scene in a motorway works canteen, the labourers stare in an embarrassed fashion at the camera, while musicians play fiddles and tin whistles in a corner of the room – a mixing of work and leisure that would never have occurred in reality.

One extended section of the film is shot underground, with the men who are working on the Victoria Line. Unlike the voice-overs or musical background to much of the rest of the film, here diegetic sound complements the visual presentation of labour. The noise of the drills is overwhelming, matching the viewer's difficulty in distinguishing the near-naked bodies of the workmen underground. The images recall the factory-based scenes in *Saturday Night, Sunday Morning*, where the Johnny Dankworth jazz score gives way to overpowering industrial noise, but in Donnellan's film there is no narrative outside the subjection to work, and no being for the labourers beyond the physical presence of flesh, muscle and bone. The underground scenes highlight the surfaces of the labourers' bodies, focusing on back, arms, chest, face, flesh in a series of extended close-ups. In these highly textured passages, it is as though the bodies themselves offer access to the memories and experiences of the labourers.[34]

---

[33] Andrew Higson, 'Space, Place, Spectacle: Landscape and Townscape in the Kitchen Sink Films', in Andrew Higson (ed.), *Dissolving Views: Key Writings on British Cinema* (London: Cassell, 1996). For critiques of Higson, see B. F. Taylor, *The British New Wave* (Manchester: Manchester University Press, 2006), and Bell, 'Envisioning the Working Class.'

[34] See Laura U. Marks, *The Skin of the Film: Intercultural Cinema, Embodiment and the Senses* (Durham, NC: Duke University Press, 2000), for a stimulating analysis of 'haptic visuality', and

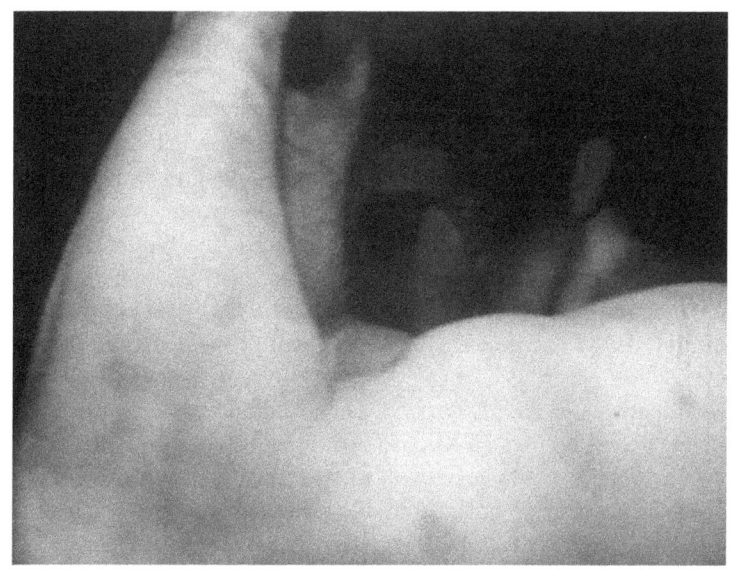

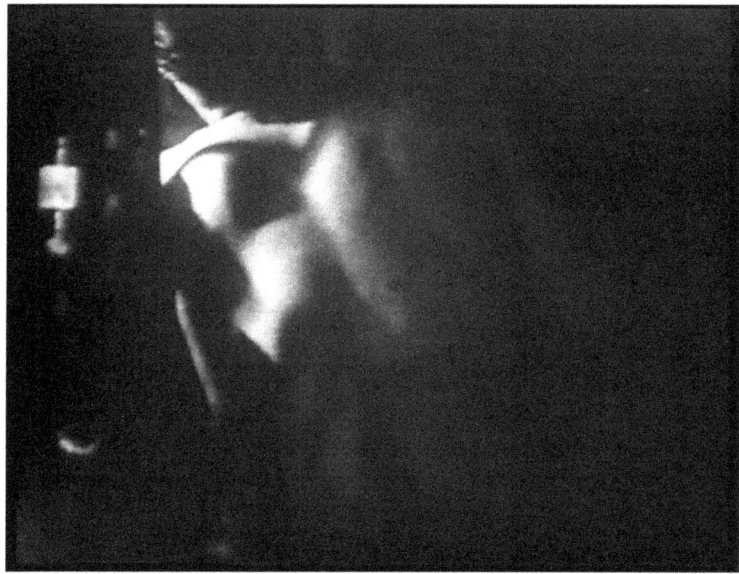

The workmen in the Underground, with its connotations of death and burial, become elemental figures, opposed to the usual associations of the Underground system with travel and time. Indeed, one of the only shots of completed buildings occurs towards the end of the underground sequence, when the men are released from the tunnel and arrive on the surface, looking towards the modern buildings across the street, but separated from them by the bars of the lift cage. Donnellan acknowledged that his decision to shoot at this particular lift-shaft was to highlight the contrast between under- and overground existence: 'There was one in Cavendish Square, a stone's throw from Broadcasting House. I chose that one because the contrasts were sharpest: the shifts of diggers, nearly all Irish, in ragged trousers stained with London clay, would come up from the tunnels in the dawn or evening straight into the glare and glitz of the West End.'[35]

In comparison to the Mallorys in David Lodge's novel, for example, or the articulate young men in Michael Campbell's London fiction, these are peasants in the city, savage outliers to the urban community which they help construct. They are associated with the anti-modern, yet in order to represent them, both Auerbach and Donnellan move beyond the conventions of realism towards a late-modernist blurring of the distinction between figure and ground. As in Tom Murphy's *A Whistle in the Dark*, the almost excessive foregrounding of a determining and determinist milieu undoes conservative naturalist modes by elevating them to the level of the poetic, the abstract and the phenomenological. In all three cases, the relationship between stereotype or caricature and historically contingent experience structures the work itself.

I have been arguing that there was a disjuncture between the stock formations in which migrant experience was represented and the contingent, varied experiences of migrants themselves. But I have also maintained that the forms in which migrant experience was represented were historically structured and constituted part of the way that 'real' experiences were interpreted and understood. The clay and earth in Auerbach and Donnellan, which swallow the workmen, the intense violence in Murphy's play, which overwhelms the action, are less realist responses to migrant lives in England than highly self-conscious explorations of the determining power of representation. In response to Charles Parker's questions during

---

experiments in intercultural cinema with attempts to portray embodied experience, through close-ups, as an alternative to 'visual mastery.'
[35] Donnellan, 'We Were the BBC', p. 152.

the research for *The Irishmen*, the labourers offered practical and pragmatic reasons for the development of the migrant workers' way of life: they drink because 'they are lonesome', 'pubs are the only places to meet.... I started with a shandy'; they fight because they are thrown together in unnatural conditions on the sites and in lodging houses: 'A dozen blokes round the table. At least twice a week there was a row, a punch-up in the dinner room'; they take on labouring work because they can't adapt themselves to offices and factories. Yet Parker's comments suggest a lingering belief that there is something inherently Irish about their choices. 'An Irishman', he observes, chooses unskilled labour because he 'takes a pride in exploiting his body – takes a pride in what his body rather than what his mind can do.'[36] Harry Carney explains his grotesque performance of an Irish stereotype as playing to the gallery: 'I wouldn't want to disappoint them.' But he also believes, unlike his brother Michael, that he has no option. The tropes of stereotype and caricature necessarily form the basis of representations which also push the boundaries of those stereotypes.

The point may be made more clearly by comparison with another 1965 film, Desmond Davis's adaptation of Edna O'Brien's short story, 'I Was Happy Here.' In 1964 Davis had directed the film of the second novel in O'Brien's trilogy, *Girl with Green Eyes*, with Rita Tushingham in the role of Kate and Lynn Redgrave as Baba. The film was marketed as an exuberant version of Tony Richardson's award-winning 1961 adaptation of Sheila Delaney's play, *A Taste of Honey*, where Tushingham had taken the role of Jo, the seventeen-year-old who becomes pregnant by a black sailor, in a film which emphasised the regional setting of Salford through a series of extended location shots. Dublin as a location for Tushingham's 1960s single woman is subject to an engaging series of looks in *Girl with Green Eyes*, arguably caught between British and Irish realisms.[37] By contrast, in *I Was Happy Here* the over-emphasised rural Irish landscape is counterposed to 1960s London, its uncompromising modernity signaled by the Post Office Tower framed by the window of Cass's bedsit, and the film as a whole offers a challenging and complex version of the relationship between milieu and character formation.

It was filmed on location in Lahinch and Liscannor; the U.S. title, *Time Lost and Time Remembered*, suggests the nostalgic, Proustian mood of the

---

[36] Donnellan Archive, MS 4000/6/1/42/19/C; MS 4000/6/1/42/12/C; MS 4000/6/1/42/8/C.

[37] *Girl with Green Eyes*, directed by Desmond Davis, Woodfall Films, 1964. 'I hate it when the boys and girls go away', Fr Kelly says to Kate after she has been dragged back home by her father. He equates moving to Dublin with emigration, but 'this hick town', as Baba calls it, fails to offer new opportunities and the girls must leave for London at the end of the film.

film, which opens on a young woman, Cass (played by Sarah Miles), who has returned to the quiet Irish coastal hotel where she once worked, in flight from her unfeeling upper-middle-class dentist husband, whom she met and married after moving to London. The film is structured as a series of flashbacks to her carefree life in rural Ireland, her romance with a local fisherman (Sean Caffrey), and her later lonely months working as a garage attendant in London, waiting for her fisherman to arrive. After she receives a letter from him announcing the end of their relationship she becomes involved with the rich, rugger-playing, Wimbledon dentist (Julian Glover), to whom she becomes unhappily married. So far, so familiar. There are certainly passages of the film which echo the description of the tourist short that Cait and Baba gate-crash in *Girl with Green Eyes*: 'All lies, about dark-haired girls roaming around Connemara in red petticoats. No wonder they had to show it in private.' In *I Was Happy Here*, Sarah Miles, a fair-haired girl, roams around the town, which is photographed in such extended and loving detail it could be a tourist promotion; she cycles and runs on the beach, and explores ruined castles with her beau, to emphasise the wild and carefree world in which she lived prior to her emigration. To cap it all, Cyril Cusack appears as the sage old hotel owner, offering gnomic rural wisdom to both husband and wife.

There are two aspects of the film which undermine the caricature of natural Ireland and natural Irish womanhood. First, Cass is the architect of her own misfortune. She insists on emigrating despite knowing that her fisherman is not sure this is what he wants, and despite the fact that she has a good job. This much fits with stereotypes of Irish women leaving Ireland less because of need than for a desire for change and new horizons. But she also mistakes her fisherman on her return, imagining that she can resume her romance, whereas he has become engaged to a local girl, who is represented as entirely down-to-earth and right for him. (It is made clear that Cass's fantasy of romance with her former boyfriend leads her not only to lose her virginity, fall pregnant and marry the Wimbledon dentist, but also subsequently to lose her baby.) In the context of such misinterpretation and misunderstanding, the nostalgic tourist viewpoint which structures the film is put into question. There is also, quite simply, too much of it. Contemporary reviewers of the film complained about the 'poetic' and excessive use of landscape, describing it, for example, as a 'pretentiously poetic little film', 'saturated with sentimentality and despair.'[38]

---

[38] Bosley Crowther, 'One More Unhappy Colleen', *New York Times*, 30 August 1966. For a later, experimental take on film's ability to capture the ways in which migrant memory, stereotype and

It is certainly possible to read the film as an indulgent excess of cliché, stereotype and sentimentality. But as in Donnellan's *The Irishmen* (which was also criticised for being pretentious), where the relationship between rural background and city life is structured in a similar narrative fashion, through repeated flashbacks, the film as a whole asks how it is possible to distinguish between figure and ground, and between image and experience. The problem with which I began this study, that of the mutually reinforcing relationship between cultural stereotypes and social experience, has become the problem of the artwork itself.

This is not to deny the twin difficulties skirted by Donnellan's film in particular: the romanticisation and aestheticisation of manual labour. As Paul Long has argued of the work of both Donnellan and Parker in the 1950s, it was heavily invested in ideas of a more 'genuine' working-class culture, in which oral tradition and popular and communal art forms, seen as more authentically rooted in communities still founded on manual labour, compared favourably to the newer commercial mass cultures whose influence was decried by left cultural theorists.[39] The uneasy relationship between nomadic, rural Irish labourers and the upwardly mobile consumerist society they were helping to build chimed neatly with this cultural-political agenda. In the process, the actuality of the labourer became lost, or submerged within a broader cultural imperative to reveal these working men as representative – of Irish men in England, and of the experience of manual labour in industrialised society.

Donnellan's film attempts to get beyond an ethnographic form of visuality, to give a sense of the emotional experience of emigration through the 'exile' narrative, and to conjure a form of embodied experience through the use of close-ups, while acknowledging that the experience remains mysterious. But it can not overcome the paradox of the labouring body represented as alienated, fractured, commodified by the social relations of capitalism but then also aestheticised and imbued with some of the aura of

experience become imbricated with one another, see the early films of Thaddeus O'Sullivan: *A Pint of Plain* (London: Royal College of Art, 1975) explores the lives of single Irish men in an environment of London pubs and seedy clubs; *On a Paving Stone Mounted* (London: British Film Institute, 1978) explores emigrant memory and the role of Irish stereotypes in shaping the way Irish experience is understood in both London and Ireland. See *Thaddeus O'Sullivan: The Early Films, 1974–1985* (Dublin: Irish Film Institute, 2014). As Lance Pettit argues, O'Sullivan's work 'expresses an extended creative response to the material conditions of Irish migrancy' ('Film Notes', p. 6).

39 Paul Long argues that traditional, masculine, working-class occupations on the railways, and in labouring, fishing and mining were chosen for the Radio Ballads because they 'involve a highly-visible and self-evident form of labour', which has a long tradition of being subject to aestheticisation. See Long, "British Radio and the Politics of Culture", p. 148.

the artwork – fractured but at the same time made whole, or meaningful, again.

By the time Auerbach and Donnellan were engaged in representing London building sites, the labourers were as likely to be from Irish towns and cities as from the small farms. But they were firmly associated with a pre-modern, rural and 'primitive' existence. Their bond with clay has a long history in modern Irish literature, building on the stock of images of clay and earth in the Catholic liturgy, from representations of the famine by William Carleton, to the lump of clay in Joyce's short story, a reminder of death, to Patrick Kavanagh's powerful reprise of the deadening and life-giving qualities of the material in 'The Great Hunger': 'clay is the word and clay is the flesh.' Mirroring the Catholic liturgy, Patrick Maguire's life is bounded by earth – the clay is inert matter which needs to be fertilised to bear fruit, but also an artistic material, which can be shaped into new forms. Kavanagh was alert to the problem of aestheticising manual labour, and his poem repeatedly switches perspective, moving from the tourist or outsider's gaze (represented by long shots reminiscent of documentary film) to a troubled 'insider's' attempt to kneel where Patrick Maguire kneels, and 'feel what he feels.' Kavanagh's dilemma gave impetus to a major preoccupation of contemporary Irish poetry, from John Montague's *The Rough Field* to Heaney's early work, or Muldoon's *Hay*: the concern to write of agricultural labour in a manner which acknowledges it as labour, even as it is narrativised. Donnellan's film and Auerbach's paintings are engaged with the same problematic, seeking an insider's rather than a detached realism, by linking the body, the hands and materials, and not just the eye, to vision.

For both Donnellan and Auerbach, clay and earth function as the raw materials of urban renewal, and of art. Their works imply that renewal is rooted in an authentic relationship with an elemental landscape, whether as labourer or artist. What is striking about Donnellan's film in particular is the way that the Irishmen are simultaneously associated with articulate expression (through song) and a mute, primitive inarticulacy. For the labourers constitute both an alternative to domesticated and respectable working-class culture, and at the same time the primitive underbelly of modern culture. The rubbed-out, overlaid figures in Auerbach's paintings and the indistinct forms peopling the underground in Donnellan's film resemble nothing so much as ghosts, toilers from another realm, the 'half-men' described by Tom Murphy, caught between worlds.

Afterword

It is as well to be reminded that the representations discussed here touch on only a small part of the Irish immigrant experience in post-war Britain. They are freighted with literary – and cinematic – history, as much as offering reflections of the 'real.' Even limiting the range to rural migrants, there is so much of the texture of 'real-life' experience which does not appear, or appears only tangentially. The rituals and rhythms of a country Catholicism transplanted to urban parishes is for the most part ignored – from the difficulties of arranging shift work to be able to get to early or late mass, to the ceremonies and celebrations of feast days and holy days, to the more private rites of daily prayer. The experience of courtship and marriage, though the majority experience for young migrants from Ireland, was for the most part absorbed, even submerged, in a larger narrative in which the state of Irish marriage stood for the state of the nation. The 1950s was a period in which a modernising Catholicism sought to harness aspirations towards companionship, and individual desire and self-fulfilment, to the ideal of the Catholic family, moving away from the prescriptions of moral theology as a means of control. Yet the national imperative required marrying in Ireland rather than marrying foreign. Though the Catholic hierarchy working with emigrants in England increasingly acknowledged the importance of supporting unions forged in Britain, and sought to meet the needs of young families for housing and schooling, these families fitted uncomfortably into the history of representations of exile and emigration and the meanings with which those representations were imbued. Thus they barely figure in the literature of the 1950s and '60s, and their experience would have to wait until a second wave of writers, some of them the children of first-generation migrants, began to explore their stories.[1]

---

[1] See Harte, *The Literature of the Irish in Britain*; Arrowsmith, 'Gender, Violence and Identity'; Murray, *London Irish Fictions*.

Narratives of domesticity are largely absent: settling down, making homes, the changing rhythms of family life. Politics is touched on only tangentially, despite the fact that the settled Irish were active in local Labour party organisations, and a minority became involved in radical left politics and republican organisations. But perhaps most striking of all are the modes of speech and silence which accompanied experiences of sex and sexuality among Irish migrants. It is obviously not the case that sex was ignored in discussions of the population crisis or in representations of emigrants. Yet sex was addressed for the most part through a series of inherited narrative modes, we might call them set-pieces or clichés, which did little to undermine or alter the persistence of cultural and gendered stereotypes. The inability of the rural Irish economy to hold its own against Britain's booming industrial expansion (and full employment) in the 1950s was figured in part through images of weak and wayward women who were unwilling to endure the rigours and discomforts of rural life. Consumerist desires and romantic aspirations moved in tandem in the models of urban affluence and social mobility promulgated from metropolitan centres in both Ireland and England, through women's magazines, campaigns to Buy Irish or Buy British, and the production and trade imperatives of both countries. Anxieties about moral weakness, sexual waywardness, contraception, illegitimacy and mixed marriages were addressed, as they were during the revival and post-independence periods, through concerns over the behaviour of women and girls. This was partly because of the assumption that male sexual urges were uncontrollable, and it was therefore the task of women to set appropriate boundaries.[2] As we have seen, women writers such as Lavin, Laverty and O'Brien deconstructed these ideological alliances with aplomb, revealing the contradictions at the heart of associations between women, romance and modernisation.

Yet it remains striking that male bodies were rarely associated with sexuality, or indeed consumerist modernity, during this period. The naked torsos in Donnellan's film represent labouring, not sexualised, flesh. Mac Amhlaigh tells a story of turning up late to find lodgings in a boarding house, where he had to climb in next to a man already in bed, and they recited the rosary together, rough but pious countrymen.[3] The all-male

---

[2] See Cronin, *Impure Thoughts*.

[3] See Mac Amhlaigh, *An Irish Navvy*, p. 73: 'two strangers in the same bed saying the rosary together.' Cowley quotes one recollection of bed-sharing: 'It's an awful feeling when you move in the night and touch another man who probably, like yourself, is sleeping in the buff.' *Men Who Built Britain*, p. 223.

groups in Murphy, Power, John B. Keane and Mac Amhlaigh are represented alternately as labouring and fighting men (drinking and fighting
when they are not labouring), suspicious and wary of domesticity, affluence, aspirationalism, but also sexual relationships in general.[4] In keeping
with this, images of heterosexual union are suppressed or shown to be
irrelevant to the lives of the migrant labourers, while at the same time
homosexuality appears equally extraneous to concerns, although stories
of fights with dandified Teddy Boys suggest an anxiety to prove manly
credentials.

The relatively narrow range of tropes which recur in representations of
both emigrants and immigrants, and in work by both Irish and non-Irish
artists, is testament to the continuing strength of associations between
Irish national survival and the qualities honed by rural Irish life, the
endurance of revivalist cultural stereotypes. From the mid-nineteenth century more Irish people lived in towns than in the countryside. Arguably,
the continuing strength and imaginative purchase of the stark oppositions
between the country and the city in mid-twentieth-century Ireland had to
do with the fact that, because of the long history of migration and emigration, the boundary between rural and urban was in reality extremely
porous. Even if Ireland could be imagined as a rural country, the people
it produced were highly urbanised. It was the processes of urbanisation –
the high levels of mobility amongst the Irish population – rather than
the experiences of rural life which were reflected in much of the folklore,
balladry and other forms of popular culture. Yet the sense that 'the finest
of our men', whose qualities of physical and moral strength could not be
replaced, were being lost to the nation was not merely a belated expression
of revivalist concerns, a last gasp of conservative corporatist Catholicism,
but an expression of ambivalence about the costs of modernity to an Irish
society ill-equipped to compete economically with her much more powerful neighbour.

Moreover, the migrants themselves carried this set of assumptions and
preoccupations with them. Images of tradition (whether valorised or not)
punctuate migrant narratives and narratives about migrants alike: the
rhythms of country life which tally uneasily with the demands of modern
industrial labour and appear to corroborate prejudices against the Irish
as unreliable workers; the naturalness of Irish girls; the spontaneity and

---

[4] The character of Harry in *A Whistle in the Dark* is an exception here, since he builds his aspiration
not on conformity to the values of the respectable working class (like his brother Michael), but on
wielding power through acting as a pimp, and go-between.

genuineness of Irish sociability compared to the forms of mass culture favoured by the English; traditional Irish song and folk culture compared to television and 'artificial' entertainments; the rituals of pre-Vatican II Catholicism; the physical strength of the 'real' working man, compared to the new modes of work associated with light industry.

The dialectic of emigration depended on these oppositions and thus affected how emigration was lived as well as how it was understood. The structural dependence between the apparently traditional, and communal, culture of the emigrant and apparently modern industrial society runs through the all the forms of representation I have discussed in this book. In the early post-war years emigration was condemned as unpatriotic by – mostly conservative – Irish clerics and politicians. Yet at the same time it was acknowledged as a 'safety-valve' against social unrest, and even a means of deferring Ireland's encounter with modernity, by displacing it elsewhere. The Irish immigrant in Britain enacted that encounter, remaining, as far as the stereotypes went, resistant to secular modernity in both positive and negative ways, but also irrevocably changed by it.

I have traced the evolution of some of these stock formations – bodied forth as types and stereotypes – through the migrant journey from Ireland to Britain, and across the genres of post-war Irish literature. In doing so I have been arguing for the value of a practice of critical reading, which pays attention to the ways in which such received discourses move and mutate across different types of texts, from records of public opinion to popular drama, literary fiction and experimental film. But I have also been arguing that the self-conscious repetition, manipulation and distortion of these formations in literature and art – broadly speaking – offer a particular form of knowledge, and a particular way of seeing. I end with one last example, which is also one of the places where I began.

At the very end of 'The Great Hunger', as life closes in on Paddy Maguire, Kavanagh offers a vision of the aged farmer caught for a moment within a frame, and poised on a threshold. It is the earth itself which speaks:

> Patrick Maguire, the old peasant, can neither be damned nor glorified:
> The graveyard in which he will lie will be just a deep-drilled potato-field
> Where the seed gets no chance to come through
> To the fun of the sun.
> The tongue in his mouth is the root of a yew.
> Silence, silence. The story is done.
> He stands in the doorway of his house
> A ragged sculpture of the wind,

October creaks the rotted mattress,
The bedposts fall. No hope. No lust.
The hungry fiend
Screams the apocalypse of clay In every corner of this land.

The idea of the bachelor farmer as moulded by forces beyond his control runs throughout the poem. He can be sculpted by the wind because, as the poem has established, he too is formed of the clay which he also works. Maguire 'grunts and spits/Through a clay-wattled moustache'; his soul is like 'a bag of wet clay' which rolls down the hill 'diverted by the angles/Where the plough missed or a spade stands, straitening the way.'

Although it was written in 1942, and therefore lies outside the period which I have been discussing, Kavanagh's poem has functioned as a touchstone in thinking through many of the issues I have explored in this book. The poem takes as its subject the lingering death of rural Irish communities, the problem of depopulation, the emptying out of isolated parishes, the solitary male, poverty of resources – for the soul as well as the body – and the question of how to survive in such conditions. Kavanagh directly targets revivalist idealisations of peasant life, which he associates with the external perspective of the 'tourist' and 'expert.' We can hear an echo of theories of racial degeneration, of the kind I discussed in Chapter 1, in his cameo of the travellers' lament for the death of civilisation:

> The travellers stop their cars to gape over the green bank into his fields: -
> There is the source from which all cultures rise,
> And all religions,
> There is the pool in which the poet dips
> And the musician.
> Without the peasant base civilisation must die,
> Unless the clay is in the mouth the singer's singing is useless.

Kavanagh's difficulty in the poem is to forge a perspective which knows the farmer from both inside and outside. He keeps shifting the viewpoint from a position within the 'mud-walled space' which is 'the blind ploughman's' habitat, where you can feel but not see, to something like the long shot in a documentary film, a vantage point which allows you to judge the relationship between figure and background, but only externally – you can't feel it.

It is precisely this form of writing – on the cusp between ethnographic and documentary explorations of environment and milieu, and imaginative creation of new ways of seeing – which I have been analysing in this book. Arguably the sociological turn in post-war Irish writing – the focus on the male labourer, the concern with distinguishing figure from ground, and the emphasis on entrapment inside a narrative not of one's own choosing (the straitened way) – can be traced back, in part, to Kavanagh's reflections on the shaping power of environment and history. The poem explores restriction, confinement, enclosure – the contours of a life determined by the long historical shadows of the famine and political, religious and cultural responses to it. Yet it also acknowledges the aspects of a life which escape determination, and explores the sense in which individuals too determine their lives despite, and through, their 'fates.' Maguire is both a figure shaped by nature and at the same time the artist of his own destiny, through the nature, and specifically the clay, which he works.

We can think of clay as raw material, which has to be shaped by experience – it is in this sense that Maguire is 'sculpted' by his environment. But clay is also the experience, the raw material of a life which, I have been arguing, gets culturally determined, and especially so at moments of historical crisis. We have seen how Irish emigrant and immigrant experience has been shaped into various stock formations, the types and stereotypes of popular literature and documentary analysis. And for Kavanagh, as for Edna O'Brien, Tom Murphy, Anthony Cronin, Frank Auerbach and Philip Donnellan, the clay – the raw material of the work – is both the life and the way it has been sculpted. Their works embody the tension between sociological and literary approaches, between analysis and revelation, for as Kavanagh reminds us, clay is the flesh but it is also the word.

Bibliography

MANUSCRIPTS

National Archives, London.
Papers of Arnold Marsh, Trinity College, Dublin.
Phillip Donnellan Archive, Birmingham Central Library.

TELEVISION, FILM AND RADIO

Boat Train to Euston. Radharc films, 1965.
The Colony. Dir. Philip Donnellan. BBC, 1964.
Girl with Green Eyes. Dir. Desmond Davis, 1964.
Hotel Chaplain. Radharc films, 1965.
I Was Happy Here. Dir. Desmond Davis, 1965.
The Irishmen: An Impression of Exile. Dir. Philip Donnellan. BBC, 1965.
Men at Lunch. Dir. Seán Ó Cualáin. Sónta Films, 2012.
Oldbury Camp. Radharc films, 1965.
On a Paving Stone Mounted. Dir. Thaddeus O'Sullivan. British Film Institute, 1978.
A Pint of Plain. Dir. Thaddeus O'Sullivan. Royal College of Art, 1975.
'Song of a Road.' Prod. Ewan McColl and Charles Parker. BBC Home Service, 1959.
Thaddeus O'Sullivan: The Early Films, 1974–1985. Irish Film Institute, 2014.

NEWSPAPERS, JOURNALS AND MAGAZINES

Birmingham Mail
Ireland's Own
Irish Democrat
Irish Digest
Irish Monthly
Irish Press
Irish Women's Journal
The Messenger of the Sacred Heart
New Statesman
New Society
New York Times

The People
Radio Times
The Standard
Studies: An Irish Quarterly Review
Tribune
Women's Life
Women's View
Women's Way
Young Woman

PUBLISHED SOURCES

Arensberg, Conrad and Solon Kimball. *Family and Community in Ireland.* Cambridge, MA: Harvard University Press, 1940.

Arrowsmith, Aidan. 'Gender, Violence and Identity in *A Whistle in the Dark*', in Christopher Murray (ed.), *Alive in Time: The Enduring Drama of Tom Murphy*. Dublin: Carysfort Press, 2012, pp. 221–238.

Auerbach, Frank. 'Fragments from a Conversation', in David Wright and Patrick Swift (eds.), *X: A Quarterly Review* 1:1 (1959), pp. 31–34.

Behan, Brendan. *The Dubbalin Man.* Dublin: A & A Farmer, 1997.

Bell, Timothy Alan. 'Envisioning the Working Class in British Fiction, 1957–1967'. PhD dissertation, Queen Mary University of London, 2012.

Bhabha, Homi. 'The Other Question – the Stereotype and Colonial Discourse', *Screen*, 24:6 (1983), pp. 18–36.

Bonnett, Alistair. *White Identities: Historical and International Perspectives.* Harlow: Pearson Education, 2000.

Bowen, Elizabeth. *A World of Love.* London: Cape, 1955.

Brannigan, John. *Race in Modern Irish Literature and Culture.* Edinburgh: Edinburgh University Press, 2009.

  Brendan Behan: Cultural Nationalism and the Revisionist Writer. Dublin: Four Courts Press, 2002.

Brown, Terence. *Ireland: A Social and Cultural History, 1922–2002*, rev. edn. London: Harper Perennial, 2004.

Brunsdon, Charlotte. '"A Fine and Private Place": The Cinematic Spaces of the London Underground', *Screen*, 47:1 (2006), pp. 1–17.

Bugler, Jeremy. 'Ireland in London', *New Society*, 14 March 1968, pp. 369–371.

Campbell, Michael. *O Mary, This London.* London: Heinemann, 1959.

Casey, Eamon. 'The Pastoral on Emigration', *The Furrow* 18:5 (1967), pp. 245–256.

Castle, Gregory. *Modernism and the Celtic Revival.* Cambridge: Cambridge University Press, 2001.

Castles, Stephen and Godula Kosack. *Immigrant Workers and Class Structures in Western Europe.* Oxford: Oxford University press, 1973.

A Catholic Handbook for Irish Men and Women Going to England. Dublin: Catholic Truth Society of Ireland, 1953.

Clear, Caitriona. '"I Can Talk About It, Can't I?": The Ireland Maura Laverty Desired, 1942–1946', *Women's Studies*, 30:6 (2001), pp. 819–835.

'"Too Fond of Going": Female Emigration and Change for Women in Ireland, 1946–1961', in Dermot Keogh, Finbarr O'Shea and Carmel Quinlan (eds.), *Ireland in the 1950s: The Lost Decade*. Cork: Mercier Press, 2004, pp. 135–146.

Women of the House: Women's Household Work in Ireland, 1922–1961. Dublin: Irish Academic Press, 2000.

Cleary, Joe. *Outrageous Fortune: Capital and Culture in Modern Ireland*. Dublin: Field Day Publications, 2007.

Coleman, Terry. 'The Elite inside the Tunnel', *New Society*, 6 January 1966, pp. 6–8.

Collis, Robert. *The State of Medicine in Ireland*. Dublin: Parkside Press, 1943.

To Be A Pilgrim. London: Secker and Warburg, 1975.

Colum, Padraic. *The Fiddler's House: A Play in Three Acts, and The Land: An Agrarian Comedy*. Dublin: Maunsel & Co., 1909.

Connolly, Tracey. 'The Commission on Emigration, 1948–1954', in Dermot Keogh, Finbarr O'Shea and Carmel Quinlan (eds.), *Ireland in the 1950s: The Lost Decade*. Cork: Mercier Press, 2004, pp. 87–104.

Commission on Emigration and Other Population Problems 1948–1954: Reports. Dublin: Stationery Office, [1955].

Coulton, Barbara. *Louis MacNeice in the BBC*. London: Faber and Faber, 1980.

Cowley, Ultan. *The Men Who Built Britain*. Dublin: Wolfhound Press, 2004.

Cronin, Anthony. *The Life of Riley*. Dublin: New Island, 2010 [1964].

Cronin, Michael G. *Impure Thoughts: Sexuality, Catholicism and Literature in Twentieth-Century Ireland*. Manchester: Manchester University Press, 2012.

Cronin, Mike, Mark Duncan and Paul Rouse. *The GAA: A People's History*. Cork: Cork University Press, 2009.

Curtis, L. P. *Apes and Angels: The Irishman in Victorian Caricature*. Ann Arbor: University of Michigan Press, 1977.

Daly, Mary E. *The Slow Failure: Population Decline and Independent Ireland*. Madison: University of Wisconsin Press, 2006.

Das, Santanu. *Touch and Intimacy in First World War Literature*. Cambridge: Cambridge University Press, 2006.

Deane, Seamus. *Celtic Revivals: Essays in Modern Irish Literature*. London: Faber and Faber, 1985.

Deevy, Teresa. 'Temporal Powers', *Journal of Irish Literature*, 14:2 (1985), pp. 18–75.

Delaney, Enda. *Demography, State and Society: Irish Migration to Britain, 1921–1971*. Liverpool: Liverpool University Press, 2000.

The Irish in Post-War Britain. Oxford: Oxford University Press, 2007.

Dobbins, Gregory. *Lazy Idle Schemers: Irish Modernism and the Politics of Idleness*. Dublin: Field Day Publications, 2010.

Dunn, Nell. *Talking to Women*. London: MacGibbon and Kee, 1965.

Ferriter, Diarmaid. *Occasions of Sin: Sex and Society in Modern Ireland*. London: Profile Books, 2010.

Finn, Tomás. *Tuairim, Intellectual Debate and Policy Formation: Rethinking Ireland, 1954–1975*. Manchester: Manchester University Press, 2012.

Finnane, Mark. *Insanity and the Insane in Post-Famine Ireland*. London: Croom Helm, 1981.

Fitzpatrick, David. 'Synge and Modernity in *The Aran Islands*', in Brian Cliff and Nicholas Grene (eds.), *Synge and Edwardian Ireland*. Oxford: Oxford University Press, 2012, pp. 121–158.

Foster, John Wilson. *Fictions of the Irish Literary Revival*. Syracuse, NY: Syracuse University Press, 1993.

Foster, Roy. *Luck and the Irish: A Brief History of Change c. 1970–2000*. London: Penguin, 2007.

Galton, Francis. *Inquiries into Human Faculty and Its Development*. London: Macmillan: 1883.

Garvin, Tom. *Preventing the Future: Why Ireland Was So Poor for So Long*. Dublin: Gill and Macmillan, 2005.

Glass, Ruth. *Newcomers: The West Indians in London*. London: Allen and Unwin, 1960.

Gretton, John. 'The Lump', *New Society*, 18 March 1970, pp. 469–470.

Grene, Nicholas. *Synge: A Critical Study of the Plays*. Basingstoke: Macmillan, 1985.
   (ed.). *Talking about Tom Murphy*. Dublin: Carysfort Press, 2002.

Griffin, Pat. *Gaelic Hearts: A History of London GAA, 1896–1996*. London: London Co. Board Gaelic Athletic Association, 2011.

Haddon, A. C. and C. R. Browne. 'The Ethnography of the Aran Islands, County Galway', *Proceedings of the Royal Irish Academy*, 2 (1891–1893), pp. 768–830.

Halsey, A. H. *A History of Sociology in Britain*. Oxford: Oxford University Press, 2004.

Harte, Liam. *The Literature of the Irish in Britain: Autobiography and Memoir*. Basingstoke: Palgrave Macmillan, 2009.
   '"You Want to be a British Paddy?": The Anxiety of Identity in Post-War Irish Migrant Writing', in Dermot Keogh, Finbarr O'Shea and Carmel Quinlan (eds.), *Ireland in the 1950s: The Lost Decade* (Cork: Mercier Press, 2004), pp. 233–51.

Healy, John. *Death of an Irish Town*. Cork: Mercier Press, 1968.

Hickey, Des and Gus Smith (eds.). *A Paler Shade of Green*. London: Leslie Frewin, 1972.

Hickman, Mary. 'Diaspora Space and National (Re)Formations', *Éire-Ireland*, 47:1&2 (2012), pp. 19–44.
   Religion, Class and Identity: The State, the Church and the Education of the Irish in Britain. Aldershot: Avebury, 1995.

Higson, Andrew (ed.). *Dissolving Views: Key Writings on British Cinema*. London: Cassell, 1996.

Hoggart, Richard. *The Uses of Literacy*. London: Penguin, 2009.

Hooton, E. A. and C. W. Dupertuis. *The Physical Anthropology of Ireland: Papers of the Peabody Museum of Archeology and Ethnology*, 30:1–2. Cambridge, MA: Peabody Museum, 1995.

Humphreys, A. J. *New Dubliners: Urbanization and the Irish Family*. London: Routledge and Kegan Paul, 1966.

Hyman, James. *The Battle for Realism: Figurative Art in Britain during the Cold War 1945–1960*. New Haven, CT: Yale University Press, 2001.

Ignatiev, Noel. *How the Irish Became White*. London: Routledge, 1995.

Irish Agricultural Institute. *West Cork Resource Survey*. Dublin: An Foras Taluntais, 1963.

Irish University Review: A Journal of Irish Studies, Special Issue on Brendan Behan, 44:1 (2014).

Jacobson, Matthew Frye. *Whiteness of a Different Colour: European Immigrants and the Alchemy of Race*. Boston: Harvard University Press, 1998.

Jackson, John A. *The Irish in Britain*. London: Routledge and Kegan Paul, 1963.

 Report on the Skibbereen Social Survey. Dublin: Human Sciences Committee, 1967.

Jones, Greta. *Social Darwinism in English Thought: The Interaction between Biological and Social Theory*. Brighton: Harvester Press, 1980.

 Social Hygiene in Twentieth Century Britain. London: Croom Helm, 1986.

Kavanagh, Patrick. 'The Great Hunger', in Antoinette Quinn (ed.), *Collected Poems* (London: Penguin, 2005).

 'Sex and Christianity', *Kavanagh's Weekly*, 24 May 1952, pp. 7–8.

 Tarry Flynn. London: Penguin Classics, 2000 [1948].

Keane, John B. *Hut 42*. Dixon, CA: Proscenium Press, 1968.

 Many Young Men of Twenty. Dublin: Progress House, 1961.

 Self-Portrait. Cork: Mercier Press, 1964.

 Three Plays: Sive, The Field, Big Maggie. Cork: Mercier Press, 1990.

Kenny, Kevin. *The American Irish: A History*. Ann Arbor: University of Michigan Press, 2000.

Kerr, Madeleine. *The People of Ship Street*. London: Routledge and Kegan Paul: 1958.

Kiberd, Declan. *Inventing Ireland: The Literature of the Modern Nation*. London: Jonathan Cape, 1995.

Kushner, Tony. *We Europeans? Mass Observation, 'Race' and British Identity in the Twentieth Century*. Aldershot: Ashgate, 2005.

Laing, Stuart. *Representations of Working-Class Life*. Basingstoke: Palgrave Macmillan, 1986.

Laverty, Maura. *Never No More: The Story of a Lost Village*. London: Longmans, Green, 1942.

Lavin, Mary. 'Sarah', in *The Stories of Mary Lavin, Vol. 2*. London: Constable, 1974.

Lee, J. J. *Ireland 1912–1985: Politics and Society*. Cambridge: Cambridge University Press, 1989.

Leitch, Maurice. *Poor Lazarus*. London: Panther, 1970.

Lennon, M., M. McAdam and J. O'Brien. *Across the Water: Irish Women's Lives in Britain*. London: Virago: 1988.

Lodge, David. *How Far Can You Go?* London: Secker & Warburg, 1980.

 The Picturegoers. London: Penguin, 1992.

Long, Paul. 'British Radio and the Politics of Culture in Post-War Britain: The Work of Charles Parker', *The Radio Journal: International Studies in Broadcast and Audio Media*, 2:3 (2004), pp. 131–152.

Lovell, Terry. 'Landscapes and Stories in 1960s British Realism', in Andrew Higson (ed.), *Dissolving Views: Key Writings on British Cinema*. London: Cassell, 1996, pp. 157–177.

Luddy, Maria. *Prostitution and Irish Society, 1800–1940*. Cambridge: Cambridge University Press, 2007.

Mac Amhlaigh, Donall. *An Irish Navvy: The Diary of an Exile*, trans. Valentine Iremonger. Cork: Collins Press, 2003 [1964].

MacCarthy, Ethna. 'Public Health Problems Created by Louse Infestation', *Irish Journal of Medical Science* (February 1948), pp. 65–78.

McDyer, James. *Fr McDyer of Glencolumbkille: An Autobiography*. Dingle: Brandon Books, 1982.

McGahern, John. *Amongst Women*. London: Faber, 1991.

—— *The Barracks*. London: Panther, 1966.

—— *The Dark*. London: Panther, 1967.

McKibbin, Ross. *Class and Cultures: England 1918–1951*. Oxford: Oxford University Press, 2000.

McLaverty, Michael. *School for Hope*. London: Jonathan Cape, 1954.

Malcolm, Elizabeth. '"The House of Strident Shadows": The Asylum, the Family and Emigration in Post-Famine Rural Ireland', in Greta Jones and Elizabeth Malcolm (eds.), *Medicine, Disease and the State in Ireland, 1650–1940*. Cork: Cork University Press, 1999, pp. 177–194.

Manning, Mary. *Mount Venus*. New York: Houghton Mifflin, 1938.

Marks, Laura U. *The Skin of the Film: Intercultural Cinema, Embodiment and the Senses*. Durham, NC: Duke University Press, 2000.

Mathews, P. J. *Revival: The Abbey Theatre, Sinn Féin, the Gaelic League and the Co-Operative Movement*. Cork: Cork University Press, 2009.

Mattar, Sinead Garrigan. *Primitivism, Science and the Irish Literary Revival*. Oxford: Oxford University Press, 2004.

Meaney, Gerardine. 'Decadence, Degeneration and Revolting Aesthetics: The Fiction of Emily Lawless and Katherine Cecil Thurston', *Colby Quarterly*, 36:2 (2000), pp. 157–175.

Miles, Robert. *Racism and Migrant Labour*. London: Routledge, 1982.

Mogey, John M. *Rural Life in Northern Ireland*. London: Oxford University Press, 1947.

Molloy, M. J. *Selected Plays of M. J. Molloy*, ed. Robert O'Driscoll. Gerrards Cross: Colin Smythe, 1998.

Moore, Brian. *The Feast of Lupercal*. Boston, MA: Little, Brown, 1957.

—— *Lonely Passion of Judith Hearne*. Boston, MA: Little, Brown, 1955.

Muckle, John. *Little White Bull: British Fiction in the Fifties and Sixties*. Bristol: Shearsman Books, 2014.

Murphy, John. *The Country Boy: A Play in Three Acts*. Dublin: Progress House, 1960.

Murphy, Tom. *A Whistle in the Dark and Other Plays*. London: Methuen, 1989.

Murray, Peter and Maria Feeney. *The Market for Sociological Ideas in Early 1960s Ireland: Civil Service Departments and the Limerick Rural Survey, 1961–1964*. Dublin: National Institute for Regional and Spatial Analysis, 2010.

Murray, Tony. *London Irish Fictions: Narrative, Diaspora and Identity*. Liverpool: Liverpool University Press, 2012.

Nash, Catherine. *Of Irish Descent: Origin Stories, Genealogy and the Politics of Belonging*. Syracuse University Press, 2008.

Newman, Jeremiah (ed.). *The Limerick Rural Survey, 1958–1964*. Tipperary: Muintir na Tíre Publications, 1964.

Noble, Virginia. *Inside the Welfare State: Foundations of Policy and Practice in Post-War Britain*. London: Routledge, 2009.

O'Brien, Edna. *Mother Ireland*. London: Penguin, 1978.

The Country Girls. London: Phoenix, 2007 [1960].

O'Brien, Flann. *At Swim-Two-Birds*. London: Longmans Green, 1939.

The Third Policeman. London: Pan Books, 1974.

O'Brien, John Anthony (ed.). *The Vanishing Irish: The Enigma of the Modern World*. London: W. H. Allen, 1954.

Ó Conaire, Pádhraic Óg. *Déirc an Díomhaointis*. Baile Átha Cliath: Sáirséal agus Dill, 1972.

Ó Conghaile, Micheál. *Conamara agus Árainn 1880–1980*. Béal an Daingin, Conamara: Cló Iar-Chonnachta, 1988.

O'Connor, Frank. *The Backward Look: A Survey of Irish Literature*. London: Macmillan, 1967.

Crab Apple Jelly: Stories and Tales. London: Macmillan, 1944.

O'Connor, Kevin. *The Irish in Britain*. London: Sidgewick and Jackson, 1972.

O'Crohan, Tomas. *The Islandman*, trans. Robin Flower. Oxford: Oxford University Press, 1977.

O'Donnell, Peadar. *The Big Windows*. London: Jonathan Cape, 1955.

The Role of Industrial Workers in the Problems of the West. Dublin: Distributed by Dochas Co-operative Society, [1965?].

O'Dowd, Liam. 'Town and Country in Irish Ideology', *Canadian Journal of Irish Studies*, 12:2 (1987), pp. 43–53.

Ó Drisceoil, Donal. *Peadar O'Donnell*. Cork: Cork University Press, 2001.

O'Faolain, Sean. *Come Back to Erin*. London: Jonathan Cape, 1940.

Ó Giolláin, Diarmuid. *Locating Irish Folklore: Tradition, Modernity, Identity*. Cork: Cork University Press, 2000.

Ó hOdhráin, Mícheál. *Sléibhte Mhaigh Eo*. Dublin: Foilseachain Naisiunta Teoranta, 1964.

O'Shea, Kieran. *The Irish Emigrant Chaplaincy Scheme in Britain, 1957–82*. Dublin: Irish Episcopal Commission for Emigrants, 1985.

O'Toole, Fintan. *Tom Murphy: The Politics of Magic*. Dublin: New Island Books, 1994.

Patterson, Sheila. *Dark Strangers: A Sociological Study of the Absorption of a Recent West Indian Migrant Group in Brixton, South London*. London: Tavistock, 1963.

Immigrants in Industry. Oxford: Oxford University Press, 1968.

Panayi, Panikos (ed.). *Racial Violence in Britain, 1840–1950*. Leicester: Leicester University Press, 1993.

Pettit, Lance. 'Philip Donnellan, Ireland and Dissident Documentary', *Historical Journal of Film, Radio and Television*, 20:3 (2001), pp. 351–365.

Screening Ireland: Film and Television Representation. Manchester: Manchester University Press, 2000.

Power, Richard. *Apple on a Treetop*, trans. Victor Power. Dublin: Poolbeg Press, 1980.

Quinn, Antoinette. *Patrick Kavanagh: A Biography*. Dublin: Gill and Macmillan, 2001.

Rafroidi, Patrick. 'The Great Brian Moore Collection', in Patrick Rafroidi and Maurice Harmen (eds.), *The Irish Novel in Our Time*. Villeneuve-d'Ascq: Publications de l'Université de Lille III, 1976, pp. 221–36.

Report of the Commission on Emigration and Other Population Problems. Dublin: Stationery Office, 1954.

Rex, John and Robert Moore. *Race, Community and Conflict: A Study of Sparkbook*. Oxford: Oxford University Press, 1967.

Robertson, Elizabeth. 'Broadcasting Ireland: The BBC Third Programme and the Cult of Nostalgia', MA research essay, Queen Mary University of London, 2008.

Rodgers, W. R. *Irish Literary Portraits*, ed. Harden Jay. London: BBC, 1971.

Roediger, David. *The Wages of Whiteness: Race and the Making of the American Working Class*. London: Verso, 1991.

Rose, E. J. B. et al. *Colour and Citizenship: A Report on British Race Relations*. London: Institute of Race Relations, 1969.

Ryan, James. 'Inadmissible Departures: Why Did the Emigrant Experience Feature so Infrequently in the Fiction of the Mid-Twentieth Century?' in Dermot Keogh, Finbarr O'Shea, Carmel Quinlan (eds.), *Ireland in the 1950s: The Lost Decade*. Cork: Mercier Press, 2004, pp. 221–32.

Scott, Joan W. 'The Evidence of Experience', *Critical Inquiry*, 17:4 (1991), pp. 773–797.

Sigerson, George. 'Irish Literature: Its Origin, Environment', in Sir Charles Gavan Duffy (ed.), *The Revival of Irish Literature*. London: Fisher Unwin, 1894.

Spark, Muriel. *The Bachelors*. London: Macmillan, 1960.

Spencer, A. E. C. W. *Arrangements for the Integration of Irish Immigrants in England and Wales*, ed. Mary Daly. Dublin: Irish Manuscripts Commission, 2011.

Spinley, B. *The Deprived and the Privileged*. London: Routledge and Kegan Paul, 1953.

Sykes, A. J. 'Navvies: Their Social Relations', *Sociology*, 3:2 (May 1969), pp. 157–172.

'Navvies: Their Work Attitudes', *Sociology* 3:1 (1969), pp. 21–34.

Synge, J. M. *The Complete Works of J. M. Synge*, ed. Aidan Arrowsmith. Ware: Wordsworth Editions, 2008.

Travels in Wicklow, West Kerry and Connemara. London: Serif, 2009 [1911].

Taylor, B. F. *The British New Wave*. Manchester: Manchester University Press, 2006.

Toner, Jerome. *Rural Ireland: Some of Its Problems*. Dublin: Clonmore and Reynolds, 1955.

Thomson, Mathew. *The Problem of Mental Deficiency: Eugenics, Democracy, and Social Policy in Britain c. 1870–1959*. Oxford: Clarendon Press, 1998.

Valiulis, Maryann. 'Neither Feminist nor Flapper: The Ecclesiastical Construction of the Ideal Irish Woman', in Mary O'Dowd and Sabine Wichert (eds.), *Chattel, Servant or Citizen: Women's Status in Church, State and Society*. Belfast: Institute of Irish Studies, Queens University of Belfast, 1995.

Varley, Tony and Chris Curtin, 'Defending Rural Interests against Nationalists in 20th-Century Ireland: A Tale of Three Movements', in John Davis (ed.), *Rural Change in Ireland*. Belfast: Institute of Irish Studies, 1999, pp. 58–83.

Walter, Bronwen. *Outsiders Inside: Whiteness, Place and Irish Women*. London: Routledge, 2000.

'Whiteness and Diasporic Irishness: Nation, Gender and Class', *Journal of Ethnic and Migration Studies*, 37:9 (2011), pp. 1295–1312.

Waters, Chris. '"Dark Strangers" in our Midst: Discourses of Race and Nation in Britain, 1947–1963', *Journal of British Studies*, 36:2 (1997), pp. 207–238.

Webster, Wendy. *Imagining Home: Gender, 'Race' and National Identity, 1945–64*. London: UCL Press, 1998.

Whitehead, Kate. *The Third Programme: A Literary History*. Oxford: Clarendon Press, 1989.

Wilk, R. 'Loggers, Miners, Cowboys, and Grab Fishermen: Masculine Work Culture and Binge Consumption', in R. Oka and I. Kuijt (eds.), *Social Economies of Greed and Excess: Lessons from Recessions, Past and Present*. New York: Altamira Press, forthcoming.

Williams, Raymond. *The Country and the City*. Nottingham: Spokesman Books, 2011.

Wills, Clair. *That Neutral Island: A History of Ireland during the Second World War*. London: Faber and Faber, 2007.

'Women Writers and the Death of Rural Ireland: Realism and Nostalgia in the 1940s', *Éire-Ireland*, 41:1 (2006), pp. 192–212.

Wilson, Thomas M. 'From Clare to the Common Market: Perspectives in Irish Ethnography', *Anthropological Quarterly*, 57:1 (January 1984), pp. 1–15.

Wright, Barnaby (ed.). *Frank Auerbach: London Building Sites, 1952–62*. London: Courtauld Gallery, 2009.

Yeats, W. B. *On the Boiler*. Dublin: Cuala Press, 1939.

Young, Robert. *The Idea of English Ethnicity*. Oxford: Blackwell, 2008.

Zweig, Ferdynand. *The British Worker*. Harmonsworth: Penguin, 1952.

Index

Milton Keynes UK
Ingram Content Group UK Ltd.
UKHW041500021224
3327UKWH00050B/856

9 781107 680876